A Guide to
Library Research
in Psychology

A Guide to Library Research in Psychology

James Edward Bell

Howard Community College

WM. C. BROWN COMPANY PUBLISHERS
Dubuque, Iowa

To Carl and Sara

Contents

Preface

Compiling this guide was indeed a difficult task; for, everytime I went to the library to check on sources referred to within this book, I became sidetracked, finding fascinating articles and books to read. I had to continually remind myself to return to the task at hand. My hope is that this guide also helps you find reading materials on psychological topics which fascinate you.

This guide is intended to help psychology students in their use of the library. The written sections, Chapters 1 through 4, are directed toward undergraduate students. I assume that most undergraduate students have been introduced to the library and are familiar with basic information about the library. Consequently, Chapter 2 on the library is very brief, focusing on but a few features. Undergraduates are usually unfamiliar with the many sources of psychological information. Thus Chapter 3 which is concerned with these sources is more detailed. However, it was not my intent to discuss every psychological source available to students; but rather, with beginning students in mind, to focus on the key sources.

To write an excellent research paper you need to be able to gather sufficient information on a topic, synthesize it, and then communicate your views in superior written form. Chapter 4, which is devoted to suggestions on writing a research paper, stresses the process of searching for sources and gathering information on a topic. Only a few suggestions for the written form of a research paper are offered. If you wish more assistance with writing and style, select an appropriate reference from Appendix I.

Lists of psychological sources compose Chapter 5. These sources are almost entirely United States publications with a few British and Canadian sources included. Reference sources are listed first. Each of these lists is an attempt to comprehensively cover the material published in a category. Particular emphasis was placed on including recent sources. Except for the two selected lists of bibliographies which contain only sources published since 1960, the other reference lists contain works published before 1960 as well as more recent publications. These lists of reference sources should be useful to undergraduate and graduate psychology students.

Besides reference sources, Chapter 5 includes textbooks, supplementary readings, theory books, books of readings, and journals of possible interest to undergraduate and beginning graduate psychology students. More technical sources, such as symposiums, conferences, and extended reports of original research, are excluded. However, lists which are "*" contain several advanced sources. The lists entitled "Readings on . . ." contain books of readings, usually reprints of important journal articles, and other edited sources that include the original works of a number of writers. Four lists, "Experimental Psychology," "History of Psychology," "Readings on the History of Psychology," and "Systems and Theories," whose references are valuable historical sources, include older as well as more recent references. All other lists are limited to sources published between 1960 and 1970. A number of 1970 sources are included.

For best results with this guide, read through the first four chapters making notes on ideas you want to try or sources you wish to explore. Then, when using the library take this guide with you for handy reference. The table of contents has been designed to direct you quickly to desired information.

In Chapter 5 the reference sources except bibliographies are numbered. In Chapters 2 through 4 reference sources are followed by a number in parentheses. This number is the assigned number from Chapter 5 where full bibliographic information is given. For example, on p. 7, *A Comprehensive Dictionary of Psychological and Psychoanalytical Terms* by English and English is followed by the number "11" in parentheses. The 11th reference source in Chapter 5 contains full bibliographic information on this dictionary. Reference sources in Chapter 5 are followed by the page in parentheses where the source is discussed in Chapters 2 through 4. For example, in Chapter 5, the English and English dictionary is followed by the page number "7" in parentheses. On page 7 the English and English dictionary is discussed. Books in Chapter 5 followed by the letters "pb" signify that a paperback edition has been published.

I wish to thank the many individuals who provided ideas for and constructive criticism of the various drafts of this guide. Particular thanks goes to librarians Karl Grisso, Hans Von Brockdorff, and Peter Fenton who stimulated my interest in this area and spent many patient hours answering my questions. I also appreciated the support of the library staffs of Elmira College and Skidmore College. Special thanks are due my wife Ruth for her help.

chapter 1

Introduction

Psychology, a young and fast-growing science, is enriched yearly by the publication of many new journals and a variety of books. Consequently, college library holdings in psychology are expanding to include increased information on traditional topics as well as discussion and research on new topics. This expansion necessitates increased competence in using the library.

This guide is designed to increase the student's proficiency in two important library skills. The first of these skills is to be able to find answers to specific questions such as "What is the definition of cognitive dissonance?" or "What did book reviewers write about *Children of the Dream*?" The second of these library skills is to be able to research a topical area finding all of the information related to that topic. For instance the student may wish to research as topics for a library research paper "the moral development of children," or "the comparison of the intelligence of identical twins."

At times psychology students are required to write a library research paper. Mastery of the two skills mentioned above aids significantly in gathering the information needed for such a paper. In addition to facilitating the library search for meaningful material, this guide also provides suggestions for the organization and proper form of a research paper.

Discussion moves from a brief overview of general library features in Chapter 2 to a description of the major types of psychological sources, both reference and nonreference, in Chapter 3. The beginning student should find the reference sources discussed in this chapter especially useful while the more advanced student may use Chapter 3 as a review.

Chapter 4 focuses on a systematic procedure for effectively using the sources of Chapter 3 to either answer specific questions or research a topic. Here are found suggestions for writing a research paper from the initial choice of a topic through the form for the final copy. The student is cautioned to verify these suggestions with his instructor as individual instructors may have their own preference for the method of approach and/or form of a research paper.

Extensive lists of reference sources, textbooks, and books of readings for the several specialized areas of psychology are found in Chapter 5. Both the undergraduate and graduate student are directed to consult the lists of reference sources while the undergraduate student will find the lists of textbooks and readings useful for supplementing class reading, answering specific questions, and providing a summarizing of an area to be researched.

Appendix I lists books on several academic areas such as studying, applying for fellowships, and gaining admission to graduate school. To supplement the use of the card catalog and to encourage browsing, Appendix II contains a detailed listing of the Library of Congress classification numbers related to psychology.

chapter 2

The College Library

Years ago the college library was housed on the top floor of the oldest building on campus. The library itself was open only a few hours a week and students were encouraged to stay away from it. Through the years, however, college libraries have increased tremendously in size and importance. Today the library contains information and sources on nearly every conceivable subject and is likely to be the most significant part of the campus, not just a musty isolated corner.

Although present college libraries vary in size, facilities, and services, they have several common features important for the purposes of this guide. These features include the circulation desk, card catalog, classification system, book stacks, reference collection, periodicals, and, of course, the librarians.

CIRCULATION DESK

Books are checked out and information dispensed at the circulation desk. Many libraries have a manual which provides an introduction to that particular library, outlining its physical arrangement, services available, procedures for checking out books, and its rules and regulations. Knowing the procedures, rules, and regulations saves time and frustration. For example, knowing how to fill out a call slip prevents having to fill out a duplicate because the first was done incorrectly and knowing the library hours prevents one from arriving only to find the building locked. Ask for such a library guide at the circulation desk. Students are advised to know or find answers to the following questions at the circulation desk.

1. What newspapers and periodicals does the library subscribe to?
2. What materials are stored on microfilm?
3. Where is the microfilm stored?

4. Where are the microfilm readers housed?

5. What types of government documents are received and how are they classified?

6. Are there special collections? What do they contain and where are they found?

7. Is a photocopying machine available?

8. What is the procedure for obtaining material through interlibrary loan?

CARD CATALOG

The library's card catalog is an index to its books with each book represented by three types of cards. These are an author card, a title card, and a subject card. Ordinarily, author, title, and subject cards are filed together under a single alphabet, although some libraries group author and title cards in one file and subject cards in another. Because the card arrangement is not the same in all libraries, determining what filing rules are used is important. Turabian* (533) suggests asking the following questions:

1. Are abbreviations alphabetized as though written in full? That is, "Dr." filed as Doctor; "Ft." filed as Fort; "St." filed as Saint; "U.S." filed as United States, etc.?

2. Are names beginning with *M'*, *Mc,* and *Mac* alphabetized as they stand or as though each were spelled *Mac?*

3. What scheme of alphabetization is used for names with prefixes such as *de, von, le, la?*

4. Are Germanic words containing vowels with an umlaut alphabetized as they appear with the umlaut or as though *ä* were *ae,* *ö* were *oe,* and *ü* were *ue?*

5. Is alphabetization word-by-word or letter-by-letter? That is, do all the entries beginning with the *word* "new" follow each other in alphabetic sequence before words of which the *first syllable* is "new-" (word-by-word); or are individual words disregarded and a strict alphabetic order maintained through a second or even a third word (letter-by-letter)? Under the word-by-word scheme "New York" would precede "Newark"; under the letter-by-letter scheme, the opposite order would obtain.

6. How are anonymous works cataloged?

7. How are the works of authors writing under pseudonyms cataloged?

8. What other filing rules are there? [pp. 9-10].

*Kate L. Turabian, *Student's Guide for Writing College Papers,* Phoenix Books, University of Chicago Press, Chicago and London. ©1963 by The University of Chicago. All rights reserved.

It is easier to find a particular book with known title and author than to locate all of the books on a given topic area. For instance, to find a book on "creativity," one would first check the heading "creativity" in the card catalog. In addition to listing books on "creativity" the card catalog might refer to related subjects. The student would then look further in the card catalog under these related subjects. But the search for all of the books pertinent to an area, such as "creativity," does not end with this first examination of the card catalog.

Two books which list synonymous subject headings are *Subject Headings Used In the Dictionary Catalogs of the Library of Congress* (534) and *Sear's List of Subject Headings* (535). Psychological dictionaries can also be used to find synonymous terms. Looking up "creativity" in these books, for example, suggests the related subject areas of "creation, creative ability, inspiration, originality, and genius." Synonymous subject areas often can be used to obtain further references from the card catalog and from other sources discussed later in this guide.

CLASSIFICATION SYSTEM

The student's knowledge of the classification system used in his college library facilitates finding books. Librarians usually use either the Dewey Decimal or the Library of Congress Classification System. Under each of these systems a book is identified by a call number which allows the book to be quickly located on the shelves. The major classifications for the psychological materials are BF in the Library of Congress Classification and 150-159 in the Dewey Decimal Classification. However, many psychology books have call numbers other than BF or 150-159. Appendix II contains a detailed listing of these and other categories of special interest to the psychology student.

BOOK STACKS

Once a student has the title, author, and call number of a pertinent volume, he needs to secure it from the stacks where most of the books are shelved. If library policy allows students to go directly to the stacks, this writer suggests that the student quickly learn the basic layout of the stacks as well as the general location of psychological materials. When the student has found a particular book in the stacks, he can scan the titles housed adjacently noting whether any of the titles seem pertinent. Books on the same subject often are shelved together so that a relevant book may be discovered by scanning.

REFERENCE COLLECTION

The reference collection is a group of sources which either contain specific information or serve as a guide to other sources. Examples of the first type of reference work are dictionaries, encyclopedias, and handbooks. Indexes, abstracts, and bibliographies are examples of the second type of reference work. The sources described in the first part of Chapter 5 belong to the reference collection and thus are shelved with other reference works. Psychology students are advised to browse through the reference collection noting which psychological reference sources are available to them.

PERIODICALS

Containing most of the original psychological research, periodicals are another source students need to consult. To facilitate quick location of a desired periodical, it is expedient to know not only what periodicals are available but also their arrangement and location.

LIBRARIANS

Librarians can be of great assistance to the student. Too often a student hesitates to make use of these valuable persons. Librarians can be especially helpful if the student has attempted to define what information he needs and if he has already searched the more common sources.

chapter 3

Library Sources
in Psychology

Psychological information is found in a variety of sources. The sources discussed in this chapter are reference works, books, periodicals, government documents, and newspapers.

I. Reference Sources.

Reference sources are to be consulted for specific information. As has been mentioned previously, there are two basic types of reference sources. One is that which contains the needed information itself. Examples are dictionaries, encyclopedia, handbooks, biographical sources, book reviews, and test information. The student who learns to use these well becomes proficient in the first basic library skill, finding answers to specific questions. The second type of reference source indicates where information can be found. Examples are indexes, abstracts, and bibliographies. These sources are useful when a student is assigned a research paper. Then, proficiency in searching for pertinent literature in an area, the second basic library skill, is necessary.

A. Dictionaries.

For most psychological library work psychological dictionaries are preferred to either general unabridged or general abridged dictionaries. The psychological dictionary which has received the strongest recommendations for general use is English and English's *A Comprehensive Dictionary of Psychological and Psychoanalytical Terms* (11). Not only does it have over 11,000 entries, but also nearly 300 subjects are accorded extended discussion. The three page preface of this dictionary helps students understand some of the difficulties inherent in psychological definitions. English and English advise readers who cannot find a particular term to look up a synonym, a deferential spelling or each of the words of a compound word. Because it was published in 1958, a newer psychological dictionary will have to be consulted for recent psychological terms.

Dictionaries are numbered 1 through 72 in Chapter 5.

Students will also find definitions in a glossary near the end of introductory textbooks and in the glossaries for some textbooks of more advanced courses.

B. Encyclopedias.

Encyclopedia articles, arranged alphabetically, cover a variety of topics. Each article is written by an expert in that area. Each article, a summary of an area, includes important definitions and a discussion of the historical background, current status, and major problems or issues in the area as well as a bibliography. Because of the long process involved in gathering the large amount of material compiled in an encyclopedia, the information is not the most recent. The student would do better to consult other sources for current information in the area. However, encyclopedias are useful in obtaining a nontechnical summary or introductory knowledge of an area.

The student may seek introductory information on some topics in a general encyclopedia such as *Encyclopedia Americana* or *Encyclopaedia Britannica*. Although these encyclopedias are published annually, not all articles within them are revised annually. The most recent reference in an article's bibliography suggests when the article was last revised.

A variety of encyclopedias, more specific to psychology than the above general encyclopedias, are more useful in the initial search for references in an area. Four recent ones are *The International Encyclopedia of the Social Sciences* (97), *The Encyclopedia of Mental Health* (76), the *Encyclopedia of Psychoanalysis* (80), and *The Encyclopedia of Human Behavior* (83). Other encyclopedias covering psychological topics are numbered 73-100. A good way to learn about these sources is to browse through them noting both the nature and depth of the topics covered. If information prior to 1946 is desired, the student will find the *Encyclopedia of Psychology* (86) useful.

C. Handbooks.

When reviewing the literature in preparation of this guide, this author discovered no general definition of "handbook," finding rather that books of varying purpose and description were referred to as "handbooks." Thus, if a publisher or a reviewer referred to a volume as a handbook or if the word "handbook" appeared in the title, the book was included in the list of handbooks in Chapter 5. But handbook volumes seem to fall into two groups. Those in the first group are oriented around theoretical and research information while those in the second group are concerned with the practical application of psychological theory and research findings. Sufficient time is required to gather information for and publish handbooks that they, like encyclopedias, are a poor source for the most recent information in an area. Despite this limitation they are useful as is indicated below.

Handbooks of the first group are sufficiently sophisticated that psychologists and advanced psychology students find them most useful. Each article within these volumes presents extended discussion of theoretical positions and research findings. Extensive bibliographies follow each article. Although generally intended for advanced students, the beginning student will find some of these handbooks useful in researching a topic. Four recent handbooks are more appropriate than the others listed in Chapter 5 for the beginning student. These are *The Handbook of Social Psychology* (198), *Handbook of Personality Theory and Research* (124), *Infancy and Early Childhood: A Handbook and Guide to Human Development* (126), and *Carmichael's Manual of Child Psychology* (220).

Human Behavior: An Inventory of Scientific Findings (115) is especially useful for the novice psychologist. The authors of this handbook reviewed the scientific knowledge of the behavioral sciences, not just of psychology. Principles or statements about human behavior which are supported by several research studies provide the framework around which the volume is organized. For example, the finding that measured intelligence increases as social class increases serves as one topical area. Behavioral science research in this area is summarized and interpretations of the major research studies discussed. The novice can understand the discussion of these statements and will find the bibliographical references helpful if he wishes to pursue the topic to a greater depth.

The second group of handbooks have certain specific applications. Many are clinically oriented, offering suggestions for dealing with specific psychological and physical problems. Some of the topics covered in this group of handbooks are alcohol and drug addiction, child discipline, mental retardation, statistical computations and testing. *The Physician's Concise Handbook of Psychiatry* (128) and *Baby and Child Care* (253) are examples of this group of handbooks.

The following advice is offered to facilitate finding information in a handbook. First, to locate an appropriate handbook, look for one meaningful to the broad subject heading which includes your more refined topic. That is, if the area of investigation is "moral development of children," look for a handbook concerned with "child development" or "socialization." Secondly, after a volume generally pertinent to the refined area of investigation has been secured, the quickest way to find the specific topic, such as "moral development of children," is through the handbook's index.

D. Biographical Sources.

Biographical information enlightens the student about the life and qualifications of an author or an individual mentioned in the readings. If the student is curious about an individual known to be an American psychologist, he should consult the most recent directory published by the American Psychological Association (271). Some of the psychologists mentioned in psychology courses can be found in the series, *A History of Psychology in Autobiography* (280, 281). Sources for biographical information on psychologists are numbered 269-285.

If the person is living but not a psychologist, recent *Who's Who* (285) and the index to current biographies *Biography Index* (273) are useful sources.

If the person is deceased, the following sources should be consulted: *Dictionary of American Biography* (294), *National Cyclopedia of American Biography* (302), *Webster's Biographical Dictionary* (306), or *Who Was Who in America* (283). Additional biographical information sources are numbered 286-307. Other sources, particularly for foreign biographies, can be found in *Guide to Reference Books* (529) or by consulting a librarian. Because a large number of people are discussed in biographic sources, it is imperative that the student have the correct spelling and full name.

E. Book Reviews.

Book reviews are an important source to consult when the student is looking for an interesting book to read or when he needs evaluative information on a book. Because book reviews reflect the preferences and particular orientation of the reviewer, reading more than one review of a specific book is recommended.

The *Mental Health Book Review Index* (312), the only index devoted entirely to book reviews on psychological topics, has listed over 4400 books since 1956. One issue which lists books alphabetically by author is published yearly. In 1969 a twelve year cumulated index for the years 1956-1967 was published (313). Book reviews for works published before 1967 are most likely included in this cumulated index. The student is directed to the recent yearly volumes for listings of reviews of recent books.

Contemporary Psychology (310), a monthly journal, reviews materials in all fields of psychology. Critical and evaluative comments are woven into an extended discussion of the book being reviewed. Because there is presently no cumulative index, the "Author and Reviewer Index" published annually in the December issue can be used to find a reference for the desired review. A student looking for a review looks first in the December issue of the year the book was published. If a review listing is not found in this issue, the student should look up the author in the two succeeding December issues, for most books are reviewed within two years of their publication.

Books on psychological measurement and testing are listed along with references for their reviews in the *Mental Measurements Yearbooks* (308). Reviews of older psychoanalytic writings are listed in *The Index of Psychoanalytic Writings* (311). Prior to 1961, *Education Index* (320) listed book reviews under the heading "Book Reviews."

Many of the psychological journals contain book reviews. The periodicals listed in Chapter 5 which are followed by an "R" contain book reviews.

If the student desires to evaluate a book on a topic of interest to those outside academic psychology, such as, aggression, child rearing, or drugs, several other sources list book review references. The *Book Review Index* (317) lists book reviews included in over 200 periodicals while the *Book Review Digest* (316) indexes a fewer number of periodicals but includes short comments from some of the reviews. Some of the book reviews listed in *Essay and General Literature Index* (321) and *An Index to Book Reviews in the Humanities* (322) are meaningful for psychologists.

Three journals which briefly review some psychology books are *Choice* (319), *Library Journal* (323), and *Science Books* (325). *Choice* reviews psychology books appropriate for college libraries. *Science Books* reviews books appropriate for freshman and sophomore college students. *Library Journal* reviews books of a more popular nature than do *Choice* or *Science Books*. Since 1967, the reviews in *Library Journal* have been cumulated annually into a book entitled *The Library Journal Book Review* (323).

F. Test Information.

Several areas of research use psychological tests. Students interested in determining the research on a particular test or concerned with locating a test for a class project should refer to the six volumes of *Mental Measurements Yearbooks* (330). These volumes list and describe thousands of tests. Research references pertaining to a test as well as books and book reviews in the field of tests and measurements can be found in *Mental Measurements Yearbooks*. *Tests In Print* (329) lists currently available tests. *Personality Tests and Reviews* (332) includes a synthesis of information from the personality sections of the six *Mental Measurements Yearbooks* and new information on personality tests. A comprehensive index of all tests, reviews, and references and an index of excerpted book reviews found in all six *Mental Measurements Yearbooks* help tie together the information in this useful set of sources. *Psychological Testing* (328) and *Essentials of Psychological Testing* (334) are two textbooks useful as reference sources on tests and testing. The use of psychological tests is a topic of much public discussion. Presentation of many of the controversies are contained in a special issue of the *American Psychologist* (327).

G. Abstracts and Indexes.

Journal articles report psychological research and topical reviews of the literature. Most psychological journals are specialized, each concerned with a subfield of psychology. For example, *Developmental Psychology* is one journal which publishes work in the field of developmental psychology and *Journal of Social Psychology* publishes in the area of social psychology. See Chapter 5 for a listing of psychological journals, grouped according to area of concern. Only rarely is an issue of a journal devoted to one topic; usually the articles within one issue cover a variety of topics. Articles are usually published in the chronological order as they are received from researchers and accepted for publication. The student researching a topic in the field of child development might find a pertinent article by going to a child development journal and thumbing through the recent issues. However, using indexes and abstracts is both more efficient and more productive. Abstracts and indexes both list references by topical area, but abstracts additionally provide brief nonevaluative summaries of the sources listed. These summaries help eliminate the references which at first appeared meaningful but in fact were not. Thus, if the student has access to both an abstract and an index, he should first use the abstract.

No one principle holds for either the organization, rate of publication, or cumulation of indexes or abstracts. Abstract and index entries are listed either alphabetically as in *Readers' Guide to Periodical Literature* (382) or nonalphabetically under broad subject categories as in *Psychological Abstracts* (372). Rate of publication varies from monthly to yearly. Some indexes cumulate yearly or at greater or lesser intervals; some do not cumulate at all. The student, thus, is directed to read the introduction and the table of contents of the index or abstract to familiarize himself with it to gain maximum benefit from the source.

Psychological Abstracts (372) is the most important abstract for psychology students. Published monthly, it includes abstracts of articles published in over 400 journals. Author and subject indexes are also included in each monthly issue. Since 1968, in June and December, a cumulated subject index and a cumulated author index for the previous six months are issued. A listing of the journals whose articles are abstracted in *Psychological Abstracts* is included at the beginning of the June and December cumulated indexes. Prior to 1968 the December issues included annual cumulated subject and author indexes. In recent years, several volumes compiling indexes of a number of annual cumulated indexes have been published (373-377). These, of course, save the time of having to go from index to index and make the work of researching an area much lighter.

Psychological Abstracts lists journal articles, books, and bibliographies. Book reviews are not listed. Books are listed under the subject entry, "Books" and bibliographies are listed under the subject entry, "Bibliographies." Complete bibliographic information is given for each entry; this enables the student to locate the original article. And, as is the nature of an abstract, a summary of the article is included. Such summaries help the student decide whether he desires to read the full article.

To find information in *Psychological Abstracts* turn first to the "Subject Index Terms" listed after the author index in the most recent semiannual cumulated index. These subject index terms are the subject categories under which references in the index are listed. From this list the student should pick a term or terms as closely related as possible to his research topic or interest. Then he should proceed to the "Cumulated Subject Index" looking up the terms chosen from "Subject Index Terms." A series of numbers follow each subject index term. These numbers are not page numbers but are abstract numbers and locate the abstracts relevant to that term within that volume of *Psychological Abstracts*.

After locating the listed abstracts, the student reads them selecting out those which are useful, copying full bibliographic information for these articles. This author recommends using several cumulated indexes before going to the journals to read the full articles. The student is also directed to begin his search with the most recent cumulated index working back to older ones. If there are monthly indexes more recent than the most recent semiannual cumulated index, these also should be checked for possible references. As references are accumulated in this manner, the student may notice particular authors' names appearing more than once. This sometimes indicates that these authors are currently researching the area and their names should be checked in the "Cumulated Author Index" for any other of their publications of interest to the student. Authors' names, arranged alphabetically in the "Cumulated Author Index," are followed by abstract numbers. These numbers are used in the same way abstract numbers following subject entries are used.

The student may find that the particular library he is using does not carry all of the periodicals for which he has references from *Psychological Abstracts*. This is not necessarily a comment on the quality of the library for few libraries have even a majority of the periodicals indexed in *Psychological Abstracts*. The student can creditably research an area if he uses the articles in the periodicals which his library does carry.

Psychological Abstracts does not index and summarize literature published before 1936. *Psychological Index* (378) lists psychological sources published between 1894 and 1936. The publication of the *Author Index to Psychological Index, 1894-1935* (373) and *Psychological Index: Abstract References* (379) has increased the usefulness of *Psychological Index*. The most comprehensive listing of psychological sources prior to 1900 is found in Rand's *Bibliography of Philosophy, Psychology, and Cognate Subjects* (478).

Specialized abstracts and indexes are numbered 341 through 406. Five examples of these sources are *Child Development Abstracts and Bibliography* (351), *Education Index* (356), *Index Medicus* (363), *Mental Retardation Abstracts* (366), and *Sociological Abstracts* (387). Under the entry "Psychology," indexes often list other entries of interest to psychologists. Thus, looking under "Psychology" and noting what other related entries are included gives the student perspective on the psychological topics covered in a particular index. As with other reference sources, the more the student uses a source the more useful the source becomes.

For most topics chosen by beginning students thorough use of *Psychological Abstracts* produces large numbers of references. The student should check with his instructor to determine whether he wishes the student to search other abstracts and indexes.

These abstracts and indexes list references in areas related to psychology. Psychological information is listed in all of these sources.

SUBJECT	ABSTRACTS AND INDEXES
Anthropology	*International Bibliography of Social and Cultural Anthropology* (364), *Social Sciences and Humanities Index* (385)
Art	*Art Index* (342)
Bibliography	*Bibliographic Index* (531), *Psychological Abstracts* (372), *Education Index* (356)
Biography	*Biography Index* (273), *Essay and General Literature Index* (357)
Biology	*Biological Abstracts* (345), *Biological and Agricultural Index* (346), *BioResearch Index* (347), *Index Medicus* (363), *Technical Book Review Index* (326)
Book Reviews	*Book Review Digest* (316), *Book Review Index* (317), *Canadian Periodical Index* (318), *Essay and General Literature Index* (321), *Index to Book Reviews in the Humanities* (322), *Technical Book Review Index* (326)
Dissertations	*Dissertation Abstracts International* (392), *Masters Abstracts* (393)
Education	*British Education Index* (348), *Canadian Periodical Index* (350), *Child Development Abstracts and Bibliography* (351), *Current Index to Journals in Education* (353), *Education Index* (356), *Poverty and Human Resources Abstracts* (371), *Public Affairs Information Service Bulletin* (381), *Research in Education* (384)
General Subjects	*Canadian Periodical Index* (350), *Readers' Guide to Periodical Literature* (382)
Government	*Monthly Catalog of United States Government Publications* (367, 407), *Public Affairs Information Service Bulletin* (381),
Humanities	*British Humanities Index* (349), *Canadian Periodical Index* (350), *Essay and General Litera-*

	ture Index (357) *Index to Book Reviews in the Humanities* (322), *Social Science and Humanities Index* (385)
Mass Communication	"Articles on Mass Communications in U.S. and Foreign Journals" (343), *Public Affairs Information Service Bulletin* (381), *Social Sciences and Humanities Index* (385)
Medicine	*Bibliography of Medical Reviews* (344), *Biological Abstracts* (345), *BioResearch Index* (347), *Excerpta Medica* (359-362), *Index Medicus* (363)
Music	*Music Index* (368)
Newspapers	*Index to the Times* (390), *New York Times Index* (389), *Subject Index to the Christian Science Monitor* (388), *Wall Street Journal: Index* (391)
Philosophy	*Philosopher's Index* (370), *Social Sciences and Humanities Index* (385)
Physiology	*Biological Abstracts* (345), *Biological and Agricultural Index* (346), *BioResearch Index* (347), *Excerpta Medica, Section 2A: Physiology* (359), *Index Medicus* (363), *Technical Book Review Index* (326)
Sociology	*Excerpta Criminologica* (358), *International Bibliography of Sociology* (365), *Poverty and Human Resources Abstracts* (371), *Social Sciences and Humanities Index* (385), *Sociological Abstracts* (387)
Technology	*Applied Science and Technology Index* (341), *Technical Book Review Index* (326)

The abstracts and indexes below list references primarily of interest to psychologists.

SUBJECT	ABSTRACTS AND INDEXES
Aging	*Adult Development and Aging Abstracts* (394), *Bibliography of Medical Reviews* (344), *Current Literature on Aging* (354), *Excerpta Medica, Section 20: Gerontology and Geriatrics* (362), *Index Medicus* (363)

Book Reviews	*Mental Health Book Review Index* (312)
Child Development	*Child Development Abstracts and Bibliography* (351)
Deafness	*DSH Abstracts* (355)
Delinquency	*Crime and Delinquency Abstracts* (352), *Excerpta Criminologica* (358)
Drugs	*Drug Dependence* (396)
Educational Psychology	*British Education Index* (348), *Child Development Abstracts and Bibliography* (351) *Education Index* (356), *Poverty and Human Resources Abstracts* (371), *Research in Education* (384)
Intelligence	*Perceptual Cognitive Development* (369)
Mental Retardation	*Mental Retardation Abstracts* (366), *Index Medicus* (363)
Psychiatry	*Bibliography of Medical Reviews* (344), *Excerpta Medica, Section 8B: Psychiatry* (360), *Schizophrenia Bulletin* (398)
Psychopharmacology	*Psychopharmacology Abstracts* (380)
Rehabilitation	*Excerpta Medica, Section 19: Rehabilitation and Physical Medicine* (361), *Rehabilitation Literature* (383), *Index Medicus* (363)
Suicide	*Bulletin of Suicidology* (395)

Psychological Abstracts (372) lists articles on all of the subjects mentioned above.

H. Bibliographies.

Bibliographies, lists of sources meaningful to a specific topic, result from a thorough search of the literature. At times the student researching an area may have to make this search himself. At other times he may avail himself of bibliographies compiled by experts. These bibliographies cover topical areas ranging from the very broad to the well circumscribed. The following demonstrates the narrowing of drug topics, all of which have bibliographies available. That is, the general, "drugs" to "hallucinogens" to "L.S.D." Some of the ready-made bibliographies are annotated, describing and sometimes evaluating the references listed. Annotated bibliographies, as abstracted references, expedite the student's decision to read or not read the reference in full.

The following three sources list psychological bibliographies. *Psychological Abstracts* (372) is the most important source for the student writing a research paper. References to bibliographies compiled by experts are listed under the index entry "Bibliographies." *Education Index* (356) lists references to bibliographies under specific topic headings. Thus the student would look under the subject heading closest in meaning to his topic. And the third, a general reference index listing bibliographies in many fields, is *Bibliographic Index* (531). The student would begin his search in this volume by looking under the subject entry "Psychology," only later looking under other subject entries related to psychology.

A complete bibliography of psychoanalytic writings for the years 1900-1960 can be found in Grinstein's *The Index of Psychoanalytic Writings* (470). This work is an expansion and updating of Rickman's *Index Psychoanalyticus, 1893-1926* (471). Bibliographies compiled prior to 1900 are found in Rand's *Bibliography of Philosophy, Psychology, and Cognate Subjects* (478). Louttit gathered all the psychological bibliographies published between 1900 and 1927 and published them in the volume entitled, *Bibliography of Bibliographies of Psychology, 1900-1927* (476).

Psychological Bulletin, Review of Educational Research, and *Annual Review of Psychology* (433) are three important sources which present evaluative surveys of well-defined areas of current psychological research. An extensive bibliography closes each of the articles in these volumes. The thoroughness of these review articles makes their bibliographies especially useful to students. These three sources are indexed in *Psychological Abstracts* (372).

The student, however, has an alternative to using *Psychological Abstracts* when looking for review articles in these sources. *Psychological Bulletin,* a monthly journal containing articles which integrate and critically evaluate original research in all fields of psychology, published its own cumulative index in the September 1967 issue. This subject and author index for reviews between 1940 and 1966 simplifies the task of locating desired articles.

Review of Educational Research reviews several areas of interest to psychology students. These are: educational and psychological testing; growth, development, and learning; guidance, counseling and personnel services; mental and physical health; and statistical methodology. If the student is interested in compiling a bibliography on topics in these areas, he is advised to look through the table of contents of recent volumes of *Review of Educational Research* for articles related to his topic.

Similarly, the student is advised to look through the table of contents of recent volumes of *Annual Review of Psychology* for articles related to any of the following areas: aesthetics, abnormal and clinical psychology, behavioral genetics, comparative psychology and ethology, developmental psychology, education and counseling, industrial psychology, learning and motivation, personality, physiological psychology, psycholinguistics, receptor processes, social psychology, and statistics.

Other sources containing articles with extensive bibliographies are handbooks and serials. Handbooks are numbered 101-268. A serial, usually an annual publication devoted to one general area, contains articles providing up-to-date surveys of narrow fields. Although the topics covered in each publication vary, the serial title remains constant. Because of the specific topical variation, the student needs to check several issues to best use the source. Some of the serials particularly of interest to undergraduate students are: *Advances in Child Development and Behavior* (425), *Advances in Experimental Social Psychology* (426), *International Review of Research in Mental Retardation* (443), *Minnesota Symposium on Child Psychology* (447), *Nebraska Symposium on Motivation* (448), and *Progress in Experimental Personality Research* (451). Serials are numbered 424-461.

Many of the sources students encounter make references to other sources. Thus, encyclopedia articles, textbooks, other books, and especially journal articles can lead to further sources of information. The compilation of a bibliography is a complex process which is more productive if done in a systematic manner. Chapter 4 contains suggestions for putting together a bibliography.

II. Books.

In any library, books of a psychological nature are found by searching the card catalog. But once a particular book has been located, the student must decide whether this indeed is a book related to his area of interest and useful for his purpose. Gathering the following information helps in evaluating the book.

A. *Title:* Are any words in the title related to the student's area of interest?

B. *Author or Editor:* Who is the author? As students become more knowledgeable in psychology, they recognize the names of key writers and researchers in particular areas. Biographical information about the author or editor is most often found on the dustjacket of the book or in the preface.

C. *Copyright Date:* This date is especially important in psychology since new information is constantly being published. And this new information can and often does modify previous conclusions. It is important to distinguish between the copyright date and the imprint date. The copyright date indicates when the book was first published, whereas the imprint date gives the year of the latest reprinting.

D. *Preface or Foreword:* Authors often state the purpose of their work, intended audience and special features or unusual limitations of the book in the preface. The preface thus may facilitate deciding whether the book meets the student's particular needs.

E. *Table of Contents:* The table of contents, whether in outline form or a simple listing of chapters, shows the organizational form and which major topics are included within the book.

F. *Index:* Many books have an index which exactly locates specific information. Usually author and subjects are indexed separately, although sometimes they may be combined into a single index. If the student finds his topic listed in either the table of contents or the index, the book should be examined carefully for relevant material.

G. *Bibliography:* The bibliographies included at the end of individual chapters or at the book's termination gives information regarding the importance of and currentness of sources used in compiling the book. Of course, the more work a student does in an area the more expert he becomes in judging the value of the cited sources.

H. *Introductory Chapter:* Some books are written so that the introductory chapter gives an overview of the book's content with the last chapter summarizing the book. If the first and last chapters are not as indicated above, reading the first and last few pages of each chapter should provide an idea of the authors concerns and discussion.

I. *Additional Information:* Footnotes, reading lists, glossary, appendices, illustrations, graphs, and tables are sources of information not to be ignored.

Textbooks, in addition to the reference works cited in the previous section, can serve as reference sources. Many of the books listed and grouped according to broad subject area in Chapter 5 have been used as textbooks in a variety of psychology courses. These books are excellent sources for a wide range of psychological information. However, because of the time involved in publishing a book, the most recent research is not included. Psychological journals must be searched for the most recent information.

Textbooks are valuable in several ways. Through the use of the book's index, answers to specific questions can be found. For example, parents often have questions related to the growth and development of their children. Some information would be found in introductory textbooks. Child development textbooks, many of which list ages at which babies begin certain activities, provide more detailed answers. Textbooks may be used also to provide an overview or summary of areas of interest to the student. The bibliographies and studies referred to within the body are references to more specialized and detailed works. This writer directs students to note carefully the studies referred to within the textbook for ordinarily the author discusses the most important studies in the area.

Textbooks also assist the student in finding the topical area to look up in a handbook. Looking through several introductory textbooks assists the students in placing his topic within one or two broader areas of psychology. For instance, the student interested in "cognitive dissonance" could look through several introductory textbooks and find the topic discussed in the chapters on social psychology and motivation. The student then pursues his search by looking up "social psychology" and "motivation" in handbooks and/or goes to textbooks on social psychology or motivation for more information on cognitive dissonance. Book reviews and their expert evaluation can help the student decide which of the books in these areas are most pertinent for his purposes.

If a student is having difficulty understanding a theory or needs to understand a particular theoretical position in greater detail than he can find in a textbook, he is advised to select a book specific to that theoretical position. These books describe, summarize, and evaluate the theories within a particular area of psychology and also refer to books or articles in which the theorists made their original statements. For example, four books in developmental psychology and five in social psychology direct themselves specifically to theories. These books are:

Developmental Psychology

Baldwin, Alfred. *Theories of Child Development.* New York: Wiley, 1967.

Langer, Jonas. *Theories of Development.* New York: Holt, Rinehart & Winston, Inc., 1969.

Muss, Rolf. *Theories of Adolescence.* (2nd ed.) New York: Random House, 1968, pb.

Maier, Henry. *Three Theories of Child Development: The Contributions of Erik H. Erikson, Jean Piaget, and Robert Sears.* (Rev. ed.) New York: Harper & Row, 1969.

Social Psychology

Abelson, Robert et al. (Eds.) *Theories of Cognitive Consistency: A Sourcebook.* Chicago: Rand McNally, 1968.

Deutsch, Martin and Krauss, R. *Theories in Social Psychology.* New York: Basic Books, 1965.

Insko, Chester. *Theories of Attitude Change.* New York: Appleton-Century-Crofts, 1967.

Kiesler, Charles et al. *Attitude Change: A Critical Analysis of Theoretical Approaches.* New York: Wiley, 1969.

Shaw, Marvin and Costanzo, P. *Theories of Social Psychology.* New York: McGraw-Hill, 1970.

To select "theory books" from the lists in Chapter 5 select ones with the word "Theory" in the title.

Books of readings, usually collections of previously published journal articles on selected topics, can be especially helpful if the library has a small journal collection. These books cover a wide variety of psychological topics, usually including the most important journal articles from many sources within a single volume. This writer advises students to peruse several books of readings on the same topic as there is surprisingly little overlap from volume to volume in the articles included.

Several books contain lists of selected psychological books varying from those of interest to the layman to those intended for professional psychologists. Students might use these sources as interesting reading or to facilitate the search for references in a particular area. *The Reader's Adviser: A Guide to the Best in Literature* (469) and *Good Reading: A Guide for Serious Readers* (477) contain annotated lists of psychology books for psychology students and the interested layman. *How to Find Out in Philosophy and Psychology* (462) lists and discusses reference sources, including foreign sources. *Professional Problems in Psychology* (463) discusses reference sources published prior to 1953.

Four books group both introductory and technical nonreference books into subject areas. *The Harvard List of Books in Psychology* (472) annotates and groups 704 books into 31 categories. Although many of the sources are technical and the list needs to be updated, this comprehensive list is the most useful for purposes of library research. The second and third sources are *Sources of Information in the Social Sciences* (483) and *A Reader's Guide to the Social Sciences* (474). Both contain fewer psychological sources than *The Harvard List of Books in Psychology* and only some of the books included are annotated. But all three direct the user to significant psychological works. The fourth source is *The New York University Lists of Books in Education* (504). Although primarily a listing of educational sources with annotations, over 50 of the 178 subject areas are on psychological topics.

A list of guides to the literature of fields related to psychology are numbered 484-529. Two examples are *Documentation in Education* (498) and *Guide to Psychiatric Books* (516). These guides can be used if a topic overlaps into other disciplines.

III. Periodicals.

Psychological information is found in both general periodicals and specialized psychological periodicals. The general periodicals, often called magazines, are written for the lay public whereas the psychological periodicals, often called journals, are a vehicle through which psychologists communicate with each other. Magazines such as *Time, Harper's Magazine, Look,* and *Ladies' Home Journal* are indexed in *Readers' Guide to Periodical Literature* (382). Instructors vary in their opinion of the usefulness of these magazines as sources for psychology research projects. The student is cautioned to check with his instructor ascertaining whether he looks upon such sources with favor or disfavor.

Articles within psychological journals generally are of two types. These are articles reporting original research and articles summarizing a specific area, its theoretical position and related research studies. The second type of article, often called a review of the literature, presents less detailed information on each study cited than was given in the original report. These reviews of the literature evaluate the cited studies, relating them to each other and a pertinent theoretical position. See pp. 19 and 20 for a discussion of the major review sources.

Because journal articles are written at a level to be understood by other psychologists, the beginning student may have difficulty completely comprehending this material. Understanding is made easier if the student first reads a summary of the area to which the article directs itself in a textbook related to the area of the article. A psychological dictionary helps the student understand the terminology used in these articles.

Of the many journals, at least five are written in a manner more easily understood by the beginning student. Scanning these journals may help the student discover a topic in which he is interested. These are *Psychology Today, Scientific American, The Journal of Social Issues, American Psychologist,* and *Transaction.*

As was discussed previously, abstracts and indexes facilitate the search for references meaningful to the student's topic. Once a reference is obtained, the student is advised to read the introduction and/or summary of the article before deciding whether to pursue reading in greater depth. If a particular article reporting original research has been selected as worthy of more detailed consideration, knowledge of the general form of such articles speeds gathering information. The general form follows:

A. *Bibliographic Information:* This information includes the title, author, journal, date and pages.

B. *Abstract:* An abstract is a brief summary of the material included in sections C through F.

C. *Introduction to the Topic:* The topic to which the author addresses himself is often termed the "problem." In this section the problem is placed in historical perspective and a statement is made as to the rationale for selecting the problem. A statement of the hypothesis or hypotheses to be tested are also included.

D. *Description of the Method Used to Test the Hypothesis:* Subjects (often abbreviated *Ss*), equipment, and procedure are discussed. Information about the subjects includes any special characteristics required, the process by which they were selected and the number used. The equipment is the material used and the procedure is a detailed description of instructions given to the subjects, how the independent variable was manipulated, the dependent variable measured, and a description of the exact sequence of events in the research.

E. *Presentation of Results:* In this section the researcher explains the relationship between his hypothesis and the data gathered. Do the data confirm or reject the hypothesis? Also included is a description of the statistical tests used to analyze the data.

F. *Discussion of the Results:* An analysis of the results and limitation of the research study are presented. Conclusions are drawn and the study's implications for future research postulated.

G. *Conclusion or Summary:* The summary may be omitted if the article began with an abstract. The summary is a brief statement of the essential information included in sections C through F.

H. *Bibliographic Citations:* References used in a survey of the literature pertinent to the study's area of investigation are listed at the close of the article. Locating these references and their citation of sources can quickly build a useful bibliography.

As a generalization, the most detailed information on a specific research study is in the journal article in which the researcher reported his work. Progressively less detail is found in review articles, handbooks, textbooks of specific areas, general introductory textbooks, psychological encyclopedias and general encyclopedias. Information originally reported in journals is used to compile these other sources. This generalization guides the student to a source commensurate with the detail he is seeking.

IV. Newspapers.

Newspapers disseminate psychological information on topics of interest to the general public. For instance, some of the topics recently discussed and reported in the *New York Times* are: aggression research, battered children, drugs, juvenile delinquency, sleep research, treatment of the mentally ill, testing and intelligence. Different newspapers often publish the same news item on the same day. Thus, an index to one newspaper can serve as a guide to other newspapers. Four of the major newspapers which publish indexes are: *The Times* (London) (390), the *New York Times* (389), the *Christian Science Monitor* (388), and the *Wall Street Journal* (391).

V. Government Documents.

The United States Government publishes a number of documents of interest to psychologists. These documents, usually issued by the Department of Health, Education, and Welfare, are on alcohol usage; developmental psychology: infants, children, adolescents, and aging; drugs; education; juvenile delinquency; mental health and mental illness; mental retardation; psychopharmacology; smoking; suicide; and violence: riots and aggression. Government psychological periodicals are listed on pages 97 and 98. Subject bibliographies published by the government are on pages 66-72. Publication lists issued by agencies of the Department of Health, Education and Welfare are on pages 81 and 82. Because of the variety of ways of classifying and shelving government documents, the interested student should see the reference librarian when he desires to use these sources.

chapter 4

The Library
Research Paper

There is no one method for producing an excellent research paper. The following outline suggests a procedure for choosing a topic, gathering information relevant to that topic, and then writing the paper. However, the suggestions and hints you receive must be modified according to your needs and particular situation.

1. Understand the assignment.

    Some students have discovered that their perception of the assignment differed from the instructor's. Prevent this frustration by carefully rereading the assignment and talking with class members or the instructor to validate your understanding.

2. Choose a topic.
    a. If you are having difficulty choosing a topic, try the following.
        (1) Keep an idea notebook during the term. Write down interesting ideas, controversies, or problems that you want to know more about.
        (2) Review your assigned readings and lecture notes.
        (3) Look over the headings and entries in *Psychological Abstracts* (372).
        (4) Browse through some of the psychological journals, particularly *Psychology Today.*
        (5) Talk with other psychology students about possible topics.
        (6) Ask yourself what is the research information relevant to statements found in newspapers, magazines, or stated on radio and TV broadcasts.

(7) Reflect on behavior you have observed, groups you have been in, or common sense sayings discussed in conversation.

b. Sometimes you will have several topics in mind and the problem then becomes selecting from the alternatives. Considering the following will help in this selection process.

(1) Is the topic psychological?

(2) How has your instructor restricted the assignment?

(3) Is the topic suitable for your level of understanding?

(4) Are you sufficiently interested in the topic to explore it in depth?

(5) Is there enough time to cover the topic well?

(6) Are a variety of sources available for your use?

(7) Can you be objective about the topic?

c. The initial topic selected is usually too broad. Some students narrow their topic before they begin the search for information. More narrow their topic after they have begun the search and can evaluate the availability of information. The four examples below demonstrate the gradual narrowing of a topic.

(1) Intelligence—twin research, identical twin research, analysis of the major studies of the intelligence of identical twins reared apart.

(2) Learning—simple types of learning, operant conditioning, partial reinforcement of operant responses, fixed ratio schedules, fixed ratio schedules with normal human subjects.

(3) Social psychology—attitudes, attitude change, cognitive consistency and attitude change, cognitive dissonance and attitude change, attitude change produced by role playing and the theory of cognitive dissonance.

(4) Mass media and violence—TV violence, effects of viewing TV violence on children, preschool children and the effects of viewing violence when the model is not punished for the violence.

d. The structure imposed on psychology by various sources provides assistance in narrowing a topic. For instance, if you

compare the classification system in Appendix II, the group-
ings in *Psychological Abstracts* (372), and the divisions used
in various textbooks, you notice that each system moves
from broad areas to specific topics. Most chapters in introductory psychology textbooks focus on a major topic. This
topic is then divided into several smaller areas. These areas, in
turn, are further divided into smaller areas. As a general statement, your topic is too large and needs further narrowing if
you find an entire book, encyclopedia article, or chapter in
an introductory text devoted to that topic.

3. Search for sources and compile a bibliography.
   a.   The outline below follows the general guideline of working
      from general to specific sources.
      (1) Begin with your textbook. It is close at hand.
      (2) Look for reference materials. These are listed in Chapter
          5 and can be located through the card catalog.
         (a) For a summary of the area use encyclopedias (73-100)
            and introductory textbooks.
         (b) For definition of key terms use psychological diction-
            aries (1-72) and glossaries.
         (c) For bibliographies see the listings of bibliographies in
            this guide. Use the entry, "Bibliography" in *Psycho-
            logical Abstracts* (372) and use subject entries in *Edu-
            cation Index* (356) and *Bibliographic Index* (531). If
            the topic is in the area of tests and measurements, see
            Mental Measurements Yearbook (308), and for topics
            in the area of psychoanalysis see *Index to Psycho-
            analytic Writings* (470).
      (3) See the lists of books arranged by subject area from
          Chapter 5 to select books in your topic area.
      (4) Gather possible subject headings for use in searching the
          card catalog, indexes, and abstracts.
         (a) Use *Subject Headings Used in the Dictionary Catalogs
            of the Library of Congress* (534). See p. 5 of this
            guide.
         (b) Use *Sear's List of Subject Headings* (535).
         (c) Use a psychological dictionary to find synonymous
            terms.
      (5) Use the card catalog to find books.

(a) Look under the subject headings found in step 4, above, to locate books and their call numbers.

(b) Look up the call number of relevant books listed in Chapter 5 of this guide.

(c) Find the call number of books listed in the bibliographies of encyclopedias and introductory textbooks.

(d) Find the call number of books listed in bibliographies.

(e) Find the call number of books mentioned in other sources.

(6) Find related government documents. See p. 27.

(7) Locate reviews of the literature. First look in handbooks (101-268), then in *Annual Review of Psychology* (433), *Review of Educational Research, Psychological Bulletin,* and pertinent serials (424-461). See pp. 19-20.

(8) Use the abstracts and indexes most appropriate to your topic.

(a) Use *Psychological Abstracts* (372) first. See pp. 13-15.

(b) Use other indexes (341-406).

(c) Begin with the most recent cumulated issue of the index and work backwards.

(d) Look through the recent noncumulated issues.

(9) Look up journal articles.

(a) Group bibliographic references found through the indexes according to journals. Read from the most recent to the oldest.

(b) Check the bibliographies closing each article for other references. This step is especially important. Many psychologists conduct a search of the literature primarily through the use of the bibliographies which close each article. They begin their search with the most recent pertinent reference they can find through *Psychological Abstracts.* This article's bibliographic references send the psychologists to other articles which in turn lead to other references. The area is searched from recent to older references.

(c) Use the procedure suggested on pages 25-26 for reading research journal articles.

(10) Search for the most recent information. Certain journals are apt to be referred to more frequently in the bibliogra-

phy you have compiled. Browse through the most recent issues of these journals to see if any further articles are pertinent.

 b. Take a moment to reflect upon where you have searched and what you have found. Where else might you look?

 c. If you have difficulty, check with the reference librarian or your instructor.

4. Systematically copy bibliographic information for possible sources.

 a. Make a preliminary bibliography card, as soon as a source is found. 3 x 5 and 4 x 6 cards are often used.

  (1) Copy the important bibliographic information for each source on a separate card.

   (a) For a book: author, title, place of publication, publisher, copyright date.

   (b) For a journal article: author, title, journal, year, volume, pages.

   (c) For a book review: reviewer, author and title of book reviewed, review publication, year, volume, pages.

   (d) For unpublished material: author, title, indicate unpublished, where material was obtained, date, pages.

   (e) For a newspaper article: author (if known), title of article, newspaper, date, pages.

  (2) Copy bibliographic information on only one side of a card.

  (3) Copy the call number for a book next to the bibliographic information.

 b. Develop a system for filing and grouping your cards, so that none are lost and each card can be located quickly.

 c. Consider using a photocopying machine for long lists of possible sources.

5. Begin reading.

 a. Read the general sources first and move to more specific material.

 b. Skim sources for major ideas, controversies, and trends.

 c. Record the usefulness of a source on the preliminary bibliography card.

 d. Book reviews (308-326) and their expert evaluation help you decide how to use a specific source.

e. Information about authors from biographical sources (269-307) assists evaluation of an author's expertness.

6. Organize your information into an outline.

Making an outline generates thoughts about organization as well as an awareness of possible gaps in collected information. Your organization is directly related to your topic, the amount and quality of information gathered, and your creative synthesis. The following approaches may be useful in stimulating your thoughts regarding organization of your paper.

a. What is the problem? Are there subdivisions of the problem? How do the research findings fit together? What criticisms have been made of the research? What conclusions do you draw about the research and the problem?

b. What have been the usual approaches to the problem? What independent variables have been studied? What dependent variables have been studied? What are the trends in the findings for each set of variables? How can the inconsistencies in the research findings be explained? If there is consistency, have significant variables or controls been overlooked?

c. What are the various ways the problem has been stated? If the problem is part of a controversy, what are the various viewpoints and the supporting research? Is there a way to unite the different viewpoints?

7. Formulate questions from your outline to be answered from careful study of your sources.

8. Begin careful study. Start with the sources which appear to be the most valuable.

9. Make content note cards.

a. Take content notes only after completing the above steps. This decreases taking irrelevant notes.

b. Summarize in your own words on the note card. It is important to guard against using information out of context or incorrectly summarizing. Study the source until the meaning is understood; then, look away while summarizing in your own words. Rechecking with the original source verifies that you have been accurate and summarized in your own words.

c. Place quotation marks around sentences or groups of words taken directly from the original source. Use direct quotes sparingly. Sentences which are idiosyncratic in their wording or the quote of an expert may be quoted.

d. Include the page number for both summarized information and direct quotes.

e. Devise meaningful headings for your note cards and place the headings in the same place on every card.

10. Be systematic.

   a. Keep all of your note cards in one container where they are secure and not likely to be lost.

   b. Whatever system you use, stick to it after starting.

   c. Do not throw away any of your material until your paper is returned or you receive a grade.

11. Rework your original outline as you find more information and better understand your topic.

12. Write a rough draft from your outline.

   Begin writing by quickly jotting down your thoughts. If you experience difficulty writing a particular section, skip that section and continue writing. Searching for just the right word or phrase at this point isn't worthwhile because you may yet change the organization as you further define your thoughts on the topic.

13. Follow the style suggested by your instructor.

   Know and use the guidelines set forth in the college's or psychology department's style manual. If you desire information on writing, see the manuals in Appendix I.

   Articles submitted for publication in journals of the American Psychological Association are required to follow the style explained in the *Publication Manual of the American Psychological Association* (532). The suggestions below are taken with slight modifications from this manual. For a more detailed explanation, see the *Publication Manual.*

   a. Use the third person rather than the first.
      "This investigator . . . ." "This researcher . . . ."
                    Not "I think . . . ."

   b. Use verb tenses as follows:

      (1) Ordinarily use the past tense. The results of research and descriptions of procedures are written in the past tense.

      (2) Use the present tense for definitions, theoretical statements, and untested hypotheses.

      (3) Avoid use of the future tense.

   c. Use the passive voice to describe procedures.

   d. Use the following abbreviations:

      (1) experimenter, *E*; experimenters, *E*s; experimenter's, *E*'s; experimenters', *E*s'.

(2) subject, S; subjects, Ss; subject's, S's; subjects', Ss'.

(3) observer, O; observers, Os; observer's, O's; observers', Os'.

(4) number of subjects, N.

e. Citations within the body of the paper differ from the citations used in the bibliography. Important words in the title of books, journals, and journal articles are capitalized. Titles of books and journals are underlined and titles of journal articles are placed within quotation marks.

f. Document your material and footnote properly.

(1) The research paper should be in your own words with footnotes or citations to indicate the source of specific information or ideas. The basic citation information is the writer's surname and the date of publication.

(a) If there is no author, use the first words of the title and the publication date in parentheses.

(*Random House Dictionary,* 1968)

(b) If there is one author, use the author's surname and publication date in parentheses.

Another study (Jackson, 1966) reported . . . .

(c) If the author is mentioned, enclose publication date in parentheses.

Jackson (1966) reported . . . .

(d) If there are two authors, use both surnames and an ampersand.

Another study (Jackson & Norm, 1967) reported . . . .

(e) If there are three or more authors, use the surnames of all authors for the first citation and only the surname of the first author plus "et al." for later citations.

Another study (Jackson, Norm, Rath, & Woek, 1968) reported . . . .

The Jackson et al. (1968) research . . . .

(f) If citing several sources at the same time, separate by semicolons and list alphabetically.

Three textbooks (Aiken, 1969; McKeachie & Doyle, 1970; Swift, 1969) . . . .

(g) If more than one source by the same author is cited, separate the publication dates by commas and do not repeat the author. List the earliest publication first.

Four studies (Jackson, 1945, 1951, 1966, 1968) reported . . . .

(h) If two or more sources in the same year by one author are cited, arrange alphabetically by titles and place the letter "a" after the year of the first source and "b" after the second source.

Two studies (Jackson, 1965a, 1965b) reported . . . .

(2) For those few times when you wish to use the exact words of a source, place quotation marks around those words and put the page number in brackets at the end of the quote.

Anderson & Jones (1966) said: ". . . in every maze [p. 12]."

(a) Quotes of less than three lines are incorporated into the text.

(b) Quotes longer than three lines are indented five spaces, single spaced, and the quotation marks are dropped.

(3) Some books on writing research papers suggest that "common knowledge" need not be footnoted. Beginning students in psychology often have difficulty knowing whether certain information is common knowledge. Also some information believed by laymen is questioned by psychologists. If there is the slightest doubt, footnote or give the citation.

g. Prepare your reference lists.

(1) Within psychology a variety of forms are used. Consistent use of form and accurate citation are both very important. The recommendations listed below follow closely those in the *Publication Manual* (532).

(a) Book: The basic information is author, title, place of publication, publisher, year of publication with the title underlined. Capitalize only the first letter of the first word of a title. Edition is abbreviated (ed.) and editor is abbreviated (Ed.).

Jackson, D.E. *Psychological problems.* New York: Find Press, 1965.

Mason, P.L. (Ed.) *Psychological illnesses in lower class males.* (3rd ed.) Waltham, Mass.: New Press, 1968. 3 vols.

Use an ampersand with more than one author. If using a chapter of an edited book, provide page numbers.

Jackson, D.E. & Norm, F.G. The problem of anxiety. In H.I. Kahl (Ed.) *Problems of psychology*. London: Oxford University Press, 1955. Pp. 20-45.

(b) Periodicals: The basic information is author, title, name of journal (underlined), year published, volume, pages without the p. or pp. Capitalize only the first letter of the first word of an article title.

Barn, J.S. Intelligence and creativity in preschool children. *American Psychologist,* 1952, 7, 33-36.

(c) Secondary sources: If you are not able to locate the original, give information for both the original and the secondary source.

Hoop, S.S. Creativity in rats. *Journal of Unusual Behavior,* 1970, 2, 345-443. (*Psychological Abstracts,* 1970, 44, No. 4433)

Martin, R.R. Perceptions. *Journal of Early Psychology,* 1901, 1, 1-2. Cited by J. Pull, *History of psychology*. Chicago: Historical Press, 1950, P. 41.

(d) Book reviews: In addition to the usual citation, add the name of the book and its author.

Larson, J. Review of D.E. Jackson, *Psychological problems. Contemporary Psychology,* 1966, 11, 13.

(e) Unpublished materials:

Dissertations: Doe, J.S. *Cognitive dissonance and anxiety.* Unpublished doctoral dissertation, University of Minnesota, 1966.

Paper read at a scientific meeting: Doe, J.E. Cognitive dissonance and role playing. Paper presented at the meeting of the Eastern Psychological Association, New York, May 1967.

Other materials: Smith, P.S. Frustration-aggression and projection. Unpublished manuscript. Elmira College Library, 1970.

(2) Grouping of sources.

Traditionally all sources footnoted or cited in the student's paper are listed in alphabetical order by authors' surname in a section entitled "Bibliography" or "References." Some writers suggest that references for sources meaningful to the student's topic though not cited within the body of his paper also be listed. At times books or journals the student wishes to use are unavailable. Thus this writer recommends four mutually exclusive listings of sources.

(a) "References Used" includes all and only references cited in the paper.

(b) "References Read" includes sources read but not cited. These sources should be annotated to show their relevance to the topic.

(c) "References Unavailable" is a listing of sources which appeared relevant but were unavailable. These entries are annotated when possible.

(d) "Other Sources" includes interviews, personal observations, and other unpublished materials.

14. Revise your paper.

Allowing a period of time to elapse between drafts of the paper provides a better perspective on your work. After the time gap rewrite and polish your paper into a superior finished product.

15. Type the final copy of the paper. Carefully proofread your paper making minor corrections in ink. The following are included in the completed product.

a. Title page: The title page includes the following information: descriptive title, your name, class, instructor's name, and date handed in.

b. Abstract: An abstract is a brief summary of what your topic is and what you found.

c. Outline: If an outline is required, it is placed on a separate page following the abstract.

d. Research paper discussion.

e. References: Start a new page for the first list of references.

16. Staple, paperclip or put your research paper in a binder to be handed in.

chapter 5

Lists of
Psychological Sources

Psychological Dictionaries

1. American Psychiatric Association. *A psychiatric glossary.* (3rd ed.) New York: Springer, 1969, pb.

2. Baker, Rachel. *Sigmund Freud.* New York: J. Messner, 1952.

3. Baldwin, James. *Dictionary of philosophy and psychology.* New York: Macmillan, 1905.

4. Brussel, James, and Cantzlaar, G. *The layman's dictionary of psychiatry.* New York: Barnes and Noble, 1967, pb.

5. California Test Bureau. *A glossary of measurement terms.* Monterey, Calif.: The Bureau, 1960, pb.

6. Chaplin, James. *Dictionary of psychology.* New York: Dell, 1968, pb.

7. Davitz, Joel et al. *Terminology and concepts in mental retardation.* New York: Teachers College Press, 1964, pb.

8. Diamond, Robert, and Woodward, J. *The amateur psychologist's dictionary.* New York: Arco, 1966, pb.

9. *A dictionary of terms in measurement and guidance.* New York: Psychological Corporation, 1939.

10. Drever, James. *A dictionary of psychology.* Revised by Harvey Wallerstein. Baltimore: Penguin, 1964, pb.

11. English, Horace, and English, A. *A comprehensive dictionary of psychological and psychoanalytical terms.* New York: McKay, 1958. (p. 7)

12. Erdelyi, M., and Grossman, F. *Dictionary of terms and expressions of industrial psychology.* New York: Pitman, 1939.

13. Ferm, Vergilius (Ed.) *A dictionary of pastoral psychology.* New York: Philosophical Library, 1955.

14. Fodor, Nandor, and Gaynor, F. (Eds.) *Freud: dictionary of psychoanalysis.* New York: Philosophical Library, 1958.

15. Fraser, D. *Basic concepts in modern psychology.* Cambridge, England: Heffer, 1963.

16. Harriman, Phillip. *Handbook of psychological terms.* (3rd ed.) Totowa, N.J.: Littlefield, Adams, 1970, pb.

17. Harriman, Philip. (Ed.) *The new dictionary of psychology.* New York: Philosophical Library, 1947.

18. Heidenreich, Charles. *A dictionary of personality: behavior and adjustment terms.* Dubuque, Iowa: Wm. C. Brown Company Publishers, 1968, pb.

19. Hinsie, Leland, and Campbell, R. *Psychiatric dictionary.* (4th ed.) New York: Oxford, 1970.

20. Hopke, William (Ed.) *Dictionary of personnel and guidance terms: including professional agencies and associations.* Chicago: J.G. Ferguson, 1968.

21. Hutchings, Richard. *A psychiatric word book.* (7th ed.) Utica, New York: State Hospital Press, 1943.

22. Kahn, Samuel. *Psychological and neurological definitions and the unconscious.* Boston: Meador, 1940.

23. Kupper, William. *Dictionary of psychiatry and psychology.* Paterson, N.J.: Colt Press, 1953.

24. Lingeman, Richard. *Drugs from A to Z: a dictionary.* New York: McGraw-Hill, 1969, pb.

25. Moore, Burness, and Fine, B. (Eds.) *A glossary of psychoanalytic terms and concepts.* (2nd ed.) New York: American Psychoanalytic Association, 1968.

26. Myers, Lou. *A psychiatric glossary: a cartoon view of the world of psychiatry.* New York: Dutton, 1962.

27. Rycroft, Charles. *A critical dictionary of psychoanalysis.* New York: Basic Books, 1968.

28. Stone, Calvin. *Abnormal psychology glossary.* Stanford, Calif.: Stanford, 1954.

29. Tuke, D. *A dictionary of psychological medicine . . .* London: Churchill, 1892.

30. Verplanck, W. *A glossary of some terms used in the objective science of behavior.* Washington: American Psychological Association, 1957.

31. Warren, Howard. *Dictionary of psychology.* New York: Houghton Mifflin, 1934.

32. Wilkening, Howard, and Van Dycke, L. *A student's psychology handbook.* San Francisco: Chandler, 1958, pb.

33. Williams, L. *A glossary for students of educational psychology.* Norman, Okla.: University of Oklahoma Book Exchange, 1965.

34. Wulfeck, J., and Bennett, E. *The language of dynamic psychology.* New York: McGraw-Hill, 1954.

Other Specialized Dictionaries

35. Abercrombie, M. et al. *A dictionary of biology.* Chicago: Aldine, 1962.

36. American Medical Association. *Current medical terminology.* (3rd ed.) Chicago: American Medical Association, 1966.

37. Armour, Richard. *A diabolical dictionary of education.* New York: World, 1969.

38. Burton, Maurice. *University dictionary of mammals of the world.* New York: Apollo, 1968.

39. Chandor, A. (Ed.) *Dictionary of computers.* Baltimore: Penguin, 1970.

40. *Dorland's illustrated medical dictionary.* (24th ed.) Philadelphia: Saunders, 1965.

41. Fairchild, Henry (Ed.) *Dictionary of sociology.* New York: Philosophical Library, 1944, pb.

42. Freund, John, and Williams, F. *Dictionary and outline of basic statistics.* New York: McGraw-Hill 1967, pb.

43. Good, Carter (Ed.) *Dictionary of education.* (2nd ed.) New York: McGraw-Hill, 1959.

44. Gould, Julius, and Kolb, W. (Eds.) *A dictionary of the social sciences.* New York: Free Press, 1964.

45. Gray, Peter. *The dictionary of the biological sciences.* New York: Van Nostrand Reinhold, 1967.

46. Henderson, Isabella, and Henderson, W. *A dictionary of biological terms.* (8th ed.) New York: Van Nostrand Reinhold, 1963.

47. Hoerr, Norman, and Osol, A. (Eds.) *Blakiston's new Gould medical dictionary.* (2nd ed.) New York: Blakiston, 1956.

48. Horn, Jack. *Computer and data processing dictionary and guide.* Englewood Cliffs, N.J.: Prentice-Hall, 1966.

49. Hoult, Thomas. *Dictionary of modern sociology.* Totowa, N.J.: Littlefield, Adams, 1969, pb.

50. Jaeger, Edmund. *A sourcebook of biological names and terms.* (3rd ed.) Springfield, Ill.: Thomas, 1955.

51. Keller, Mark, and McCormick, M. *A dictionary of words about alcohol.* New Brunswick, N.J.: Rutgers Center of Alcohol Studies, 1968.

52. Kendall, Maurice, and Buckland, W. *Dictionary of statistical terms.* (2nd ed.) New York: Hafner, 1960.

53. Leftwich, A. *A dictionary of zoology.* (2nd ed.) New York: Van Nostrand Reinhold, 1967.

54. Mihanovich, Clement et al. *Glossary of sociological terms.* Milwaukee: Bruce, 1957.

55. Mitchell, Geoffrey (Ed.) *A dictionary of sociology.* Chicago: Aldine, 1968.

56. Nice, Richard (Ed.) *Dictionary of criminology.* New York: Philosophical Library, 1965.

57. Panunzio, Constantine. *A student's dictionary of sociological terms.* Berkeley, Calif.: University of California Press, 1941.

58. Parr, John, and Young, R. (Eds.) *Parr's concise medical encyclopaedia.* Amsterdam, N.Y.: Elsevier, 1965.

59. Pennack, Robert. *Collegiate dictionary of zoology.* New York: Ronald, 1964.

60. Poser, Charles. *International dictionary of drugs used in neurology and psychiatry.* Springfield, Ill.: Thomas, 1962.

61. Reissner, Albert, and Wade, C. *Dictionary of sexual terms.* Bridgeport, Conn.: Associated Booksellers, 1967.

62. Runes, Dagobert (Ed.) *Dictionary of philosophy.* New York: Philosophical Library, 1942.

63. Sippl, Charles. *Computerman's dictionary.* Los Angeles: Trio Management Science Publications, 1965.

64. Sippl, Charles. *Computer dictionary and handbook.* Indianapolis, Ind.: Howard W. Sams, 1966.

65. Stedman, Thomas. *Stedman's medical dictionary.* (21st ed.)Baltimore: Williams and Wilkins, 1966.

66. Taber, Clarence. *Taber's cyclopedic medical dictionary.* (10th ed.)Philadelphia:Davis, 1965.

67. Theodorson, George, and Theodorson, A. *A modern dictionary of sociology.* New York: Crowell, 1969, pb.

68. Thompson, William. *Black's medical dictionary.*(28th ed.) London: Black, 1969.

69. Winick, Charles. *Dictionary of anthropology.* New York: Greenwood, 1969, pb.

70. Winn, Ralph. *Dictionary of hypnosis.* New York: Philosophical Library, 1965.

71. Young, Earl. *Dictionary of social welfare.* New York: Social Sciences, 1948.

72. Zadrozny, John (Ed.) *Dictionary of social sciences.* Washington: Public Affairs Press, 1959.

Encylopedias

73. Beigel, Hugo. *Encyclopedia of sex education.* New York: Stephen Daye Press, 1952.

74. Blishen, Edward (Ed.) *Encyclopedia of education.* New York: Philosophical Library, 1970.

75. Branham, Vernon, and Kutash, S. (Eds.) *Encyclopedia of criminology.* New York: Philosophical Library, 1949.

76. Deutsch, Albert (Ed.) *Encyclopedia of mental health.* New York: Franklyn Watts, 1963. 6 vols. (p. 8)

77. Dublin, Louis. *Factbook on man: from birth to death.* (2nd ed.) New York:Macmillan, 1965.

78. Ebel, Robert (Ed.) *Encyclopedia of educational research.*(4th ed.) New York: Macmillan, 1969.

79. Edwards, Paul et al. (Eds.) *Encyclopedia of philosophy.* New York: Macmillan, 1967. 8 vols.

80. Eidelberg, Ludwig (Ed.) *Encyclopedia of psychoanalysis.* New York: Free Press, 1968. 2 vols. (p. 8)

81. Ellis, Albert, and Abarbanel, A. (Eds.) *Encyclopedia of sexual behavior.* (2nd ed.) New York:Hawthorn Books, 1967. 2 vols., pb.

82. Fodor, Nandor. *Encyclopaedia of psychic science.* New Hyde Park, New York: University Books, 1966.

83. Goldenson, Robert (Ed.) *The encyclopedia of human behavior: psychology, psychiatry, and mental health.* New York: Doubleday, 1970. 2 vols. (p. 8)

84. Gray, Peter (Ed.) *The encyclopedia of the biological sciences.* (2nd ed.)New York: Van Nostrand Reinhold, 1970.

85. Gruenberg, Sidonie (Ed.) *The new encyclopedia of child care and guidance.* New York: Doubleday, 1968.

86. Harriman, Philip (Ed.) *Encyclopedia of psychology.* New York: Philosophical Library, 1946. (p. 8)

87. Hastings, James (Ed.) *Encyclopaedia of religion and ethics.* New York: Scribner, 1908-1927. 12 vols.

88. Jordain, Philip. *Condensed computer encyclopedia.* New York: McGraw-Hill, 1969.

89. Koch, Sigmund (Ed.) *Psychology: a study of a science.* New York: McGraw-Hill, 1954-1963. 7 vols.

90. *McGraw-Hill encyclopedia of science and technology, The.* (Rev. ed.)New York: McGraw-Hill, 1967. 15 vols.

91. Monroe, Paul (Ed.) *Cyclopedia of education.* New York: Macmillan, 1913. 5 vols.

92. Narramore, Clyde. *Encyclopedia of psychological problems.* Grand Rapids, Mich.: Zondervan, 1966.

93. Podolsky, Edward. *Encyclopedia of aberrations: a psychiatric handbook.* New York: Philosophical Library, 1966.

94. Rivlin, Harry, and Schueler, H. (Eds.) *Encyclopedia of modern education.* New York: Philosophical Library, 1943.

95. Roman, Klara et al. (Eds.) *Encyclopedia of the written word: a lexicon for graphology and other aspects of writing.* New York: Ungar, 1968.

96. Seligman, E., and Johnson, A. (Eds.) *Encyclopaedia of the social sciences.* New York: Macmillan, 1930-1935. 15 vols.

97. Sills, David et al. (Eds.) *The international encyclopedia of the social sciences.* New York: Macmillan, 1968. 17 vols. (p. 8)

98. Smith, Edward et al. *The educator's encyclopedia.* Englewood Cliffs, N.J.: Prentice-Hall, 1961.

99. Watson, Foster (Ed.) *The encyclopaedia and dictionary of education.* London: Pitman, 1921-1922. 4 vols.

100. Winn, R. (Ed.) *Encyclopedia of child guidance.* New York: Philosophical Library, 1943.

Handbooks

101. Abelson, Robert et al. (Eds.) *Theories of cognitive consistency: a sourcebook.* Chicago: Rand McNally, 1968.

102. Agranowitz, Aleen, and McKeown, M. *Aphasia handbook: for adults and children.* (2nd ed.) Springfield, Ill.: Thomas, 1970.

103. Allen, Robert, and Allen, S. *Intellectual evaluation of the mentally retarded child: a handbook.* Beverly Hills, Calif: Western Psychological Services, 1967, pb.

104. American Medical Association. *Mental retardation: a handbook for the primary physician.* Chicago: The Association, 1965, pb.

105. American Physiological Society. *Handbook of physiology.* Baltimore: Williams and Wilkins, 1959-1968. 15 vols.

106. Andrews, T. (Ed.) *Methods of psychology.* New York: Wiley, 1948.

107. Ard, Ben, and Ard, C. (Eds.) *Handbook of marriage counseling.* Palo Alto, Calif.: Science and Behavior, 1969.

108. Arieti, Silvano. *American handbook of psychiatry.* New York: Basic Books, 1959-1966. 3 vols.

109. Avedon, Elliot, and Arje, F. *Socio-recreative programing for the retarded: a handbook for sponsoring groups.* New York: Teachers College Press, 1964.

110. Backstrom, Charles, and Hursh, G. *Survey research.* Evanston, Ill.: Northwestern University Press, 1963.

111. Barnes, Charles, and Eltherington, L. *Drug dosage in laboratory animals: a handbook.* Berkeley: University of California Press, 1964, pb.

112. Beizmann, Cecile. *Handbook for scorings of Rorschach responses.* New York: Grune and Stratton, 1970.

113. Bellack, Leopold (Ed.) *Handbook of community psychiatry and community mental health.* New York: Grune and Stratton, 1963.

114. Bensberg, Gerard (Ed.) *Teaching the mentally retarded: a handbook for ward personnel.* Southern Regional Education Board, 1965.

115. Berelson, Bernard, and Steiner, G. *Human behavior: an inventory of scientific findings.* New York: Harcourt, Brace and World, 1964. (p. 9)

116. Berger, Henry. *Encyclopedic diagnosis of nervous and mental diseases.* (9th ed.) St. Louis: Od Peacock Sulton Co., 1943.

117. Bergin, Allen, and Garfield, S. (Eds.) *Handbook of psychotherapy and behavior change: an empirical analysis.* New York: Wiley, 1970.

118. Bernstein, Allen. *A handbook of statistics solutions for the behavioral sciences.* New York: Holt, Rinehart & Winston, 1964.

119. Bindman, Arthur, and Spiegel, A. *Perspectives in community mental health.* Chicago: Aldine, 1969.

120. Birren, James (Ed.) *Handbook of aging and the individual.* Chicago: University of Chicago Press, 1959.

121. Blinkov, Samuil, and Glezer, L. *The human brain in figures and tables: a quantitative handbook.* New York: Plenum Press, 1968.

122. Bloodstein, Oliver. *A handbook on stuttering.* Chicago: National Easter Seal Society for Crippled Children and Adults, 1969, pb.

123. Bonime, Walter. *The clinical use of dreams.* New York: Basic Books, 1962.

124. Borgatta, Edgar, and Lambert, W. (Eds.) *Handbook of personality theory and research.* Chicago: Rand McNally, 1968. (p. 9)

125. Braceland, Francis, and Stock, M. *Modern psychiatry: a handbook for believers.* Garden City, N.Y.: Doubleday, 1963, pb.

126. Brackbill, Yvonne (Ed.) *Infancy and early childhood: a handbook and guide to human development.* New York: Free Press, 1967. (p. 9)

127. Bruning, James, and Kintz, B. *Computational handbook of statistics.* Glenview, Ill.: Scott, Foresman and Company, 1968, pb.

128. Brussel, James. *The physician's concise handbook of psychiatry.* New York: Brunner/Mazel, 1969. (p. 10)

129. Burgess, Ernest (Ed.) *Aging in western culture.* Chicago: University of Chicago Press, 1960.

130. Burington, Richard, and May, D. *Handbook of probability and statistics with tables.* (2nd ed.) New York: McGraw-Hill, 1970.

131. Callis, Robert et al. *The counselor's handbook: profile interpretations of the Strong Vocational Blanks.* Urbana, Ill.: Parkinson and Associates, 1965.

132. Campbell, David. *Handbook for the Strong Vocational Interest blank.* Stanford, Calif.: Stanford University Press, 1970.

133. Cantril, Hadley. *Public opinion: 1935-1946.* Princeton: Princeton University Press, 1951.

134. Carkhuff, Robert et al. *The counselor's handbook: scale and profile interpretations of the MMPI.* Urbana, Ill.: Parkinson and Associates, 1965.

135. Carter, Charles (Ed.) *Medical aspects of mental retardation.* Springfield, Ill.: Thomas, 1965.

136. Carter, Charles (Ed.) *Handbook of mental retardation syndromes.*(2nd ed.)Springfield, Ill.: Thomas, 1970.

137. Cattell, Raymond (Ed.) *Handbook of multivariate experimental psychology.* Chicago: Rand McNally, 1966.

138. Cattell, Raymond (Ed.) *Handbook of modern personality study.* Chicago: Aldine, 1971.

139. Chakravarti, Indra. *Handbook of methods of applied statistics.* New York: Wiley, 1967.

140. Christensen, Harold (Ed.) *Handbook of marriage and the family.* Chicago: Rand McNally, 1964.

141. Cole, Michael, and Maltzman, I. (Eds.) *Handbook of contemporary Soviet psychology.* New York: Basic Books, 1969.

142. Costello, Charles (Ed.) *Symptoms of psychopathology: a handbook.* New York: Wiley, 1970.

143. Cuddon, Eric. *The meaning and practice of hypnosis.* New York: Citadel, 1965, pb.

144. Dahlstrom, W., and Welsh, G. *An MMPI handbook: a guide to use in clinical practice and research.* Minneapolis: University of Minnesota Press, 1960.

145. Damm, Henry (Ed.) *The handbook of biochemistry and biophysics.* Cleveland: World, 1966.

146. Davies, Ida. *Handbook for volunteers in mental hospitals.* Minneapolis: University of Minnesota Press, 1950.

147. Davis, Ross, and Huffman, R. *A stereotaxic atlas of the brain of the baboon (Papio).* Austin: University of Texas Press, 1968.

148. DeGroot, J. *The rat forebrain in stereotaxic co-ordinates.* Amsterdam: North Holland Publishing Company, 1959.

149. DeLucchi, M. *A stereotaxic atlas of the chimpanzee brain (Pan satyrus).* Berkeley: University of California Press, 1965.

150. Dichter, Ernest. *Handbook of consumer motivation.* New York: McGraw-Hill, 1964.

151. Dorcus, Roy, and Jones, M. *Handbook of employee selection.* New York: McGraw-Hill, 1950.

152. Dreikurs, Rudolph, and Grey, L. *Logical consequences: a handbook of discipline.* New York: Meredith, 1968.

153. Ellis, Norman (Ed.) *Handbook of mental deficiency: psychological theory and research.* New York: McGraw-Hill, 1963.

154. Emmers, Raimond, and Akert, K. *A stereotaxic atlas of the brain of the squirrel monkey (Saimiri sciureus).* Madison, Wis.: University of Wisconsin Press, 1963.

155. Eysenck, Hans (Ed.) *Handbook of abnormal psychology.* New York: Basic Books, 1961.

156. Falkner, Frank (Ed.) *Human development.* Philadelphia: Saunders, 1966.

157. Faris, Robert (Ed.) *Handbook of modern sociology.* Chicago: Rand McNally, 1964.

158. Farris, E. (Ed.) *The care and breeding of laboratory animals.* New York: Wiley, 1950.

159. Foshay, Arthur (Ed.) *The Rand McNally handbook of education.* Chicago: Rand McNally, 1963.

160. Fraenkel, William. *The mentally retarded and their vocational rehabilitation: a resource handbook.* New York: National Association for Retarded Children, 1961.

161. Freedman, Alfred, and Kaplan, H. (Eds.) *Comprehensive textbook of psychiatry.* Baltimore: Williams and Wilkins, 1967.

162. Fross, Garland. *Handbook of hypnotic techniques.* Irvington, N.J.: Power Publications, 1966.

163. Fryer, Douglas, and Henry, E. (Eds.) *Handbook of applied psychology.* New York: Rinehart, 1950. 2 vols.

164. Fusfeld, Irving (Ed.) *A handbook of readings in education of the deaf and postschool implications.* Springfield, Ill.: Thomas, 1967.

165. Gage, N. (Ed.) *Handbook of research on teaching.* Chicago: Rand McNally, 1963.

166. Gergen, John, and MacLean, P. *A stereotaxic atlas of the squirrel monkey's brain (Saimiri sciureus).* Bethesda, Md.: Public Health Service Publication No. 933, 1962.

167. Gilberstadt, Harold, and Duker, J. *A handbook of clinical and acturial MMPI interpretations.* Philadelphia: Saunders, 1965.

168. Gordon, Jesse (Ed.) *Handbook of clinical and experimental hypnosis.* New York: Macmillan, 1967.

169. Goslin, David (Ed.) *Handbook of socialization theory and research.* Chicago: Rand McNally, 1969.

170. Greulich, William et al. *A handbook of methods for the study of adolescent children.* Washington: Society for Research in Child Development, National Research Council, 1938.

171. Griffith, John, and Farris, E. (Eds.) *The rat in laboratory investigations.* Philadelphia: Lippincott, 1942.

172. Gutheil, Emil. *Handbook of dream analysis.* New York: Liveright, 1970, pb.

173. Hankoff, L. *Emergency psychiatric treatment: handbook of secondary prevention.* Springfield, Ill.: Thomas, 1969.

174. Hare, Paul. *Handbook of small group research.* New York: Free Press, 1962.

175. Harms, Ernest (Ed.) *The handbook of child guidance.* (2nd ed.) New York: Child Care Publications, 1947.

176. Harms, Ernest, and Schreiber, P. (Eds.) *Handbook of counseling techniques.* New York: Macmillan, 1964.

177. Hart, Jane, and Jones, B. *Where's Hannah? a handbook for parents and teachers of children with behavior disorders.* New York: Hart Publishing Co., 1968.

178. Herma, Hans, and Kurth, G. (Eds.) *A handbook of psychoanalysis.* Cleveland: World, 1963, pb.

179. Herron, William et al. *Contemporary school psychology.* Scranton, Pa.: International Textbook, 1970.

180. Hoffman, Martin, and Hoffman, L. (Eds.) *Review of child development research.* New York: Russell Sage, 1964, 1966. 2 vols.

181. Hunt, J. (Ed.) *Personality and the behavior disorders.* New York: Ronald, 1944. 2 vols.

182. Huskey, Harry, and Korn, G. (Eds.) *Computer handbook.* New York: McGraw-Hill, 1962.

183. Jasper, H., and Ajmone-Marson, C. *A stereotaxic atlas of the diencephalon of the cat.* Ottawa: National Research Council of Canada, 1954.

184. Jolles, Isaac, and Southwick, S. *A clinical approach to training the educable mentally retarded: a handbook.* Beverly Hills, Calif.: Western Psychological Services, 1969, pb.

185. Karten, Harvey, and Hodos, W. *A stereotaxic atlas of the brain of the pigeon.* Baltimore: The John Hopkins Press, 1967.

186. Katz, Jay et al. (Eds.) *Psychoanalysis, psychiatry, and law.* New York: Free Press, 1967.

187. Klemer, Richard (Ed.) *Counseling in marital and sexual problems: a physician's handbook.* Baltimore: Williams and Wilkins, 1965.

188. Kline, Nathan. *Handbook of psychiatric treatment in medical practice.* Philadelphia: Saunders, 1962.

189. Koch, R., and Dobson, J. (Eds.) *The mentally retarded child and his family: a multidisciplinary handbook.* New York: Brunner/Mazel, 1970.

190. Lafayette Clinic, Detroit. *Handbooks in psychiatry.* Detroit: Wayne State University Press, 1967.

191. Lamb, Richard et al. (Eds.) *Handbook of community mental health practice.* San Francisco: Jossey-Bass, 1969.

192. Lanyon, Richard. *A handbook of MMPI group profiles.* Minneapolis: University of Minnesota Press, 1969.

193. Laughlin, Henry. *The neuroses.* New York: Appleton-Century-Crofts, 1967.

194. Levitas, G. (Ed.) *The world of psychoanalysis.* New York: Braziller, 1965. 2 vols.

195. Levitas, G. (Ed.) *The world of psychology*. New York: Braziller, 1963. 2 vols.

196. Linder, Robert, and Seliger, R. (Eds.) *Handbook of correctional psychology*. New York: Philosophical Library, 1947.

197. Lindzey, Gardner (Ed.) *Handbook of social psychology*. Reading, Mass.: Addison-Wesley, 1954. 2 vols.

198. Lindzey, Gardner, and Aronson, E. (Eds.) *The handbook of social psychology*. (2nd ed.) Reading, Mass.: Addison-Wesley, 1968-1969. 5 vols. (p. 9)

199. Linn, Louis. *A handbook of hospital psychiatry: a practical guide to therapy*. New York: International Universities Press, 1969, pb.

200. Luce, Robert et al. (Eds.) *Handbook of mathematical psychology*. New York: Wiley, 1963-1965. 3 vols.

201. MacDonald, Elizabeth (Ed.) *Occupational therapy in rehabilitation: a handbook.* Baltimore: Williams and Wilkins, 1965.

202. McGrath, Joseph, and Altman, I. *Small group research.* New York: Holt, Rinehart & Winston, 1966.

203. Magary, James (Ed.) *School psychological services in theory and practice: a handbook*. Englewood Cliffs, N.J.: Prentice-Hall, 1967.

204. Manocha, Sohan et al. *A stereotaxic atlas of the brain of the Debus monkey (Cebus Apella)*. New York: Oxford, 1969.

205. March, James (Ed.) *Handbook of organizations*. New York: Rand McNally, 1965.

206. Miller, Delbert. *Handbook of research design and social measurement.*(2nd ed.)Glenview, Ill.: Scott, Foresman, 1970, pb.

207. Miller, Emanuel (Ed.) *Foundations of child psychiatry*. Elmsford, N.Y.: Pergamon, 1968.

208. Miller, Richard, and Burack, E. *Atlas of the central nervous system of man.* Baltimore: Williams and Wilkins, 1968.

209. Milt, Harry. *Basic handbook on alcoholism.* Fair Haven, N.J.: Scientific Aids Publications, 1967.

210. Milt, Harry. *Basic handbook on mental illness.* Fair Haven, N.J.: Scientific Aids Publications, 1967.

211. Moreno, Jacob (Ed.) *The international handbook of group psychotherapy*. New York: Philosophical Library, 1966.

212. Muensterberger, W., and Axelrad, S. (Eds.) *Psychoanalytic study of society.* New York: International Universities Press, 1960-1967. 4 vols.

213. Munn, Norman (Ed.) *Handbook of psychological research on the rat.* Boston: Houghton Mifflin, 1950.

214. Murchison, Carl (Ed.) *Foundations of experimental psychology.* Worcester, Mass.: Clark University Press, 1929.

215. Murchison, Carl (Ed.) *Handbook of child psychology.* (2nd ed.) Worcester, Mass.: Clark University Press, 1933.

216. Murchison, Carl (Ed.) *Handbook of general experimental psychology.* Worcester, Mass.: Clark University Press, 1934.

217. Murchison, Carl (Ed.) *Handbook of social psychology.* Worcester, Mass: Clark University Press, 1935.

218. Murstein, Bernard (Ed.) *Handbook of projective techniques.* New York: Basic Books, 1965.

219. Mussen, Paul (Ed.) *Handbook of research methods in child development.* New York: Wiley, 1960.

220. Mussen, Paul (Ed.) *Carmichael's manual of child psychology.* (3rd ed.) New York: Wiley, 1970. 2 vols. (p. 9)

221. Napier, John, and Napier, P. *A handbook of living primates.* London: Academic Press, 1967.

222. National Council on the Aging. *Resources for the aging: an action handbook.* New York: National Council on the Aging. n.d.

223. National Mental Health Foundation. *Handbook for psychiatric aides.* Philadelphia: National Mental Health Foundation, 1946.

224. Neel, Ann. *Theories of psychology: a handbook.* Boston: Schenkman, 1968, pb.

225. Nice, Richard. *A handbook of abnormal psychology.* New York: Philosophical Library, 1955.

226. North, Robert et al. *Content analysis: a handbook with applications for the study of international crisis.* Evanston, Ill.: Northwestern University Press, 1963, pb.

227. Nylen, D. et al. *Handbook of staff development and human relations training: materials developed for use in Africa.* Washington: National Training Laboratories, 1967.

228. Ogdon, Donald. *Psychodiagnostics and personality assessment: a handbook.* Beverly Hills, Calif.: Western Psychological Services, 1967.

229. Olszewski, J. *The thalamus of the Macaca mulatta: an atlas for use with the stereotaxic instrument.* New York: S. Karger, 1952.

230. Osgood, Charles. *Method and theory in experimental psychology.* New York: Oxford, 1953.

231. Owen, Donald. *Handbook of statistical tables.* Reading, Mass.: Addison-Wesley, 1962.

232. Pearson, Gerald (Ed.) *Handbook of child psychoanalysis.* New York: Basic Books, 1968.

233. Pelligrino, Louis, and Cushman, A. *A stereotaxic atlas of the rat brain.* New York: Appleton-Century-Crofts, 1967.

234. Pillsbury, W., and Pennington, L. *Handbook of general psychology.* New York: Dryden, 1944.

235. Reuter, Edward. *Handbook of sociology.* New York: Dryden, 1941.

236. Robertiello, Richard. *A handbook of emotional illness and treatment.* Larchmont, N.Y.: Argonaut, 1962.

237. Roberts, Melville, and Hanaway, J. *Atlas of the human brain in section.* Philadelphia: Lea and Febiger, 1970.

238. Rosevar, John. *Pot: a handbook of marijuana.* New Hyde Park, N.Y.: University Books, 1967.

239. Scheinfeld, Amram. *The human heredity handbook.* Philadelphia: Lippincott, 1956.

240. Scheinfeld, Amram. *Your heredity and environment.* Philadelphia: Lippincott, 1965.

241. Schimel, John. *The parent's handbook on adolescence.* New York: World, 1969.

242. Schwab, John. *Handbook of psychiatric consultation.* New York: Appleton-Century-Crofts, 1968.

243. Scientific Staff of the Universities Federation for Animal Welfare (Eds.) *The UFAW handbook on the care and management of laboratory animals.* (3rd ed.) Baltimore: Williams and Wilkins, 1967.

244. Shea, Daniel. *A handbook on mental illness for the Catholic layman.* New York: Vantage Press, 1958.

245. Shouksmith, George. *Assessment through interviewing: a handbook for individual interviewing and group selection techniques.* New York: Pergamon, 1968, pb.

246. Siegel, Ernest. *Helping the brain-injured child: a handbook for parents.* New York: New York Association for Brain-injured Children, 1961

247. Silvan, James. *Raising laboratory animals: a handbook for biological and behavioral research.* Garden City, N.Y.: Doubleday, 1966.

248. Slobin, Dan (Ed.) *Handbook of Soviet psychology.* White Plains, N.Y.: International Arts and Science Press, 1966.

249. Snider, Ray, and Lee, J. *A stereotaxic atlas of the monkey brain (Macaca mulatta).* Chicago: University of Chicago Press, 1961.

250. Snider, Ray, and Niemer, W. *A stereotaxic atlas of the cat brain.* Chicago: University of Chicago Press, 1961.

251. Solomon, Philip, and Patch, V. (Eds.) *Handbook of psychiatry.* Los Altos, Calif.: Lange Medical Publications, 1969.

252. Southern Regional Education Board. *Recreation for the mentally retarded: a handbook for ward personnel.* Atlanta: Southern Regional Education Board, 1964.

253. Spock, Benjamin. *Baby and child care.* (Rev. ed.) New York: Pocket Books, 1968, pb. (p. 10)

254. Stevens, Harvey, and Heber, R. (Eds.) *Mental retardation: a review of research.* Chicago: University of Chicago Press, 1964.

255. Stevens, S. (Ed.) *Handbook of experimental psychology.* New York: Wiley, 1951.

256. Szebenyi, Emil. *Atlas of Macaca mulatta.* Rutherford, N.J.: Fairleigh Dickinson University Press, 1970.

257. Thorman, George. *Family therapy: a handbook.* Los Angeles: Western Psychological Services, 1965.

258. Tibbitts, Clark (Ed.) *Handbook of social gerontology.* Chicago: University of Chicago Press, 1960.

259. Travis, Lee (Ed.) *Handbook of speech pathology.* New York: Appleton-Century-Crofts, 1957.

260. Von Hilsheimer, George. *The special child: a handbook for behavior change.* Washington: Acropolis Books, 1970.

261. Von Witsen, Betty. *Perceptual training activities handbook.* New York: Teachers College Press, 1967.

262. Walsh, John. *Handbook of nonparametric statistics.* New York: Van Nostrand Reinhold, 1962.

263. Warden, C. et al. *Comparative psychology.* New York: Ronald, 1935-1940. 3 vols.

264 Watson, Robert. *The clinical method in psychology.* New York: Wiley, 1951, pb.

265. Whitla, Dean (Ed.) *Handbook of measurement and assessment in behavioral sciences.* Reading, Mass.: Addison-Wesley, 1968.

266. Wolman, Benjamin (Ed.) *Handbook of clinical psychology.* New York: McGraw-Hill, 1965.

267. Wolman, Benjamin (Ed.) *Psychoanalytic techniques: a handbook for the practicing psychoanalyst.* New York: Basic Books, 1967.

268. Wolman, Benjamin (Ed.) *Manual of childhood psychopathology.* New York: McGraw-Hill, 1970.

Biographical Sources and Directories

Psychologists

269. *American men of science—social and behavioral sciences.* New York: Bowker, 1962-.

270. *American Psychoanalytic Association roster.* New York: The American Psychoanalytic Association, 1970.

271. American Psychological Association. *Directory, 1916-.* Washington: American Psychological Association, 1916-. (p. 10)

272. American Psychiatric Association. *Biographical directory of the American Psychiatric Association.* (4th ed.) New York: Bowker, 1968.

273. *Biography Index: A Cumulative Index to Biographical Material in Books and Magazines.* New York: Wilson, 1947-. Quarterly. Annual and larger cumulations. Alphabetical arrangement. Also has index with individuals grouped according to professions and occupations. (p. 10, 16)

274. *Canadian Psychological Association: directory.* Ottawa: The Association, 1965.

275. *Current biography.* New York: Wilson, 1940-.

276. Duijker, H., and Jacobson, E. (Eds.) *International directory of psychologists, exclusive of the U.S.A.* (2nd ed.) New York: Humanities Press, 1966.

277. *McGraw-Hill modern men of science.* New York: McGraw-Hill, 1966-1968. 2 vols.

278. *Membership roster: American Association of Mental Deficiency.* Willimantic, Conn.: American Association of Mental Deficiency, n.d.

279. *Mental health directory.* Washington: Government Printing Office, Division of Public Documents, 1970.

280. Murchison, Carl (Ed.) *A history of psychology in autobiography.* Worcester, Mass.: Clarke University Press, 1930, 1932, 1936, 1952. 4 vols. (p. 10)

281. Boring, Edwin, and Lindzey, G. (Eds.) *A history of psychology in autobiography.* New York: Appleton-Century-Crofts, 1967. (p. 10)

282. Murchison, Carl (Ed.) *Psychological register.* Worcester, Mass.: Clark University Press, 1929-1932. vols. 2 and 3 only.

283. *Who was who in America.* Chicago: Marquis—Who's Who, 1943-. (p. 10)

284. *Who's who.* London: Black, 1849-.

285. *Who's who in America. Who's who in the East. Who's who in the Mid-west. Who's who in the West. Who's who in the South and Southwest. Who's who of American women.* Chicago: Marquis—Who's Who, Inc., 1899-. (p. 10)

Nonpsychologists

286. *American medical directory.* Chicago: American Medical Association, 1906-.

287. *American men of medicine.* (3rd ed.) Farmingdale, N.Y.: Institute for Research in Biography, 1961.

288. *American men of science—physical and biological sciences.* New York: Bowker, 1906-.

289. *American Educational Research Association: directory of members.* Washington: American Educational Research Association, 1970.

290. *American Sociological Association membership directory.* Washington: American Sociological Association. Biennial.

291. *Biographical dictionaries and related works: an international bibliography.* Detroit: Gale, 1967.

292. *Biographical directory of parapsychology.* New York: Helix Press, 1964.

293. *Chamber's biographical dictionary.* (Rev. ed.) New York: St. Martin's Press, 1969.

294. *Dictionary of American biography.* New York: Scribner, 1928-. (p. 10)

295. *Directory of American scholars.* New York: Bowker, 1942-.

296. *Directory of statisticians and others in allied professions.* Washington: American Statistical Association. Triennial.

297. *Essay and general literature index.* New York: Wilson, 1934-.

298. Gauld, Alan. *The founders of psychical research.* New York: Schocken, 1968.

299. Hyamson, Albert. *A dictionary of universal biography of all ages and people.* New York: Dutton, 1951.

300. *International directory of philosophy and philosophers.* New York: Humanities, 1966.

301. *Leaders in education: a biographical directory.* Lancaster, Pa.: The Science Press, 1932-1948.

302. *National cyclopedia of American biography.* New York: White, 1892-. (p. 10)

303. *National Institute of Health scientific directory and annual bibliography.* Washington: Government Printing Office, Division of Public Documents, 1970.

304. *The New York Times biographical edition.* New York: The New York Times, 1970-.

305. Thornton, John et al. *A select bibliography of medical biography.* London: Library Association, 1961.

306. *Webster's biographical dictionary.* Springfield, Mass.: Merriam, 1969. (p. 10)

307. *Who's who in American education.* Hattiesburg, Miss.: Who's Who in American Education. Biennial.

Book Reviews

Psychological Listings

308. Buros, Oscar (Ed.) *Mental measurements yearbooks.* Highland Park, N.J.: Gryphon, 1938-1965. 6 vols. See Book and Reviews section. Many of the books listed are followed by quotes from book reviews. The books in the most recent yearbook were

grouped into the following categories: "General," "Achievement," "For Examinees," "Intelligence," "Miscellaneous," "Personality," and "Vocations." (pp. 11, 30)

309. *Child Development Abstracts and Bibliography.* Lafayette, Ind.: Purdue University, Society for Research in Child Development, 1927-. Published three times a year. Contains book reviews on developmental topics.

310. *Contemporary Psychology: A Journal of Reviews.* Washington: American Psychological Association, 1956-. Monthly journal of book reviews. Annual author-reviewer index. (p. 11)

Prior to 1956 four journals published by the American Psychological Association contained book reviews. They were *Journal of Abnormal and Social Psychology, Journal of Applied Psychology, Journal of Consulting Psychology* and *Psychological Bulletin.*

311. Grinstein, Alexander (Ed.) *The Index of Psychoanalytic Writings.* New York: International Universities Press, 1956-1966. 9 vols.   (pp. 11, 19, 30)

312. *Mental Health Book Review Index.* New York: Council on Research in Bibliography, 1956-. Annual alphabetical listing by the author of the book reviewed. An index to book reviews in the behavioral sciences. (pp. 11, 18)

313. Bry, Isle, and Afflerbach, L. (Eds.) *Mental Health Book Review Index: An Annual Bibliography of Books and Book Reviews in the Behavioral Sciences. Cumulative Author-Title Index, Volumes 1-12, 1956-1967.* New York: Council on Research in Bibliography, 1969. (p. 11)

314. *Psychiatry and Social Science Review.* New York: Psychiatry and Social Science Review, 1967-. Monthly.

315. *Rehabilitation Literature.* Chicago: National Society for Crippled Children and Adults, 1956-. Monthly. See "Book Reviews" for short book reviews.

Listings Containing Some Psychology Books

316. *Book Review Digest.* New York: Wilson, 1905-. Monthly. Annual and larger cumulations. Index to book reviews arranged alphabetically by author of the book reviewed. Includes quotes from some of the reviews. (pp. 12, 16)

317. *Book Review Index.* Detroit: Gale Research, 1965-. Monthly. Annual cumulations. Index to book reviews arranged alphabetically by author of the book reviewed. (pp. 12, 16)

318. *Canadian Periodical Index.* Ottawa: Canadian Library Association, 1949-. Monthly. Annual and larger cumulations. Lists book reviews under "Book Reviews." (p. 16)

319. *Choice.* Chicago: American Library Association, 1964-. Monthly. Contains brief book reviews arranged by academic subject areas. See "Psychology." (p. 12)

320. *Education Index.* New York: Wilson, 1932-. Monthly. Annual cumulations. Book reviews are listed under "Book Reviews" until 1961. Since 1961, book reviews have not been listed. (p. 11)

321. *Essay and General Literature Index.* New York: Wilson, 1934-. Semiannual. Annual and larger cumulations. Alphabetical author-subject arrangement. (pp. 12, 16)

322. *Index to Book Reviews in the Humanities.* Detroit: Phillip Thomson, 1960-. Annual. Arranged alphabetically by author of the book reviewed. (pp. 12, 16, 17)

323. *Library Journal Book Review, The.* New York: Bowker, 1967-. Annual cumulation of monthly reviews in the *Library Journal.* Arranged by academic subject areas. See "Psychology." Many of the psychology books reviewed are on popular topics. (p. 12)

324. *New York Times Index, The.* New York: The New York Times, 1913-. Biweekly subject index. Annual cumulations. Alphabetical listing. Lists book reviews under "Book Reviews."

325. *Science Books: A Quarterly Review.* Washington: American Association for the Advancement of Science, 1965-. Quarterly. Arranged by academic subject areas. Books reviewed are neither popular books nor specialized research reports. (p. 12)

326. *Technical Book Review Index.* New York: Special Libraries Association, 1935-. Monthly index to book reviews in the sciences. Alphabetical arrangement by author of the book reviewed. Includes quotes from some of the reviews. Ordinarily psychology books are not listed here. (pp. 16, 17)

Test Information

327. Amrine, M. (Ed.) *American Psychologist,* Nov. 1965. Entire issue. (p. 12)

328. Anastasi, Anne. *Psychological Testing.* (3rd ed.) New York: Macmillan, 1968. (p. 12)

329. Buros, Oscar. (Ed.) *Tests in print: a comprehensive bibliography of tests for use in education, psychology, and industry.* Highland Park, N.J.: Gryphon, 1961. (p. 12)

330. Buros, Oscar (Ed.) *Mental measurements yearbook.* Highland Park, N.J.: Gryphon, 1938-1965. 6 vols. (p. 12)

331. Buros, Oscar (Ed.) *Reading tests and reviews: including a classified index to the mental measurements yearbooks.* Highland Parks, N.J.: Gryphon, 1968. (p. 12)

332. Buros, Oscar (Ed.) *Personality tests and reviews: including an index to the mental measurements yearbooks.* Highland Park, N.J.: Gryphon, 1970. (p. 12)

333. Burt, Cyril. *Mental and scholastic tests.* (4th ed.) London: Stapes Press, 1962.

334. Cronbach, Lee. *Essentials of psychological testing.* (3rd ed.) New York: Harper & Row, 1970. (p. 12)

335. Goheen, Howard, and Kavruck, S. *Selected references on test construction, mental test theory, and statistics, 1929-1949.* Washington: Government Printing Office, 1950.

336. Hildreth, Gertrude. *Bibliography of mental tests and rating scales.* (2nd ed.) New York: Psychological Corporation, 1939.

337. Hildreth, Gertrude. *Bibliography of mental tests and rating scales: 1945 supplement.* New York: Psychological Corporation, 1946.

338. Kuhlman, Frederick. *A handbook of mental tests.* Baltimore: Warwick and York, 1922.

339. South, Earl. *An index to periodical literature on testing . . . 1921-1936.* New York: Psychological Corporation, 1937.

340. Wang, Charles. *An annotated bibliography of mental tests and scales.* Peiping: Catholic University Press, 1939-1940. 2 vols.

Abstracts and Indexes

To Books and Periodicals

341. *Applied Science and Technology Index* (formerly entitled *Industrial Arts Index*). New York: Wilson, 1913-. Monthly.

Annual cumulations. Alphabetical subject index of periodical articles. (p. 17)

342. *Art Index.* New York: Wilson, 1933-. Quarterly. Annual and larger cumulations. Alphabetical author-subject index of periodical articles. Lists book reviews. (p. 16)

343. Articles on mass communications in U.S. and foreign journals: a selected annotated bibliography. In *Journalism Quarterly,* v. 7-, 1930-. Quarterly abstracts. Subject arrangement of periodical articles. (p. 17)

344. *Bibliography of Medical Reviews.* Washington: National Library of Medicine, 1961-. Monthly. Annual cumulations. Alphabetical subject arrangement to reviews of the literature. (pp.17, 18)

345. *Biological Abstracts.* Philadelphia: Biological Abstracts, 1926-. Semimonthly abstracts. Subject arrangement of books and periodicals. Indexes cumulate annually. (pp. 16, 17)

346. *Biological and Agricultural Index: A Cumulative Subject Index to Periodicals in the Fields of Biology, Agriculture, and Related Sciences* (formerly *Agricultural Index*). New York: Wilson, 1964-. Monthly. Annual cumulations. Subject index of periodical articles. Lists book reviews under "Book Reviews." (pp. 16, 17)

347. *BioResearch Index* (formerly *BioResearch Titles*). Philadelphia: BioScience Information Service of Biological Abstracts, 1968-. Monthly index. Keyword subject arrangement of periodical articles and other sources. Annual cumulative index. (pp.16, 17)

348. *British Education Index.* London: Library Association, 1961-. Published three times a year. Biennial cumulation. Subject and author indexes to periodical articles. (pp. 16, 18)

349. *British Humanities Index.* London: Library Association, 1962-. Quarterly. Annual cumulations. Alphabetical subject index to periodical articles. Annual author index. Lists book reviews. (p. 16)

350. *Canadian Periodical Index.* Ottawa: Canadian Library Association, 1949-. Monthly. Annual and larger cumulations. Subject index to periodical articles. Lists book reviews under "Book Reviews." (p. 16)

351. *Child Development Abstracts and Bibliography.* Lafayette, Ind.: Purdue University, Society for Research in Child Development, 1927-. Published three times a year. Abstracts books and

periodicals. Subject arrangement. Annual author and subject indexes. Contains book reviews. (pp. 15, 16, 18)

352. *Crime and Delinquency Abstracts* (formerly *International Bibliography on Crime and Delinquency*). Washington: Government Printing Office, 1963-. Monthly. Abstracts of periodicals articles and books. Subject index each issue. Annual subject index. (p. 18)

353. *Current Index to Journals in Education.* New York: CCM Information Co., 1969-. Monthly annotated alphabetical subject index to periodical articles. Semiannual and annual cumulations of the subject and author indexes. (p. 16)

354. *Current Literature on Aging.* New York: National Council on the Aging. Annual list of books, pamphlets, and periodical articles on aging. (p. 17)

355. *DSH Abstracts.* Washington: Deafness Speech and Hearing Publications, 1960-. Quarterly abstracts to periodical articles. Subject arrangement. Author and subject indexes cumulate annually. (p. 18)

356. *Education Index.* New York: Wilson, 1932-. Monthly. Annual cumulations. Alphabetical author-subject index to educational sources, primarily periodicals. (pp. 15, 16, 18, 19, 30)

357. *Essay and General Literature Index.* New York: Wilson, 1934-. Semiannual. Annual and larger cumulations. Indexes collections of essays, articles and speeches. Alphabetical author-title-subject index. Lists book reviews. (pp. 16, 17)

358. *Excerpta Crimonologica.* New York: Excerpta Medica Foundation, 1961-. Monthly abstracts. Subject arrangement with annual author and subject index. (pp. 17, 18)

359. *Excerpta Medica, Section 2A: Physiology.* New York and Amsterdam, Excerpta Medica Foundation, 1948-. Monthly abstracts. Subject arrangement. Author and subject indexes cumulate annually. (p. 17)

360. *Excerpta Medica, Section 8B: Psychiatry.* New York and Amsterdam: Excerpta Medica Foundation, 1948-. Monthly abstracts. Subject arrangement. Author and subject indexes cumulate annually. (pp. 17, 18)

361. *Excerpta Medica, Section 19: Rehabilitation and Physical Medicine.* New York and Amsterdam: Excerpta Medica Founda-

tion, 1958-. Monthly abstracts. Subject arrangement. Author and subject indexes cumulate annually. (pp. 17, 18)

362. *Excerpta Medica, Section 20: Gerontology and Geriatrics.* New York and Amsterdam: Excerpta Medica Foundation, 1958-. Monthly abstracts. Subject arrangement. Author and subject indexes cumulate annually. (p. 17)

363. *Index Medicus.* Washington: National Library of Medicine, 1960-. Cumulated annually in *Cumulated Index Medicus.* 1960-. Monthly index. Alphabetical subject and author indexes to periodical articles. (pp. 15, 16, 17, 18)

364. *International Bibliography of Social and Cultural Anthropology.* Paris: UNESCO; London: Tavistock; Chicago: Aldine. 1958-. Annual. Subject arrangement with author and subject indexes to books and periodical articles. Lists book reviews by "C.R." (p. 16)

365. *International Bibliography of Sociology.* London, Tavistock: Chicago, Aldine, 1952-. Annual. Subject arrangement with author and subject indexes to books and periodical articles. Lists book reviews by "C.R." (p. 17)

366. *Mental Retardation Abstracts.* Washington: Government Printing Office, 1964-. Quarterly abstracts of books and periodical articles. Subject arrangement. Subject and author indexes cumulate annually.(pp. 15, 18)

367. *Monthly Catalog of United States Government Publications.* Washington: Government Printing Office, 1895-. Monthly. Annual and 10 year cumulations. Subject index listed by government agency which issued the document. (p. 16)

368. *Music Index.* Detroit: Information Service, 1949-. Monthly. Annual cumulations. Author-subject index to periodical articles. Lists book reviews under "Book Reviews." (p. 17)

369. *Perceptual Cognitive Development.* Los Angeles, Galton Institute, 1965-. Bimonthly. Key word in context index to articles on intellectual functioning. Contains large number of book reviews. (p. 18)

370. *Philosopher's Index.* Bowling Green Ohio: Bowling Green University, 1967-. Quarterly. Biannual cumulations. Abstracts of periodical articles listed alphabetically by authors. Subject and author indexes. (p. 17)

371. *Poverty and Human Resources Abstracts.* Ann Arbor, Mich.: University of Michigan, 1966-. Bimonthly abstracts of books and periodical articles. Subject arrangement with author and subject index each issue. (pp. 16, 17, 18)

372. *Psychological Abstracts.* Lancaster, Pa.: American Psychological Association, 1927-. Monthly abstracts to periodical articles. Subject arrangement. Author and subject indexes cumulate semiannually. Lists books under "Books" and bibliographies under "Bibliographies." Larger cumulations are listed below. (pp. 13, 14, 15, 16, 18, 19, 28, 30, 31)

373. *Author Index to Psychological Index 1894-1935 and Psychological Abstracts 1927-1958.* Boston: G.K. Hall, 1960. 5 vols. (pp. 14, 15)

374. *Cumulative Author Index. . . . First Supplement, 1959-1963.* Boston: G.K. Hall, 1965. (p. 14)

375. *Cumulative Author Index. . . . Second Supplement, 1964-1968.* Boston: G.K. Hall, 1971 (p. 14)

376. *Cumulated Subject Index to Psychological Abstracts, 1927-1960.* Boston: G.K. Hall, 1966. 2 vols. (p. 14)

377. *Cumulated Subject Index. . . . First Supplement 1961-1965.* Boston: G.K. Hall, n.d. (p. 14)

378. *Psychological Index, 1894-1935, An Annual Bibliography of the Literature of Psychology and Cognate Subjects.* Princeton, N.J.: Psychological Review Co., 1895-1936, 42 vols. Index to books and periodical articles. Subject arrangement. Alphabetical author index. (p. 15)

379. Ansbacher, H. (Ed.) *Psychological Index: Abstract References.* Columbus, Ohio: American Psychological Association, 1940-1941. 2 vols. (p. 15)

380. *Psychopharmacology Abstracts.* Washington: Government Printing Office, 1961-. Monthly abstracts to periodical articles. Author and subject indexes cumulate annually. (p. 18)

381. *Public Affairs Information Service Bulletin.* New York: Public Affairs Information Service, 1915-. Weekly. Annual cumulations. Alphabetical subject index. Lists some government documents. (pp. 16, 17)

382. *Readers' Guide to Periodical Literature.* New York: Wilson, 1905-. Semimonthly. Annual and larger cumulations. Author-

subject index to general and popular periodical articles listed alphabetically. (pp. 13, 16, 24)

383. *Rehabilitation Literature.* Chicago: National Society for Crippled Children and Adults, 1956-. Monthly abstracts. Classified subject arrangement to books and periodical articles. Author index cumulates annually. Includes short book reviews and articles (p. 18)

384. *Research in Education.* Washington: Government Printing Office, 1966-. Monthly abstracts of books, pamphlets and research in progress. Author and subject indexes cumulate annually. See the *Thesarus of ERIC Descriptors,* (2nd ed.) [Washington: Government Printing Office, 1969] when using the subject indexes. (pp. 16, 18)

385. *Social Sciences and Humanities Index* (formerly *International Index*). New York: Wilson, 1916-. Quarterly. Annual cumulations. Alphabetical author-subject index to periodical articles. Lists book reviews. (pp. 16, 17)

386. *Science Citation Index.* Philadelphia: Institute for Scientific Information, 1963-. Quarterly. Annual cumulations. Lists periodical articles and book reviews.

387. *Sociological Abstracts.* New York: Sociological Abstracts, 1952-. Semimonthly abstracts. Subject arrangement. Author and subject indexes cumulate annually. (pp. 15, 17)

To Newspapers

388. Christian Science Monitor. *Subject Index to the Christian Science Monitor.* Boston, 1960-. (pp. 7, 27)

389. *New York Times Index, The.* New York: The New York Times, 1913-. (pp. 7, 27)

390. Times, London. *Index to the Times.* London: Times, 1907-. (p. (pp. 7, 27)

391. *Wall Street Journal: Index.* New York: Dow, Jones and Co., 1958-. (pp. 7, 27)

To Dissertations

392. *Dissertation Abstracts International* (formerly *Dissertation Abstracts*). Ann Arbor, Mich.: University Microfilms, 1952-. v. 12-. (p. 16)

393. *Masters Abstracts: Abstracts of Selected Masters Theses on Microfilm.* Ann Arbor, Mich.: University Microfilms, 1962-. (p. 16)

Government (Experimental Publications)

Five government abstracts have recently been issued on a trial basis. Although the format is subject to change, each publication presently uses a subject arrangement and includes a subject and an author index.

394. *Adult Development and Aging Abstracts* (p. 17)

395. *Bulletin of Suicidology* (p. 18)

396. *Drug Dependence* (p. 18)

397. *Reproduction and Population Research Abstract*

398. *Schizophrenic Bulletin* (p. 18)

Recent Abstracts and Indexes

399. *Behavior and Physiology Index.* Kansas City, Missouri: Science Search Associates, 1967-.

400. *Behavioral Science in Progress.* Washington: American Psychological Association, 1971.

401. *Current Contents: Behavioral, Social and Management Sciences.* Philadelphia: Institute for Scientific Information, 1969-.

402. *Exceptional Child Education Abstracts.* New York: Council for Exceptional Children, 1969-.

403. *Information Resources Center Recommends.* New York: Mental Health Materials Center, 1969-.

404. *Geriatrics Digest: A Summary of the World's Literature on Preventive Geriatrics.* Northfield, Ill.: Geriatrics Digest, Inc., 1968.

405. *Language and Language Behavior Abstracts.* New York: Appleton-Century-Crofts, 1967-.

406. *Selected Highlights of Crime and Delinquency Literature.* New York: National Council on Crime and Delinquency, 1968-.

**Selected Bibliographies Published by
the United States Government**

Listed below are some of the bibliographies published by the United States Government. The list contains bibliographies issued by the U.S. Department of Health, Education, and Welfare (HEW) since 1960. Because these bibliographies are published by the Government Printing Office in Washington, D.C., just the Superintendent of

Documents classification number, issuing department, title, and date of publication are listed.

FS 1.2:H19—U.S. Department of Health, Education, and Welfare (HEW). *Programs for the handicapped, abstracts of mental retardation research projects funded by the vocational rehabilitation administration.* 1967.

FS 1.18:C43—HEW, Office of Child Development. *Bibliography on early childhood, July 30, 1969.* 1969.

FS 2.21:—HEW, Public Health Service. *National Institutes of Health, scientific directory (year), and annual bibliography.* 1959-.

FS 2.21:37—HEW, Public Health Service. *The treatment of psychiatric disorders with insulin: a selected bibliography, 1939-1960.* 1962.

FS 2.21:39—HEW, Public Health Service. *The treatment of psychiatric disorders with metrazol, 1935-1960, a selected annotated bibliography.* 1963.

FS 2.21:40,52,59,67—HEW, Public Health Service. *Animal research in psychopharmacology: psychopharmacology handbook.* 1963-.

FS 2.21:45/4—HEW, Public Health Service. *Bibliography on smoking and health with English language abstracts of foreign items, 1969 cumulation.* 1969.

FS 2.21:60—HEW, Public Health Service. *Bibliography on clinical psychopharmacology, 1958-1960.* 1965.

FS 2.21:64—HEW, Public Health Service. *Studies on electroconvulsive therapy 1939-1963, a selected annotated bibliography.* 1966.

FS 2.21:65—HEW, Public Health Service. *A bibliography in neuropsychology, reviews, and books, 1960-1965.* 1966.

FS 2.21:66—HEW, Public Health Service. *The community general hospital as a mental health psychiatric resource, a selected annotated bibliography.* 1966.

FS 2.21:69—HEW, Public Health Service. *Community care of the mentally ill, a selected annotated bibliography.* 1966.

FS 2.21:71—HEW, Public Health Service. *Animal research in psychopharmacology, decennial index for psychopharmacology handbooks.* 1967.

FS 2.22:G31/3/965—HEW, Public Health Service. *Geronto-psychiatric literature in the postwar period.* 1969.

FS 2.22/4:3/4—HEW, National Institute of Health. *Introductory readings in mental health, selected reading list.* 1961.

FS 2.22/4:6/3—HEW, National Institute of Health. *Advanced readings in mental health, selected reading list.* 1963.

FS 2.22/4:7—HEW, National Institute of Health. *Mental retardation: a selected reading list.* 1962.

FS 2.22/13:A14—HEW, National Institute of Mental Health. *Social aspects of alienation: an annotated bibliography.* 1969.

FS 2.22/13:An8/955-66—HEW, Public Health Service. *Anti-depressant drug studies 1955-1966, bibliography and selected abstracts.* 1969.

FS 2.22/13:B73—HEW, Public Health Service. *Translations in the brain sciences, a bibliography.* 1967.

FS 2.22/13:D84/928-66—HEW, National Institute of Mental Health. *Bibliography on drug dependence and abuse, 1928-1966.* 1969.

FS 2.22/13:F21—HEW, Public Health Service. *Family therapy, a selected annotated bibliography.* 1966.

FS 2.22/13:M52/2—HEW, National Institute of Mental Health, Public Health Service. *Bibliography of informational publications issued by state mental health agencies.* 1964.

FS 2.22/13:M52/3—HEW, Public Health Service. *A selected bibliography on occupational mental health.* 1965.

FS 2.22/13:M52/4—HEW, Public Health Service. *A bibliographic index of evaluation in mental health.* 1967.

FS 2.22/13:M52/5—HEW, Public Health Service. *Bibliography on religion and mental health, 1960-1964.* 1967.

FS 2.22/13:M52/6/947-61—HEW, National Institute of Health. *Publications resulting from National Institute of Mental Health Research Grants, 1947-1961.* 1968.

FS 2.22/13:M52/8—HEW, National Institute of Mental Health. *The comprehensive community mental health center: an annotated bibliography.* 1969.

FS 2.22/13:M52/9—HEW, National Institute of Mental Health. *Consultation in mental health and related fields, a conference guide.* 1969.

FS 2.22/13:P95—HEW, Public Health Service. *Bibliography on psychotominetics, 1943-1966.* 1968. \

FS 2.22/13:Su3—HEW, Public Health Service. *Bibliography on suicide and suicide prevention.* 1969.

FS 2.22/13:T22—HEW, National Institute of Health. *Educational technology and teaching-learning process, selected bibliography.* 1968.

FS 2.22/13:T52—HEW, National Institute of Mental Health. *Psychological and social aspects of human transplantation, annotated bibliography.* 1969. Supp. 1. 1969.

FS 2.22/13:V88—HEW, National Institute of Mental Health. *Volunteer services in mental health, an annotated bibliography 1965-1969.* 1969.

FS 2.22/59-2:947-67/pt.1,2—HEW, Public Health Service. *Epilepsy abstracts, a review of the published literature 1947-1967.* 1969.

FS 2.24:M52—HEW, Public Health Service. *Annotated bibliography on inservice training for allied professionals and nonprofessionals in community mental health.* 1969.

FS 2.24:M52/2—HEW, National Institute of Health. *Annotated bibliography on inservice training in mental health for staff in residential institutions.* 1969.

FS 2.24:M52/3—HEW, National Institute of Health. *Annotated bibliography on inservice training for key professionals in community mental health.* 1969.

FS 2.24:T68/pt.1—HEW, Public Health Service. *Training methodology, part I: background theory and research, an annotated bibliography.* 1969.

FS 2.24:T68pt.2—HEW, Public Health Service. *Training methodology, part II: planning and administration, an annotated bibliography.* 1969.

FS 2.24:T68pt.3—HEW, Public Health Service. *Training methodology, part III: instructional methods and techniques, an annotated bibliography.* 1969.

FS 3.220/2:2—HEW, Social Security Administration, Children's Bureau. *Research relating to juvenile delinquents.* 1962.

FS 3.222:960/3—HEW, Social Security Administration, Children's Bureau. *Selected annotated readings on group services in the treatment and control of juvenile delinquency.* 1960.

FS 5.77:—HEW, Office of Education. *Research in education.* 1966-.

FS 5.210:10060—HEW, Office of Education. *Education, literature of the profession, bibliography . . . .* 1969.

FS 5.212:12028/Indexes—HEW, Office of Education. *Office of education research reports 1956-65 indexes.* 1967.

FS 5.212:12029/Resumes—HEW, Office of Education. *Office of education research reports 1956-65 resumes.* 1967.

FS 5.214:14031-38—HEW, Office of Education. *The education of disadvantaged children, a bibliography.* 1966

FS 5.237:37001—HEW, Office of Education. *Catalog of selected documents on the disadvantaged.* 1966.

FS 5.237:37019—HEW, Office of Education. *Literature for disadvantaged children, a bibliography.* 1968.

FS 5.237:37045—HEW, Office of Education. *Books related to compensatory education.* 1969.

FS 13:130:8—HEW, Food and Drug Administration. *Fact sheet 8, hallucinogens, a selected bibliography.* 1967.

FS 13:130:9—HEW, Food and Drug Administration. *Fact sheet 9, bibliography of selected popular references on hallucinogenic drugs.* 1967.

FS 13:130:10—HEW, Food and Drug Administration. *Fact sheet 10, stimulants and depressants, a bibliography, 1964-1967.* 1967.

FS 13:202:R31/3/965—HEW, Vocational Rehabilitation Administration. *Research and demonstration projects, an annotated listing, 1965.* 1966.

FS 13.218:P95/950-61—HEW, Vocational Rehabilitation Administration. *Psychiatric index for interdisciplinary research, guide to literature 1960-1961.* 1964.

FS 14.9/4:G31—HEW, Welfare Administration. *Selected references on aging: basic reference books and journals in gerontology.* 1963.

FS 14.13:Ag4—HEW, Welfare Administration. *Aging in the modern world, an annotated bibliography.* 1964.

FS 14.111:430—HEW, Children's Bureau. *Phenylketonuria, a comprehensive bibliography, 1964.* 1967.

FS 14.112:B32/965—HEW, Children's Bureau. *Bibliography on battered child.* 1965.

FS 14.112:C43—HEW, Children's Bureau. *Children who need protection, an annotated bibilography.* 1966.

FS 14.112:D37—HEW, Children's Bureau. *Selected bibliography on juvenile delinquency.* 1964.

FS 14.112:G13—HEW, Children's Bureau. *Galactosemia, a selected bibliography.* 1963.

FS 14.112:M52—HEW, Children's Bureau. *Selected annotated bibliography on mental retardation for social workers.* 1963.

FS 14.114:1—HEW, Children's Bureau. Welfare Administration. *Research relating to children.* 1948-.

FS 14.114/2:1—HEW, Children's Bureau. *Research relating to mentally retarded children.* 1966.

FS 15.12/2:1-4—HEW, Administration on Aging. *Selected references on aging.* 1965.

FS 17.212:B32—HEW, Social and Rehabilitation Service, Children's Bureau. *Bibliography on the battered child.* 1969.

FS 17.212:Em6—HEW, Children's Bureau. *Research relating to emotionally disturbed children.* 1968.

FS 17.212:J98—HEW, Children's Bureau. *Prevention of juvenile delinquency, selected annotated bibliography.* 1968.

FS 17.212:M52—HEW, Children's Bureau. *Selected reading suggestions for parents of mentally retarded children.* 1968.

HE 20.2417:C73—HEW, National Institute of Mental Health. *Computer applications in psychotherapy: bibliography and abstracts.* 1970.

HE 20.2417:D84/2—HEW, Public Health Service, National Institute of Mental Health. *Selected bibliography on drugs of abuse.* 1970.

HE 20.2417:H88—HEW, Public Health Service, National Institute of Mental Health. *Bibliography on human intelligence: an extensive bibliography.* 1970.

HE 20.2417:Url—HEW, Public Health Service. National Institute of Mental Health. *Bibliography on the urban crisis.* 1969.

HE 20.2759:M41—HEW, Public Health Service. *Annotated bibliography on maternal nutrition.* 1970.

HE 20.2759:Sp3/900-68—HEW, Public Health Service. *Bibliography on speech, hearing and language in relation to mental retardation, 1900-1968.* 1969.

HE 20.3012:D75—HEW, Public Health Service. *Down's syndrome (mongolism), a reference bibliography.* 1969.

HE 20.3361:D34—HEW, Public Health Service, National Institute of Health. *Selected bibliography on death and dying.* 1970.

The next three bibliographies were issued by the President's Executive Office.

PrEx 10.15:C83—U.S. Executive Office of the President, Economic Opportunity Office. *Selected references in the field of early childhood education.* 1968.

Pr 35.8:M52/L71—U.S. President. *Bibliography of world literature on mental retardation, January 1940-March 1963.* 1963. 2 vols.

Pr 35.8:M52/L71/supp.—U.S. President. *Bibliography of world literature on mental retardation, March 1963-December 1964.* 1965.

Other Bibliographies

Adjustment to blindness and severe visual impairment: a selected bibliography. New York: IRIS, American Foundation for the Blind, 1967.

Aldous, Joan, and Hill, R. *International bibliography of research in marriage and the family, 1900-1964.* Minneapolis: University of Minnesota Press, 1967.

A list of books relevant to behavior therapy. *Journal of Behavior Therapy and Experimental Psychiatry,* 1970, 1(1), 95-96.

Alvarez, Walter. *Minds that came back.* Philadelphia: Lippincott, 1961. Contains list of autobiographical accounts of physical and psychological illness.

American Psychiatric Association. *Sources of information on behavioral problems of adolescence.* Washington: The American Psychiatric Association, 1960.

American Society for Psychical Research. *Parapsychology in print,* 1970. New York: The Society, 1970.

Ammons, C., and Ammons, R. Motor skills bibliography. *Perceptual and Motor Skills.* See annual indexes.

Ammons, C., and Ammons, R. Perception bibliography. *Perceptual and Motor Skills.* See annual indexes.

Anderson, J. *Research design and analysis in the behavioral sciences: an annotated bibliography.* University Park, New Mexico: New Mexico State University, Research Center, 1967.

Andrews, Thomas. Statistical methods and research design: index of reviews and notes in the *Psychological Bulletin,* 1940-1966. *Psychological Bulletin,* 1967, 68(3), 213-220.

Andrews, Thomas, and Kerr, F. Index of literature reviews and summaries in the *Psychological Bulletin,* 1940-1966. *Psychological Bulletin,* 1967, 68(3), 178-212.

Appleton, William A guide to the use of psychoactive agents. *Diseases of the Nervous System* 1967, 28(9), 609-613.

Ard, Ben. Basic books for the marriage counselor. In B. Ard and C. Ard (Eds.) *Handbook of marrige counseling.* Palo Alto, Calif.: Science and Behavior, 1969.

Berkowitz, M., and Johnson, J. *Social scientific study of religion: a bibliography.* Pittsburg: Pittsburg University Press, 1967.

Berlin, I. *Bibliography of child psychiatry.* Psychiatric Bibliographies, No. 1. Washington: American Psychiatric Association, 1963.

Bertone, C. (Ed.) *Soviet psychology 1950-1966: a continuing bibliography.* North Hollywood;: Western Periodicals, 1969.

Bickford, Reginald et al. (Eds.) *A KWIC index of EEG literature.* New York: American Elsevier, 1965.

Bindman, Arthur. Bibliography on consultation. *Journal of Education,* 1964, 146(3), 56-60.

Blostein, Stanley. *Prevention in mental health: selected annotated bibliography.* Canada's Mental Health Supplement, 1969, No. 61.

Bobren, H. et al. *A bibliography of literature relevant to the Semantic Differential.* Urbana, Ill.: University of Illinois, 1968, pb.

Booth, Robert et al. (Eds.) *Culturally disadvantaged: a bibliography and key-word-out-of-context (KWOC) index.* Detroit: Wayne State Press, 1967.

Brackbill, Yvonne (Ed.) *Research in infant behavior: a cross-indexed bibliography.* Baltimore: Williams and Wilkins, 1964.

Child Study Association of America. *Recommended readings about children and family life, 1969.* New York: The Association, 1969.

Clevenger, Lemar et al. Malnutrition and mental retardation: An annotated bibliography. *Mental Retardation Abstracts,* 1970, 7(1), 1-24.

Committee on Professional Development. New York State Teachers of the Mentally Handicapped. *Materials for use with mentally handicapped children.* Albany, New York: N.Y. State Teachers of the Mentally Handicapped, 1970.

Cooley, G., and Parnes, S. *Bibliography re nature and nurture of creative behavior.* Buffalo, N.Y.: Creative Education Foundation, 1964.

DeBoer, D. (Ed.) Annotated bibliography on early child learning. *Education,* 1968, 89, 40-42.

Driver, Edwin. *The sociology and anthropology of mental illness: a reference guide.* Amherst: University of Massachusetts Press, 1965.

Duker, Sam *Listening bibliography.* New York: Scarecrow Press, 1964.

Durham L., and Gibb, J. A bibliography of research: 1947-1960. Part II of *Explorations I and II,* 1967. Washington: National Training Laboratory, 1967. On training group research.

Emotionally disturbed children. Albany, N.Y.: The State Education Department, 1968.

Evans, R., and Roselle, R. (Eds.) *Social psychology in life.* Boston: Allyn and Bacon, 1970, pb. Contains bibliography on social psychological analyses of problems in real-life settings.

Feldstein, Donald (Ed.) *An annotated bibliography of books and short stories on childhood and youth.* New York: Council on Social Work Education, 1969.

Ferguson, Donald, and Smith, D. School psychology (1960-1963): an annotated bibliography. *Journal of School Psychology,* 1963-1964, 2(1), 72-81.

Fine, Bernard et al. A bibliography on the psychological aspects of smoking: January 1940 through September 1965. *Psychological Reports,* 1966, 18(3), 783-787.

Forrester, Gertrude. *Occupational literature: an annotated bibliography.* New York: Wilson, 1964.

Foster, Teddy. A bibliography of experimental studies related to persuasion published in English language journals: 1941-1964. *Dissertation Abstracts,* 1968, 29(2-A), 672.

Freeman, Harrop, and Freeman, R. *Counseling: a bibliography with annotations.* New York: Scarecrow Press, 1964.

Gamage, J., and Zerkin, E. *A comprehensive guide to the English-Language literature on Cannabis (marihuana).* Beloit, Wis.: Stash Press, 1970.

Gardner, James, and Watson, L. Behavior modification of the mentally retarded: an annotated bibliography. *Mental Retardation Abstracts,* 1969, 6(2), 181-193.

Golann, Stuart. *Coordinate index reference guide to community mental health.* New York: Behavioral, 1969, pb.

Goldberg, I. *Selected bibliography of special education.* New York: Teachers College, Columbia University, 1967, pb.

Gottlieb, David, and Reeves, J. *Adolescent behavior in urban areas.* New York: Free Press, 1963.

Gowan, John. *An annotated bibliography on the academically talented.* Washington: National Education Association, 1961.

Gowan, John. *An annotated bibliography on creativity and giftedness.* Washington: National Education Association, 1965.

Gray, Philip. Checklist of papers since 1951 dealing with imprinting in birds. *Psychological Record,* 1963, 13(4), 445-454.

Green, Edward, and O'Connell, J. *An annotated bibliography of visual discrimination learning.* New York: Teachers College Press, 1969, pb.

Haley, Jay, and Glick, I. *Psychiatry and the family: an annotated bibliography of articles published 1960-1964.* Palo Alto, Calif.: Family Process, 1965

Hansen, Donald, and Parsons, H. (Eds.) *Mass communication: a research bibliography.* (New ed.) Berkeley, Calif.: Glendessary Press, 1970.

Hendershot, Carl. *Programmed learning.* (4th ed.) Bay City, Mich.: The Author, 1967.

Hungerland, Helmut (Ed.) Selective current bibliography for aesthetics and related fields. *Journal of Aesthetics and Art Criticism.* 1945-. See annual indexes.

International bibliography of social and cultural anthropology. Chicago: Aldine, 1955-.

International bibliography of studies on alcohol. New Brunswick, N.J.: Rutgers Center of Alcohol Studies, 1966-.

Jack, Jeweldine. A bibliography on Howler monkeys. *Primates,* 1967, 8(3), 271-290.

Jondito, Jean. Drugs: Part 1. *Bulletin of Bibliography,* 1969, 26(4), 89-100.

Kalish, Richard. Death and bereavement: a bibliography. *Journal of Human Relations,* 1965, 13(1), 118-141.

Kellam Constance. *A literary bibliography on aging.* New York: Council on Social Work Education, 1969.

Kendall, Maurice, and Doig, A. *Bibliography of statistical literature.* New York: Hafner, 1962.

Kiell, Norman (Ed.) *Psychoanalysis, psychology and literature: a bibliography.* Madison, Wis.: University of Wisconsin Press, 1963.

Kiell, Norman (Ed.) *Psychiatry and psychology in the visual arts and aesthetics: a bibliography.* Madison, Wis.: University of Wisconsin Press, 1965.

Knowles, E. A bibliography of research: 1960-67. Part II of *Explorations I & II,* 1967. Washington: National Training Laboratory. 1967. On training group research.

Lesh, Terry. Zen and psychotherapy: a partially annotated bibliography. *Journal of Humanistic Psychology,* 1970, 10(1), 75-83.

Levy, C. et al. The psychology of memory 1960-. *Perceptual and Motor Skills,* 1967-.

Lubin, B., and Lubin, A. *Group psychotherapy: a bibliography of the literature from 1956 through 1964.* East Lansing, Mich.: Michigan State University Press, 1966.

McGrath, J., and Altman, I. *Small group research: a synthesis and critique of the field.* New York: Holt, Rinehart & Winston, 1966.

MacLennan, B., and Levy, N. The group psychotherapy literature 1967. *International Journal of Group Psychotherapy,* 1968, 18(3), 375-401.

Margulis, Stephen, and Songer, E. Cognitive dissonance: a bibliography of its first decade. *Psychological Reports,* 1969, 24(3), 923-935.

Martin, L. *Psychological investigations in creativity: a bibliography (1954-1965).* Greensboro, N.C.: The Richardson Foundation, Inc., 1965.

May, Rollo (Ed.) *Existential psychology.* New York: Random House, 1968, pb.

Meissner, William. *Annotated bibliography in religion and psychology.* New York: Academy of Religion and Mental Health, 1961.

Michels, K. et al. Odor and olfaction: a bibliography 1948-1960. *Perceptual and Motor Skills,* 1962, 15(2), 475-529.

Miley, Charles. Birth order research 1963-1967: bibliography and index. *Journal of Individual Psychology,* 1969, 25(1), 64-70.

National Academy of Sciences. National Research Council, Disaster Research Group. *Field studies of disaster behavior: an inventory.* Washington: National Academy of Sciences. National Research Council, 1961.

National Council on the Aging. *A general bibliography on aging.* New York: The Council, 1963, pb. The National Council on the Aging publishes 15 other bibliographies on specific topics of aging.

National Easter Seal Society for Crippled Children and Adults. *A library on the rehabilitation of the physically handicapped: a selective checklist of publications in print.* Chicago: The Society 1970. The National Easter Seal Society for Crippled Children and Adults publishes 15 other bibliographies on specific topics of rehabilitation of the physically handicapped.

National Training Laboratory. *Reading book—1970 revision— annual summer laboratories in human relations training.* Washington: NTL Institute for Applied Behavioral Science, 1970.

Newton, Mary. *Books for deaf children: a graded annotated bibliography.* Washington: Alexander Graham Bell Association for the Deaf, 1963.

New York University, Creative Science Program. *Bibliography on creativity.* New York: New York University, 1966.

Our stoned age: drugs, their use, misuse, effects and influence on our society. Sante Fe, N.M.: New Mexico Research Library of the Southwest, 1970.

Parnes, Sidney. *Compendium of research on creative imagination.* Buffalo, N.Y.: The Creative Education Foundation, 1960.

Parnes, Sidney. *Creative behavior guidebook.* New York: Scribner, 1967, pb.

Pearlman, Samuel. The college drug scene. *Choice,* 1969, 6, 181-187.

Petras, John, and Curtis, J. The current literature on social class and mental disease in America: critique and bibliography. *Behavioral Science,* 1968, 13(5), 382-398.

Philbrick, B. Selected readings on perceptual-motor learning. *Journal of Health, Physical Education and Recreation,* 1968, 39, 34-36

Pursglove, Paul. A selected bibliography of books and articles relevant to Gestalt theory. In Paul Pursglove (Ed.), *Recognition in Gestalt therapy.* New York: Funk and Wagnalls, 1968.

Quarantelli, E. A selected annotated bibliography of social science studies on disasters. *American Behavioral Scientist,* 1970, 13(3), 452-456.

Razik, T. *A bibliography of creativity studies and related areas.* Buffalo, N.Y.: University Bookstore, State University of New York at Buffalo, 1965.

Raven, B. *A bibliography of publications relating to the small group.* Los Angeles: Student Bookstore, University of California at Los Angeles, 1965.

Savage, I. *Bibliography of nonparametric statistics.* Cambridge, Mass.: Harvard University Press, 1963.

Savage, Noel. *The drug dilemma.* New York: Bowker, 1970.

Scheerenberger, R. Bibliography of recent books and monographs on mental retardation. *Mental Retardation,* 1968, 6(4), 38-48.

Schein, Jerome. Current research in deafness: where to find it. *American Annals of the Deaf,* 1965, 110(1), 190-192.

Schlesinger, Benjamin. *The multi-program family: a review and annotated bibliography.* (2nd ed.) Toronto: University of Toronto Press, 1965.

Schlesinger, Benjamin. Selected mental health pocketbooks and paperbacks 1967-1968. *Canada's Mental Health Supplement,* 1968, No. 58.

Schlesinger, Benjamin. Selected mental health pocketbooks and paperbacks 1968-1969. *Canada's Mental Health Supplement,* 1969, No. 16.

Schwebel, Milton, and Krim, M. Human survival: A selected bibliography. *American Journal of Orthopsychiatry,* 1963, 33(1), 183-191.

Selected and annotated bibliography of the gifted, A. Columbus, Ohio: Ohio Department of Public Instruction, 1960.

Sells, Helen. *A bibliography on drug dependence.* Fort Worth Texas: Texas Christian University Press, 1967.

Shane, Grant. *Contemporary thought with implications for counseling and guidance: a bibliography.* Bloomington, Ind.: Bulletin of the School of Indiana, Indiana University, 1967, 43(4), 1-106.

Shock, Nathan. *A classified bibliography of gerontology and geriatrics.* Stanford, Calif.: Stanford University Press, 1951. Supplements, 1957, 1963.

Signori, Edro et al. Bibliography on attitudes toward hiring socially disadvantaged persons. *Psychological Reports,* 1967, 20(2), 643-656.

Slater, Nancy. The annotated bibliography on research on planarians: X. *Journal of Biological Psychology,* 1967, 9(1), 49-55.

Stein, M., and Heinze, S. *Creativity and the individual.* Glencoe, Ill.: Free Press, 1960.

Stevenson, Harold. Studies of children's learning: A bibliography. *Psychonomic Monographs Supplements,* 1968, 2(11), 191-218.

Stubbins, Joseph. *Workshops for the handicapped: an annotated bibliography: V.* Washington: National Association of Sheltered Workshops and Homebound Programs, 1968.

Tart, Charles. Guide to the literature on psychedelic drugs. In Charles Tart (Ed.) *Altered states of consciousness: a book of readings.* New York: Wiley, 1969, Pp. 477-483.

Tilton, James et al. *Annotated bibliography on childhood schizophrenia, 1955-1964.* New York: Grune and Stratton, 1966.

Tompkins, Dorothy. *Drug addiction: a bibliography.* Berkeley, Calif.: University of California, Bureau of Public Administration, 1960.

Torrance, E. *Publications in open sources related to the Minnesota studies of creative thinking.* Minneapolis, Minn.: University of Minnesota, 1965.

Treadwell, Yvonne. Bibliography of empirical studies of wit and humor. *Psychological Reports,* 1967, 20(3), 1079-1083

Tunkl, Judy. The annotated bibliography of research on planarians: XII. *Journal of Biological Psychology,* 1968, 10(1), 74-79.

Tunkl, Judy. A bibliography on "chemical transfer of training" in vertebrates. *Journal of Biological Psychology,* 1968, 10(1), 80-89.

Weinstein, Sidney et al. Bibliography of sensory and perceptual deprivation, isolation and related areas. *Perceptual and Motor Skills,* 1968, 26(3), 1119-1163.

Williams, Frank. *Selected publications on creative thinking.* St. Paul, Minn.: Creativity Project, Macalester College, 1966.

Williams, Robert, and Webb, W. *Sleep therapy: a bibliography and commentary.* Springfield, Ill.: Thomas, 1966.

Young, Morris. *Bibliography of memory.* Philadelphia: Chilton 1961.

Goverment Publications
Published by the United States Government

407. U.S. Superintendent of Documents. *Monthly Catalog of United States Government Publications. 1895-.* Washington: Government Printing Office, 1895-. Lists government publications according to the department which issued the publication. Both monthly and annual indexes are issued. (p. 16)

408. *Decennial Cumulative Index, 1941-1950 . . .* Washington: Government Printing Office, 1953.

409. *Decennial Cumulative Index, 1951-1960. . . .* Washington: Government Printing Office, 1968.

410. U.S. Superintendent of Documents. *Price Lists.* Washington: Government Printing Office, 1898-.

     Gives prices for materials grouped according to subject fields. Education is list 31; Animal Industry is 38, Health Hygiene is 51; Diseases is 51A; Children's Bureau is 71.

411. U.S. Superintendent of Documents. *Selected United States Government Publications.* Washington: Government Printing Office, 1928-. Biweekly list anyone can receive.

Books About Government Documents

412. Androit, John. *Guide to popular U.S. government publications.* McLean, Va.: Documents Index, 1960.

413. Androit, John. *Guide to U.S. government statistics.* (3rd ed.) Arlington, Va.: Documents Index, 1961.

414. Androit, John. *Guide to United States government serials and periodicals.* McLean, Va.: Documents Index, 1966. 4 vols.

415. Androit, John. *Selected United States government publications, 1968 annual compilation and index.* McLean, Va.: Author, 1969.

416. Body, Alexander. *Annotated bibliography of bibliographies on selected government publications.* Ann Arbor, Mich.: Western Reserve University, 1967. *Supplement 1968. Supplement 1970.*

417. Boyd, Ann. *United States government publications.* (3rd ed.) Revised by Rae Rips. New York: Wilson, 1949.

418. *Congressional Information Service/Index.* Bethesda, Md.: Congressional Information Service, 1970. Indexes and summaries of Congressional publications. Multiple-access index.

419. Hirshberg, Herbert, and Melinat, C. *Subject guide to United States government publications.* Chicago: American Library Association, 1947.

420. Jackson, Ellen. *Subject guide to major United States government publications.* Chicago: American Library Association, 1968.

421. *Legally available U.S. government information.* Arlington, Va.: Output Systems, 1970. 2 vols.

422. Leidy, William *A popular guide to government publications.* (3rd ed.) New York: Columbia University Press, 1968.

423. Schmeckebier, Laurence, and Eastin, R. *Government publications and their use.* (2nd rev. ed.) Washington: Brookings Institute, 1969.

Publication Lists Issued by Agencies of the Health, Education and Welfare Department

FS 1.18:M52/969—U.S. Department of Health, Education, and Welfare, Office of the Secretary. *Mental retardation publications of the department of Health, Education, and Welfare, January 1969.* 1969. Annotated.

FS 2.21:55—HEW, Public Health Service. *Public health service numbered publications, a catalog 1950-1962.* 1964.

FS 2.21:55/supp.1—HEW, Public Health Service. *Public health service numbered publications 1963-1964.* Supplement No. 1, to a catalog 1950-1962. 1965.

FS 2.22/13-9:—HEW, Public Health Service. *NIH quarterly publications list.*

FS 2.24/2:—HEW, Public Health Service. *List of publications issued by PHS.*

FS 5.211:11000E—HEW, Office of Education. *Publications of the office of education, 1967.* 1967.

FS 5.235:35050—HEW, Education Office. *Office of Education publications on exceptional children and youth.* 1963.

FS 17.212:P96/970—HEW, Children's Bureau. *Publications of the children's bureau.* 1970.

FS 17.212:P96/912—HEW Children's Bureau. *Children's bureau publications, an index to publications by number, title, author, and subject, 1912-.* 1970.

HE 20.2417:D84—HEW, National Institutes of Mental Health. *Government publications on drug abuse.* 1970.

Serials

424. *Advances in Behavior Therapy.* New York: Academic Press, 1967-.

425. *Advances in Child Development and Behavior.* New York: Academic Press, 1963-. (p. 20)

426. *Advances in Experimental Social Psychology.* New York: Academic Press, 1964-. (p. 20)

427. *Advances in Psychological Assessment.* Palo Alto, Calif.: Science and Behavior Books, 1968-.

428. *Advances in Sex Research.* New York: Harper & Row, 1963-.

429. *Advances in the Psychology of Learning and Motivation Research and Theory.* New York: Academic Press, 1967-.

430. *Advances in the Study of Behavior.* New York: Academic Press, 1965-.

431. *Annual Progress in Child Psychiatry and Child Development.* New York: Brunner/Mazel, 1968-.

432. *Annual Review of Physiology.* Stanford, Calif.: Annual Reviews, 1939-.

433. *Annual Review of Psychology.* Stanford, Calif.: Annual Reviews, 1950-. (pp. 19, 20, 31)

434. *Annual Survey of Psychoanalysis.* New York: International Universities Press, 1952-.

435. *Cognitive Studies.* New York: Brunner/Mazel, 1970-.

436. *Contributions to Sensory Physiology.* New York: Academic Press, 1965-.

437. *Current Concerns in Clinical Psychology.* Chicago: Aldine, 1965-.

438. *Current Topics in Clinical and Community Psychology.* New York: Academic Press, 1969-.

439. *Current Psychiatric Therapies.* New York: Grune and Stratton, 1961-.

440. *Disadvantaged Child.* New York: Brunner/Mazel, 1969-.

441. *Eugenics Society Symposia.* New York: Plenum, 1965-.

442. *Exceptional Infant.* New York: Brunner/Mazel, 1970-.

443. *International Review of Research in Mental Retardation.* New York: Academic Press, 1966-. (p. 20)

444. *International Series of Monographs on Experimental Psychology.* New York: Pergamon, 1964-.

445. *Langley Porter Child Psychiatry Series, The.* Palo Alto, Calif.: Science and Behavior, 1966-.

446. *Mental Retardation.* New York: Grune and Stratton, 1969-.

447. *Minnesota Symposia on Child Psychology.* Minneapolis: University of Minnesota Press, 1967-. (p. 20)

448. *Nebraska Symposium on Motivation.* Lincoln: University of Nebraska Press, 1953-. 1969 volume contains list of all articles since 1953. (p. 20)

449. *New Directions in Mental Health.* New York: Grune and Stratton, 1968-.

450. *Progress in Clinical Psychology.* New York: Grune and Stratton, 1956-.

451. *Progress in Experimental Personality Research.* New York: Academic Press, 1964-. (p. 20)

452. *Progress in Learning Disabilities.* New York: Grune and Stratton, 1968-.

453. *Progress in Neurology and Psychiatry.* New York: Grune and Stratton, 1944-.

454. *Progress in Physiological Psychology.* New York: Academic Press, 1966-.

455. *Psychoanalytic Study of the Child.* New York: International Universities Press, 1945-.

456. *Psychological Issues Monograph Series.* New York: International Universities Press, 1959-.

457. *Recent Advances in Biological Psychiatry.* New York: Plenum, 1962-.

458. *Research Annual on Intergroup Relations.* Chicago: Quadrangle Books, 1966-.

459. *Science and Psychoanalysis.* New York: Grune and Stratton 1958-.

460. *Society for Research in Child Development: Monographs.* Chicago: University of Chicago Press, 1935-.

461. *The World Biennial of Psychiatry and Psychotherapy.* New York: Basic Books, 1970-.

Lists of Selected Sources in Psychology

Reference Sources

462. Borchardt, D. *How to find out in philosophy and psychology.* New York: Pergamon Press, 1968, pb. Discusses American and foreign reference sources. (p. 24)

463. Daniel, Robert, and Louttit, C. *Professional problems in psychology.* New York: Prentice-Hall, 1953. Contains comprehensive list of reference sources and annotated list of 331 psychological journals. (p. 24)

464. Louttit, Chauncey. *Handbook of psychological literature.* Bloomington, Ind.: Principia Press, 1932. Expanded and updated by Daniel and Louttit's *Professional problems in psychology* (1953). Contains list of 1000 journals which contain psychological information.

465. Sarbin, Theodore, and Coe, W. *The student psychologist's handbook: a guide to sources.* Cambridge, Mass.: Schenkmen, 1969, pb. 21 major reference sources and 36 psychological journals are listed and annotated.

Nonreference Sources

466. British Psychological Society. *Psychology: a selected list of books.* Cambridge, England: Cambridge University Press, 1951 Annotated list of almost 400 books arranged in 19 categories.

467. Buros, Oscar (Ed.) *Mental measurements yearbook.* Highland Park, N.J.: Gryphon, 1938-1965. 6 vols. Contains comprehensive list of books on tests and measurements.

468. *Choice.* Chicago: American Library Association, 1964-. The February 1970 issue lists 90 books important for undergraduate libraries.

469. Courtney, Winifred (Ed.) *The reader's adviser: a guide to the best in literature.* (11th ed.) New York: Bowker, 1969. 2 vols. Books listed here are for "thoughtful and mature readers." In the chapter on psychology the sections on "Works on Modern Psychology and Psychoanalysis" and "Psychologists" contain suggested readings. Many of the 400 psychology titles are annotated. (p. 24)

470. Grinstein, Alexander. *The Index of Psychoanalytic Writings.* New York: International Universities Press, 1956-1966. 9 vols. A complete listing of psychoanalytic writings from 1900 to 1960 arranged alphabetically by author. An expansion and updating of the next source. (pp. 11, 19, 30)

471. Richman, John. *Index Psycho-Analyticus, 1893-1926.* London: Hogarth Press, 1928. (International Psycho-Analytical Library, No. 14) (p. 19)

472. *Harvard list of books in psychology.* (3rd ed.) Cambridge, Mass.: Harvard University Press, 1964, pb. Annotated list of 704 books grouped into 31 categories. (p. 24)

Although many of the sources are technical and the list needs to be updated, this is the best listing of psychological books for purposes of library research.

473. Hawkins, R. (Ed.) *Scientific, medical, and technical books.* (2nd ed.) Washington: National Academy of Sciences, 1958.

Over 400 books are divided into 12 areas. The contents and a paragraph about the importance of each book are given. More textbooks are listed here than in the *Harvard List of Books in Psychology* (472).

474. Hoselitz, Bert (Ed.) *A reader's guide to the social sciences.* (2nd ed.) Glencoe, Ill.: Free Press, 1970. Contains essay on broad areas of psychology with citation of articles and books representative of important trends. (p. 24)

475. Klein, Bernard (Ed.) *Guide to American educational directories.* New York: Klein and Company, 1969. An example of a directory listed here: *Directory for exceptional children.* (6th ed.) Boston: Porter Sargent, 1969.

476. Louttit, Chauncey. *Bibliography of bibliographies of psychology, 1900-1927.* Washington: National Research Council, 1928. (National Research Council Bulletin, No. 65) Contains complete listing of bibliographies from 1900 to 1927 arranged alphabetically by authors with a subject index. (p. 19)

477. Obler, Paul. Psychology. In J. Weber (Ed.) *Good reading: a guide for serious reading.* New York: Weybright and Talley, 1969, Pp. 241-250. Contains annotated list of 50 books grouped into four areas. (p. 24)

478. Rand, Benjamin. *Bibliography of philosophy, psychology and cognate subjects.* New York: Macmillan, 1905. New edition, 1928. Published in 1905 as volumes 3 and 4 of Baldwin, James. *Dictionary of philosophy and psychology* . . . Most comprehensive listing of early psychological sources. (pp. 15, 19)

479. Ryan, M. *PACAF basic bibliographies for base libraries: psychology.* San Francisco: Commander in Chief, Pacific Air Forces, 1966. Annotated list of books selected as important for military base libraries.

480. Solso, Robert, and Johnson, J. A survey of recommended readings in psychology. *Psychological Reports,* 1967, 20, 855-857. Lists the 33 most frequently recommended psychology books obtained from a 1966 survey of graduate departments.

481. Sundberg, Norman. Basic readings in psychology. *American Psychologist,* 1960, 15, 343-345. Lists the 30 most frequently recommended psychology books obtained from 1953-1954 and 1958-1959 surveys of graduate departments.

482. Voight, Melvin, and Treyz, J. *Books for college libraries.* Chicago: American Library Association, 1967. Lists over 800 psychology books chosen as being important for undergraduate libraries.

483. Watson, Robert et al. Psychology. In Carl White et al. *Sources of information in the social sciences.* Totowa, N.J.: Bedminster Press, 1964. Pp. 273-309. 249 books are grouped into 16 subject areas. A few French and German books are listed with trends in areas discussed. Also contains annotated list of 53 reference sources. (p. 24)

Lists of Selected Sources in Fields Related to Psychology
Anthropology

484. Beckham   Rexford. Anthropology. *Library Trends,* 1967, 15(4), 685-703. Annotated.

485. *Biennial reviews of anthropology, 1959-.* Stanford, Calif.: Stanford University Press, 1959-.

486. *International bibliography of social and cultural anthropology.* Chicago: Aldine, 1955-.

487. Kelsey, Cynthia, and Pelto, P. *Guide to cultural anthropology.* (Rev. ed.) Glenview Ill.: Scott, Foresman, 1969, pb.

488. Keesing, Felix. Anthropology. In Carl White et al. *Sources of information in the social sciences.* Totowa, N.J.: Bedminster Press, 1964. Pp. 229-272. Annotated.

489. Kelly, Gail. Anthropology. In Bert Hoselitz (Ed.) *A reader's guide to the social sciences.* New York: Free Press, 1959, Pp. 188-209, pb. Annotated.

490. Mandelbaum David et al. (Eds.) *Resources for the teaching of anthropology: including a basic list of books and periodicals for college libraries.* Berkeley: University of California, 1963, pb.

Biology

491. Bamber, Lyle. Biology. *Library Trends,* 1967, 15(4), 829-835.

492. Kerker, Ann, and Schlundt, E. *Literature sources in the biological sciences.* Lafayette, Inc.: Purdue University Libraries, 1961.

493. Smith, P.oger, and Painter, R. *Guide to the literature of the zoological sciences.* (7th ed.) Minneapolis: Burgess, 1967, pb.

Computers

494. Carter, C. *A guide to reference sources in the computer sciences.* New York: CCMIC, 1970.

495. Pritchard, Alan. *Guide to computer literature: an introductory survey of the sources of information.* Hamden, Conn.: Archon, 1969.

Education

496. Anderson, Vivienne. *Paperbacks in education.* New York: Teachers College Press, 1966, pb.

497. Brickman, William. Education. In Carl White et al. *Sources of information in the social sciences.* Totowa, N.J.: Bedminster Press, 1964. Pp. 310-357. Annotated.

498. Burke, Arvid, and Burke, M. *Documentation in education.* New York: Teachers College Press, 1967. Annotated. (p. 24)

499. Forman, Sidney and Collins, R. Education. *Library Trends,* 1967, 15(4), 648-669. Annotated.

500. Foskett, D. *How to find out: educational research.* Oxford, N.Y.: Pergamon Press, 1965, pb. Annotated.

501. Hillway, Tyrus. *Handbook of educational research: a guide to methods and materials.* Boston: Houghton Mifflin, 1969, pb.

502. Klein, Bernard (Ed.) *Guide to American educational directories.* (3rd ed.) New York: Klein and Company, 1969. Annotated.

503. Manheim, Theodore et al. *Sources in educational research.* Detroit: Wayne State University, 1969, pb. Annotated.

504. Marks, Barbara (Ed.) *The New York University lists of books in education.* New York: Citation Press, 1968, pb. Annotated list of almost 3000 sources, many relevant to psychology. (p. 24)

505. Renetzsky, Alvin, and Kaplan, P. (Eds.) *Standard education almanac, 1968.* Los Angeles: Academic Media, 1968.

506. Samples, G. *A guide to basic reference books in education.* (Rev. ed.) San Diego:Library, San Diego State College, 1966.

507. Van Dalen, Deobold, and Meyer, W. *Understanding educational research.*(Rev. ed.) New York: McGraw-Hill, 1966. Annotated.

Mass Media

508. Bluemer, Paul. Mass media. *Choice,* 1969, 5, 1554-1559.

509. Blum, Eleanor. *Reference books in the mass media.* Urbana, Ill.: University of Illinois Press Urbana, 1963.

510. Brockett, Oscar et al. *A bibliographic guide to research in speech and dramatic arts.* Chicago: Scott, Foresman, 1964.

Medicine and Psychiatry

511. Alexander, Raphael (Ed.) *Sources of medical information.* New York: Exceptional Books, 1969.

512. Blake, John, and Roos, C. (Eds.) *Medical reference works, 1679-1966: a selected bibliography.* Chicago: Medical Library Association, 1967.

513. Brodman, Estelle, and Ohta, M. Medicine. *Library Trends,* 1967, 15(4), 896-908.

514. Ebert, Myrl. *An introduction to the literature of the medical sciences.* Chapel Hill, N.C.: University of North Carolina Book Exchange, 1967, pb.

515. Medical Library Association. *Handbook of medical library practice.* (3rd ed.) Chicago: American Library Association, 1970.

516. Menninger, Karl. *A guide to psychiatric books.* (2nd ed.) New York: Grune and Stratton, 1956. Several of the lists are important in psychology. Almost 3000 books are listed. (p. 24)

517. Morton, Leslie. *How to use a medical library.* (4th ed.) London: Heinemann, 1964.

518. Sanazaro, Paul, and Chatton, M. (Eds.) *Current medical references.* (4th ed.) Los Altos, Calif.: Lange Medical Publication, 1965.

519. Woods, J. et al. Basic psychiatric literature. *Medical Library Association Bulletin,* 1968a, 58, 295-309. Lists 104 books most often recommended by psychiatry departments.

520. Woods, J. et al. Basic psychiatric literature. *Medical Library Association Bulletin,* 1968b, 56, 404-427. Lists 307 important psychiatric articles.

Philosophy

521. Arnold, Charles. Philosophy and religion. *Library Trends,* 1967, 15(3), 459-477.

522. Borchardt, D. *How to find out in philosophy and psychology.* New York: Pergamon Press, 1968, pb.

523. Koren, Henry. *Research in philosophy.* Pittsburg: Duquesne University Press, 1966.

Sociology

524. Blau, Peter, and Moore, J. Sociology. In Bert Hoselitz (Ed.) *A reader's guide to the social sciences.* New York: Free Press, 1959, Pp. 158-187, pb.

525. Einstadter, Werner. Criminology: A bibliographic selection. *Choice,* 1970, 7(2), 195-202.

526. *International bibliography of sociology.* Chicago: Aldine, 1951-.

527. Zetterberg, Hans. Sociology. In Carl White et al. *Sources of information in the social sciences.* Totowa, N.J.: Bedminster Press, 1964, Pp. 183-228.

Guides to Reference Sources in All Fields

528. Walford, Albert (Ed.) *Guide to reference materials.* (2nd ed.) London: The Library Association, 1966-1970.

529. Winchell, Constance. *Guide to reference books.* (8th ed.) Chicago: American Library Association, 1967. First supplement 1965-1966. 1968. Second supplement 1967-1968. 1970. (p. 11)

Bibliographies of Bibliographies

530. Besterman, Theodore. *A world bibliography of bibliographies.* (4th ed.) Lausanne: Societas Bibliographica, 1965. 5 vols. Contains few recent psychological bibliographies.

531. *The Bibliographic Index: A Cumulative Bibliography of Bibliographies.* New York: Wilson, 1938-. A subject index listing bibliographies separately published and included in books and periodicals. Turn first to the subject "Psychology" and then to related entries. (pp. 16, 19, 30)

Miscellaneous

532. *Publication manual of the American Psychological Association.* Washington: American Psychological Association, 1967, pb. (pp. 34, 36)

533. Turabian, Kate. *Student's guide for writing college papers.* Chicago: University of Chicago Press, 1963. (p. 4)

534. U.S. Library of Congress. Subject Cataloging Division. *Subject headings used in the dictionary catalogs of the Library of Congress.* (7th ed.) Edited by Marguerite Quattlebaum. Washington: Government Printing Office, 1966. (pp. 5, 30)

535. Westby, Barbara (Ed.) *Sears list of subject headings.* (9th ed.) New York: Wilson, 1965. (pp. 5, 30)

Lists of Published Books

Current Books

536. *The ABS guide to recent publications in the social and behavioral sciences.* New York: American Behavioral Scientist, 1965-. Annual cumulation of annotated listing of selected

journals, pamphlets, and books which appeared in New Studies in the *American Behavioral Scientist.*

537. *American book publishing record.* New York: Bowker, 1960-. Lists books published in the United States according to Dewey Decimal Classification.

538. *Cumulative book index.* New York: Wilson, 1898-. Lists books published in English alphabetically, according to title, author, and subject.

539. *Forthcoming books.* New York: Bowker, 1966-. Lists forthcoming and recently published books according to titles and authors.

540. *Quarterly check-list of psychology: an international index of current books, monographs, brochures and separates.* Darien, Conn.: American Bibliographic Service, 1961-. Lists by authors.

Older Books

541. *The ABS guide to recent publications in the social and behavioral sciences.* New York: American Behavioral Scientist, 1965-. Annual cumulations.

542. *American book publishing record.* New York: Bowker, 1960-. Annual cumulations.

543. *Books in print: an author-title-series index to the publishers trade list annual.* N.Y.: Bowker, 1948-. 2 vols.

544. *Cumulative book index.* New York: Wilson, 1898-. Annual cumulations.

545. *Library of Congress catalog books: subjects.* Publisher varies, 1950-.

546. *National union catalog: a cumulative author list.* Washington: Library of Congress, Card Division, 1956-.

547. *Library of Congress author catalog: a cumulative list of works represented by Library of Congress printed cards, 1948-1952.* Ann Arbor, Mich.: Edwards, 1953, 24 vols.

548. U.S. Library of Congress. *A catalog of books. Supplement: cards issued August 1, 1942-December 31, 1947.* Ann Arbor, Mich.: Edwards, 1948, 42 vols.

549. U.S. Library of Congress. *A catalog of books represented by Library of Congress printed cards, issued to July 31, 1942.* Ann Arbor, Mich.: Edwards, 1942-1946. 167 vols.

550. U.S. Library of Congress. *The national union catalog: a cumulative author list representing Library of Congress printed cards . . . 1953-1957.* Ann Arbor, Mich.: Edwards, 1958.

551. *Subject guide to Books in Print.* New York: Bowker, 1957-.

Paperback Books

552. *Annual paperbound book guide for colleges.* New York: Bowker, 1959-.

553. *Paperbound books in print.* New York: Bowker, 1955-.

Psychology Paperback Books

554. *Contemporary Psychology* has reviewed and listed paperbacks on psychological topics. Listed here are the years and pages for those reviews.

1956	291-294	1964	10-17, 59-61, 452-461
1957	275-278	1965	216-223, 500-506
1958	119-120	1966	290-295, 477-484
1959	262-267	1967	248-250, 565-567
1960	331-334	1968	305-308, 605-607
1961	341-347	1969	654-657
1962	262-268		
1963	9-12		

Lists of Periodicals

All Periodicals

555. Garry, Leon (Ed.) *The standard periodical directory.* New York: Oxbridge, 1969.

556. *Irregular serials and annuals: an international directory.* New York: Bowker, 1967.

557. *Ulrich's international periodicals directory.* (13th ed.) New York: Bowker, 1969-1970, 2 vols.

558. *Union list of serials.* (3rd ed.) New York: Wilson, 1965. 5 vols. *New serials titles* is an updating of the *Union list of serials.*

Psychology Periodicals

559. Publications represented. *Psychological Abstracts.* Lancaster, Pa.: American Psychological Association, 1927-. Included in

the index volumes is a list of the journals searched for psychological articles.

560. *Psychology: world list of specialized periodicals.* New York: Humanities, 1967.

561. Tomkins, Margaret, and Shirley, N. *A checklist of serials in psychology and allied fields.* Troy, N.Y.: Whitston, 1969.

Education Periodicals

562. Camp, William. *Guide to periodicals in education.* Metuchen, N.J.: Scarecrow 1968.

563. *Current index to journals in education.* New York: CCM Information Corporation, 1969-.

564. Educational Press Association of America. *A classified list of educational periodicals.* Glassboro, N.J.: The Association 1963.

565. Harvard University Library. *Education and education periodicals.* Cambridge, Mass.: Harvard University Press, 1968, 2 vols.

566. Lins, Leon, and Rees, R. *Scholars' guide to journals of education and educational psychology.* Madison, Wis. Dembar Educational Research Services, 1965.

567. Thurman, Robert. *An annotated bibliography of education periodicals in William Allen White Library.* Emporia, Kansas: Kansas State Teachers College, 1960.

Journals ("R" following a journal indicates that books are reviewed in the journal.)

Abnormal Psychology

American Journal of Orthopsychiatry, 1930-. **R**

American Journal of Psychiatry, 1944-. **R**

American Journal of Psychotherapy, 1946. **R**

Behavior Therapy, 1970-.

British Journal of Social and Clinical Psychology, 1962-. **R**

Journal of Abnormal and Social Psychology, 1906-1964.

Journal of Abnormal Psychology, 1965-.

Journal of Autism and Childhood Schizophrenia, 1971-.

Journal of Clinical Psychology, 1945-. **R**

Journal of Consulting Psychology, 1937-1967.

Journal of Consulting and Clinical Psychology, 1968-.

Journal of Counseling Psychology, 1954-. **R**

Journal of Nervous and Mental Diseases, 1874-. **R**

Mental Health, 1940-. **R**

Mental Health Digest, 1969-.

Mental Hygiene, 1917-. **R**

Psychiatry, 1938-. **R**

Psychoanalytic Review, 1913-. **R**

Review of Existential Psychology and Psychiatry, 1961-. **R**

Developmental Psychology

Adolescence, 1966-. **R**

Aging, 1951-.

Aging and Human Development, 1970-.

Child Care Quarterly, 1971-.

Child Development, 1930-.

Child Psychiatry and Human Development, 1970-.

Children, 1954-.

Developmental Psychology, 1969-.

Developmental Psychobiology, 1969-.

Exceptional Children, 1934-. **R**

Genetic Psychology Monographs, 1926-.

Gifted Child Quarterly, 1957-. **R**

Journal of Child Psychology and Psychiatry and Allied Disciplines, 1960-. **R**

Journal of Experimental Child Psychology, 1964-.

Journal of Geriatric Psychiatry, 1967-.

Merrill-Palmer Quarterly of Behavior and Development, 1954-.

Monographs of the Society for Research in Child Development, 1935-.

Research Relating to Children, 1954-.

Youth and Society, 1969-.

Educational Psychology

American Educational Research Journal, 1964-. **R**

British Journal of Educational Psychology, 1931-. **R**

Educational and Psychological Measurement, 1941-. **R**

Harvard Educational Review, 1931-. **R**

Journal of Educational Measurement, 1964-.

Journal of Educational Research, 1920-. **R**

Journal of Educational Psychology, 1910-.

Journal of Experimental Education, 1932-.

Phi Delta Kappa, 1918-.

Review of Educational Research, 1931-.

Sociology of Education, 1927-.

Experimental Psychology

American Journal of Psychology, 1887-. **R**

Behavior Genetics, 1970-.

British Journal of Psychology, 1904-. **R**

Cognitive Psychology, 1970-.

International Journal of Psychobiology, 1970-.

Journal of Comparative and Physiological Psychology, 1908-.

Journal of Experimental Psychology, 1916-.

Journal of General Psychology, 1927-.

Journal of Neurophysiology, 1938-.

Journal of Psychology, 1936-.

Journal of the Experimental Analysis of Behavior, 1958-. **R**

Journal of Physiology, 1878-.

Journal of Verbal Learning and Verbal Behavior, 1962-.

Learning and Motivation, 1970-.

Perceptual and Motor Skills, 1941-.

Psychological Bulletin, 1904-.

Psychological Monographs, 1895-1968.

Psychological Record, 1951-. **R**

Psychological Reports, 1955-. **R**

Psychological Review, 1894-.

Psychophysiology, 1964-. **R**

Psychonomic Science, 1964-.

Quarterly Journal of Experimental Psychology, 1948-. **R**

Personality and Social Psychology

British Journal of Social and Clinical Psychology, 1962-. **R**

Human Relations, 1947-.

Journal of Abnormal and Social Psychology, 1906-1964.

Journal of Applied Behavioral Science, 1965-. **R**

Journal of Applied Social Psychology, 1971-.

Journal of Conflict Resolution, 1957-. **R**

Journal of Creative Behavior, 1967-. **R**

Journal of Experimental Research in Personality, 1965-.

Journal of Experimental Social Psychology, 1965-.

Journal of Personality, 1932-.

Journal of Personality and Social Psychology, 1965-.

Journal of Projective Techniques and Personality Assessment, 1937-. **R**

Journal of Social Issues, 1945-.

Journal of Social Psychology, 1929-.

Sociometry, 1937-.

Other Psychological Journals

American Imago, 1939-. **R**

American Psychologist, 1946-.

Behavioral Science, 1956-. **R**

Canadian Journal of Behavioral Science, 1969-.

Canadian Journal of Psychology, 1947-.

Canadian Psychologist, 1951-.

Contemporary Psychology, 1956-. **R**

Existential Psychiatry, 1959-. **R**

Human Factors, 1958-.

International Journal of Psychology, 1966-.

Journal of Applied Behavioral Analysis, 1968-.

Journal of Applied Psychology, 1917-.

Journal of Humanistic Psychology, 1961-. **R**

Journal of Individual Psychology, 1940-. **R**

Journal of Learning Disabilities, 1968-. **R**

Journal of Mathematical Psychology, 1964-.

Journal of Motor Behavior, 1969-.

Journal of Parapsychology, 1937-. **R**

Journal of Psychedelic Drugs, 1968-.

Journal of Vocational Behavior, 1971-.

Organizational Behavior and Human Performance, 1966-.

Personnel Psychology, 1948-. **R**

Professional Psychology, 1970-. **R**

Psychology Today, 1967-. **R**

Psychometrika, 1936-. **R**

Nonpsychological Journals

American Scientist, 1913-. **R**

Daedalus, 1958-.

Literature and Psychology, 1951-.

Nature, 1869-. **R**

New York Times Magazine, 1896-.

Science, 1880-. **R**

Science News, 1921-. **R**

Scientific American, 1845-. **R**

Social Problems, 1953-. **R**

Time, "Behavior" 1969-.

Trans-action, 1963-. **R**

U.S. Government Psychological Periodicals

Adult Development and Aging Abstracts, 1969-. Experimental (Issued to determine if sufficient need exists to warrant a publication of this nature.)

Aging, 1951-.

American Education, 1965-.

Bulletin of Suicidology, 1967-. Experimental.

Children, 1954-.

Crime and Delinquency Abstracts, 1963-.

Drug Dependence (includes abstracts), 1969-. Experimental.

Epilepsy Abstracts, 1968-.

Index Medicus, includes *Bibliography of Medical Reviews,* 1960-.

Mental Health Digest, 1969-.

Mental Retardation Abstracts, 1964-.

Occupational Mental Health Notes (includes abstracts), 1967-.

Psychopharmacology Abstracts, 1963-.

Reproduction and Population Research Abstracts, 1969-. Experimental.

Research in Education, 1966-.

Research Relating to Children, 1954c-.

The Schizophrenia Bulletin, 1969-. Experimental.

Lists of Textbooks and Books of Readings
Introductory Textbooks

Ahmavaara, Y. *Psychology as a natural science.* Boston: Houghton Mifflin, 1970.

Aiken, Lewis. *General psychology.* San Francisco: Chandler, 1970.

Branca, Albert. *Psychology: the science of behavior.* Rev. (ed.) Boston: Allyn and Bacon, 1968.

Bugelski, Bergen. *An introduction to the principles of psychology.* New York: Holt, Rinehart & Winston, 1960.

Calvin, Allen et al. (Eds.) *Psychology.* Boston: Allyn and Bacon, 1961.

Candland, Douglas, and Campbell, J. *Exploring behavior: an introduction to psychology.* New York: Basic Books, 1961.

Cohen, John. *New introduction to psychology.* New York: Hillary, 1966, pb.

Cohen, Jozef. *The eyewitness series in psychology.* Chicago: Rand McNally, 1969-1971, pb.

Cox, Frank. *Psychology.* Dubuque, Iowa: Wm. C. Brown Company Publishers, 1970.

Dallett, Kent. *Problems of psychology.* New York: Wiley, 1969.

Das, S. *General psychology.* New York: Taplinger, 1964.

Deese, James. *Principles of psychology.* Boston: Allyn and Bacon, 1964.

Deese, James. *General psychology.* Boston: Allyn and Bacon, 1967.

Dember, William, and Jenkins, J. *General psychology: modeling behavior and experience.* Englewood Cliffs, N.J.: Prentice Hall, 1970.

Edwards, David. *General psychology.* New York: Macmillan, 1968.

Engle, T., and Snellgrove, L. *Psychology: its principles and applications.* (5th ed.) New York: Harcourt, Brace and World, 1969.

Evans, Idella, and Smith, P. *Psychology for a changing world: an applied introduction.* New York: Wiley, 1970.

Ferster, C., and Perrott, M. *Behavior principles.* New York: Appleton-Century-Crofts, 1968.

Fitch, Stanley. *Insights into human behavior.* Boston: Holbrook, 1970.

Galanter, Eugene. *Textbook of elementary psychology.* San Francisco: Holden-Day, 1966.

Gallup, Howard. *An invitation to modern psychology.* New York: Free Press, 1969, pb.

Gardiner, W. *Psychology: a story of a search.* Belmont, Calif.: Brooks/Cole, 1970.

Garrett, Henry. *Psychology and life.* (3rd ed.) New York: Social Science Press, 1969.

Geldard, Frank. *Fundamentals of psychology.* New York: Wiley, 1962.

Giorgi, A. *Psychology as a human science: a phenomenologically based approach.* New York: Harper & Row, 1970, pb.

Greeno, James. *Elementary theoretical psychology.* Reading, Mass.: Addison-Wesley, 1968, pb.

Hahn, John. *An introduction to psychology.* New York: Doubleday, 1962, pb.

Hall, Calvin. *Psychology: an introductory textbook.* Cleveland: Allen, 1960.

Hebb, Donald. *Textbook of psychology.* (2nd ed.) Philadelphia: Saunders, 1966.

Heckel, Robert, and Peacock, L. *Textbook of general psychology.* St. Louis: Mosby, 1966.

Hershey, Gerald, and Lugo, J. *Living psychology: an experiential approach to behavior.* New York: Macmillan, 1970.

Hilgard, Ernest, and Atkinson, R. *Introduction to psychology.* (4th ed.) New York: Harcourt, Brace and World, 1967.

Hill, Winfred. *Psychology: principles and problems.* Philadelphia: Lippincott, 1970.

Hutt, Max et al. *Psychology: the science of interpersonal behavior.* New York: Harper & Row, 1966.

Isaacson, Robert et al. *Psychology: the science of behavior.* New York: Harper & Row, 1965.

Johnson, Donald. *Psychology: a problem-solving approach.* New York: Harper & Row, 1961.

Kagan, Jerome, and Havemann, E. *Psychology: an introduction.* New York: Harcourt, Brace and World, 1968.

Kalish, Richard. *Psychology of human behavior.* (2nd ed.) Belmont, Calif.: Brooks/Cole, 1970.

Kendler, Howard. *Basic psychology.* (2nd ed.) New York: Appleton-Century-Crofts, 1968.

Kimble, Gregory, and Garmezy, N. *Principles of general psychology.* (3rd ed.) New York: Ronald, 1968.

Krech, David et al. *Elements of psychology.* New York: Knopf, 1969.

Krech, David et al. *Elements of psychology: a briefer course.* New York: Knopf, 1970, pb.

Lazarus, Richard (Ed.) *The foundations of modern psychology series.* Englewood Cliffs, N.J.: Prentice-Hall, 1963-1967, pb.

Leuba, Clarence, and John, W. *Man: a general psychology.* New York: Holt, Reinhart & Winston, 1961.

Lewis, Donald. *Scientific principles of psychology.* Englewood Cliffs, N.J.: Prentice-Hall, 1963.

Lindgren, Henry et al. *Psychology: an introduction to a behavioral science.* (3rd ed.) New York: Wiley, 1970.

McKeachie, Wilbert, and Doyle, C. *Psychology.* (2nd ed.) Reading, Mass.: Addison-Wesley, 1970.

McKeller, Peter. *Experience and behavior.* Baltimore: Penguin, 1968, pb.

Millenson, John. *Principles of behavioral analysis.* New York: Macmillan, 1967.

Miller, George. *Psychology: the science of mental life.* New York: Harper & Row, 1962, pb.

Mohsin, Syed. *Elementary psychology.* New York: Taplinger, 1967.

Morgan, Clifford, and King, R. *Introduction to psychology.* (3rd ed.) New York: McGraw-Hill, 1966.

Moskowitz, Merle, and Orgel, A. *General psychology: a core text in human behavior.* Boston: Houghton Mifflin, 1969.

Munn, Norman et al. *Basic psychology: an adaptation of introduction to psychology.* (2nd ed.) Boston: Houghton Mifflin, 1969, pb.

Munn, Norman et al. *Introduction to psychology.* (2nd ed.) Boston: Houghton Mifflin, 1969.

Naylor, G. *Psychology: an evolutionary introduction.* St. Lucia, Queensland: University of Queensland Press, 1968, pb.

Notterman, Joseph. *Behavior: a systematic approach.* New York: Random House, 1970.

Nurnberger, John et al. *An introduction to the science of human behavior.* New York: Appleton-Century-Crofts, 1963.

Psychology today: an introduction. Del Mar, Calif.: CRM Books, 1970.

Ray, William. *The science of psychology: an introduction.* New York: Macmillan, 1964.

Ruch, Floyd. *Psychology and life.* (7th ed.) Glenview, Ill.: Scott, Foresman, 1967.

Ruch, Floyd. *Psychology and life: brief seventh edition.* Glenview, Ill.: Scott, Foresman, 1967, pb.

Salzinger, Kurt. *Psychology: The science of behavior.* New York: Springer, 1969, pb.

Sanford, Fillmore, and Wrightsman, L. *Psychology: a scientific study of man.* (3rd ed.) Belmont, Calif.: Brooks/Cole, 1970.

Sartain, Aaron et al. *Psychology: understanding human behavior.* (3rd ed.) New York: McGraw-Hill, 1967.

Sells, Saul. *Essentials of psychology.* New York: Ronald, 1962.

Stagner, Ross, and Solley, C. *Basic psychology: a perceptual-homeostatis approach.* New York: McGraw-Hill, 1969.

Swartz, Paul. *Psychology: the study of behavior.* New York: Van Nostrand Reinhold, 1963.

Swift, W. *General psychology.* New York: McGraw-Hill, 1969.

Telford, Charles, and Sawrey, J. *Psychology: a concise introduction to the fundamentals of behavior.* Belmont, Calif.: Brooks/Cole, 1968.

Thompson, William and De Bold, R. *Psychology.* New York: McGraw-Hill, 1970.

Vernon, J. (Ed.) *Introduction to general psychology: a self-selection textbook.* Dubuque, Iowa: Wm. C. Brown Company Publishers, 1966-1969, pb.

Vinacke, W. *Foundations of psychology.* New York: Van Nostrand Reinhold, 1968.

Von Haller Gilmer, B. *Psychology.* New York: Harper & Row, 1970.

Walker, Edward (Ed.) *Basic concepts in psychology series: a basic textbook series of coordinated paperback volumes.* Belmont, Calif.: Brooks/Cole, 1965-1970, pb.

Whittaker, James. *Introduction to psychology.* (2nd ed.) Philadelphia: Saunders, 1970.

Wickens, Delos, and Meyer, D. *Psychology.* (Rev. ed.) New York: Holt, Rinehart & Winston, 1961.

Williams, Griffith. *Psychology: a first course.* New York: Harcourt, Brace and World, 1960.

Wrench, David. *Psychology: a social approach.* New York: McGraw-Hill, 1969.

Wright, D. et al. *Introducing psychology: an experimental approach.* Baltimore: Penguin, 1970, pb.

Readings on Introductory Psychology

Aronson, Elliot (Ed.) *Voices of modern psychology.* Reading, Mass.: Addison-Wesley, 1969, pb.

Baker, Robert (Ed.) *Psychology in the wry.* New York: Van Nostrand Reinhold, 1963, pb.

Bartz, Wayne (Ed.) *Readings in general psychology.* Boston: Allyn and Bacon, 1968, pb.

Blough, Donald, and Blough, P. *Experiments in psychology.* New York: Holt, Rinehart & Winston, 1964, pb.

Bugental, James (Ed.) *Challenges of humanistic psychology.* New York: McGraw-Hill, 1967, pb.

Cohen, John (Ed.) *Readings in psychology.* New York: Hillary, 1964.

Coopersmith, Stanley (Ed.) *Frontiers of psychological research: readings from Scientific American.* San Francisco: Freeman, 1964, pb.

Daniel, Robert (Ed.) *Contemporary readings in general psychology.* (2nd ed.) Boston: Houghton Mifflin, 1965, pb.

Drever, James (Ed.) *Sourcebook in psychology.* New York: Philosophical Library, 1960.

Dulany, Don et al. (Eds.) *Contributions to modern psychology.* (2nd ed.) New York: Oxford, 1963, pb.

Dyal, James (Ed.) *Readings in psychology.* (2nd ed.) New York: McGraw-Hill, 1967, pb.

Farberow, Norman (Ed.) *Taboo topics.* New York: Atherton, 1966, pb.

Foley, John et al. (Eds.) *Contemporary readings in psychology.* New York: Harper & Row, 1970, pb.

Foss, Brian (Ed.) *New horizons in psychology.* Baltimore: Penguin, 1966, pb.

Gibbons, Don, and Connelly, J. (Eds.) *Selected readings in psychology.* St. Louis: Mosby, 1970, pb.

Goode, Erich (Ed.) *Marijuana.* New York: Atherton, 1969, pb.

Guthrie, Robert (Ed.) *Psychology in the world today.* Reading, Mass.: Addison-Wesley, 1968, pb.

Guthrie, Robert (Ed.) *Encounter: issues of human concern.* Menlo Park, Calif.: Cummings, 1970, pb.

Hartley, Eugene, and Hartley, R. (Eds.) *Readings in psychology.* (3rd ed.) New York: Crowell, 1965, pb.

King, Richard (Ed.) *Readings for an introduction to psychology.* (2nd ed.) New York: McGraw-Hill, 1966, pb.

Kintz, B., and Bruning, J. (Eds.) *Research in psychology.* Glenview, Ill.: Scott, Foresman, 1970, pb.

Lockhart, R. et al. (Eds.) *Readings for general psychology.* New York: Johnson Reprints, 1967.

McGaugh, James et al. (Eds.) *Psychobiology: the biological bases of behavior: readings from Scientific American.* San Francisco: Freeman, 1967, pb.

McKinney, Fred (Ed.) *Psychology in action.* New York: Macmillan, 1967, pb.

Messick, David (Ed.) *Mathematical thinking in behavioral sciences: readings from Scientific American.* San Francisco: Freeman, 1968, pb.

Miller, George (Ed.) *Mathematics and psychology.* New York: Wiley, 1964, pb.

Newcomb, Theodore (Ed.) *New directions in psychology.* New York: Holt, Rinehart and Winston, 1962, 1965, 1967, 1970, pb.

Notterman, Joseph (Ed.) *Readings in behavior.* New York: Random House, 1970, pb.

Perez, Joseph et al. (Eds.) *General psychology: selected readings.* New York: Van Nostrand Reinhold, 1967, pb.

Powers, Grady, and Baskin, W. (Eds.) *New outlooks in psychology.* New York: Philosophical Library, 1968.

Pronko, Nicholas (Ed.) *Panorama of psychology.* Belmont, Calif.: Brooks/Cole, 1969, pb.

Readings in psychology today. Del Mar, Calif.: CRM Books, 1969.

Russell, Roger (Ed.) *Frontiers in psychology.* Glenview, Ill.: Scott, Foresman, 1964, pb.

Sanford, Fillmore, and Capalidi, E. (Eds.) *Advancing psychological science.* Belmont, Calif.: Wadsworth, 1964. 3 vols., pb.

Schmeidler, Gertrude (Ed.) *Extrasensory perception.* New York: Atherton, 1969, pb.

Scientific American Resource Library. *Readings in psychology.* San Francisco: Freeman, 1969. 2 vols.

Severin, Frank (Ed.) *Humanistic viewpoints in psychology.* New York: McGraw-Hill, 1965, pb.

Shoben, Edward, and Ruch, F. (Eds.) *Perspectives in psychology.* Glenview, Ill.: Scott, Foresman, 1963, pb.

Singer, James, and Whaley, F. (Ed.) *Patterns of psychological research.* Boston: Allyn and Bacon, 1966, pb.

Sjule, Gerald (Ed.) *Contemporary psychology.* Belmont, Calif.: Dickenson, 1970, pb.

Slucki, H. (Ed.) *Readings in psychology and human behavior.* New York: Selected Academic Readings, 1966, pb.

Spielberger, Charles et al. (Eds.) *Contributions to general psychology.* New York: Ronald, 1968, pb.

Sutich, Anthony, and Vich, M. (Eds.) *Readings in humanistic psychology.* New York: Free Press, 1969, pb.

Teevan, Richard, and Birney, R. (Eds.) *Readings for introductory psychology.* New York: Harcourt, Brace and World, 1965, pb.

Ulrich, Roger et al. (Eds.) *Control of human behavior.* Glenview, Ill.: Scott, Foresman, 1966, 1970. 2 vols., pb.

Vinacke, W. (Ed.) *Readings in general psychology* New York: Van Nostrand Reinhold, 1968, pb.

Walters, Annette (Ed.) *Readings in psychology.* Westminster, Md.: Newman, 1963, pb.

Weaver, Herbert (Ed.) *Selected readings for introductory psychology.* Berkeley, Calif.: McCutchan, 1968, pb.

Wertheimer, Michael (Ed.) *Confrontation: psychology and the problems of today.* Glenview, Ill.: Scott, Foresman, 1970, pb.

Whittaker, James (Ed.) *New research in psychology.* Boston: Blaisdell, 1970.

Wrenn, Robert (Ed.) *Basic contributions to psychology.* (2nd ed.) Belmont, Calif.: Brooks/Cole, 1970, pb.

Introductions to Psychological Research

Agnew, Neil, and Pyke, S. *The science game: an introduction to research in the behavioral sciences.* Englewood Cliffs, N.J.: Prentice-Hall, 1969, pb.

Anderson, Barry. *The psychology experiment: an introduction to the scientific method.* Belmont, Calif.: Wadsworth, 1966, pb.

Bachrach, Arthur. *Psychological research: an introduction.* (2nd ed.) New York, Random House, 1965, pb.

Doherty, Michael, and Shemberg, K. *Asking questions about behavior: an introduction to what psychologists do.* Glenview, Ill.: Scott, Foresman, 1970, pb.

Dustin, David. *How psychologists do research.* Englewood Cliffs, N.J.: Prentice-Hall, 1969, pb.

Fincher, Cameron. *A preface to psychology.* New York: Harper & Row, 1964, pb.

Henneman, Richard. *The nature and scope of psychology.* Dubuque, Iowa: Wm. C. Brown Company Publishers, 1966, pb.

Hyman, Ray. *The nature of psychological inquiry.* Englewood Cliffs, N.J.: Prentice-Hall, 1964, pb.

Kaufmann, Harry. *Introduction to the study of human behavior.* Philadelphia: Saunders, 1968, pb.

McCain, Garvin, and Segal, E. *The game of science.* Belmont, Calif.: Brooks/Cole, 1969, pb.

Developmental Psychology

Adams, James (Ed.) *Understanding adolescence: current developments in adolescent psychology.* Boston: Allyn and Bacon, 1968.

Alexander, Theron. *Children and adolescents: a biocultural approach to psychological development.* New York: Atherton, 1969.

Ames, Louis. *Child care and development.* Philadelphia: Lippincott, 1970.

Ausubel, David, and Sullivan, E. *Theories and problems of child development.* (2nd ed.) New York: Grune and Stratton, 1970.

Baldwin, Alfred. *Theories of child development.* New York: Wiley, 1967.

Baller, Warren, and Charles, D. *The psychology of human growth and development.* (2nd ed.) New York: Holt, Rinehart & Winston, 1968.

Bandura, Albert, and Walters, R. *Social learning and personality development.* New York: Holt, Rinehart & Winston, 1963.

Berkowitz, Leonard. *The development of motives and values in the child.* New York: Basic Books, 1964.

Bernard, Harold. *Human development in Western culture.* (3rd ed.) Boston: Allyn and Bacon, 1970.

Bijou, Sidney, and Baer, D. *Child development, volume I: a systematic and empirical theory.* New York: Appleton-Century-Crofts, 1961, pb.

Bijou, Sidney, and Baer, D. *Child development volume II: universal stages of infancy.* New York: Appleton-Century-Crofts, 1965, pb.

Birren, James. *The psychology of aging.* Englewood Cliffs, N.J.: Prentice-Hall, 1964.

Bischof, Ledford. *Adult psychology.* New York: Harper & Row, 1969.

Blos, Peter. *On adolescence: a psychoanalytical interpretation.* New York: Macmillan, 1962, pb.

Bossard James, and Boll, E. *The sociology of child development.* (4th ed.) New York: Harper & Row, 1966.

Bowlby, John. *Child care and the growth of love.* (2nd ed.) Baltimore: Penguin, 1965, pb.

Breckenridge, Marian, and Murphy, M. *Growth and development of the young child.* (8th ed.) Philadelphia: Saunders, 1969.

Breckenridge, Marian, and Vincent, E. *Child development.* (5th ed.) Philadelphia: Saunders, 1965.

Bromley, D. *The psychology of human aging.* Baltimore: Penguin, 1969, pb.

Church, Joseph (Ed.) *Three babies: biographies of cognitive development.* New York: Random House, 1968, pb.

Clarke, Paul. *Child-adolescent psychology.* Columbus, Ohio: Merrill, 1968.

Cole, Luella, and Hall, N. *Psychology of adolescence.* (7th ed.) New York: Holt, Rinehart & Winston, 1969.

Comfort, Alex. *The process of aging.* New York: Signet, 1964, pb.

Committee on Adolescence, Group for the Advancement of Psychiatry. *Normal adolescence.* New York: Scribner, 1968.

Cratty, Bryant. *Perceptual and motor development in infants and children.* New York: Macmillan, 1970, pb.

Crow, Lester, and Crow, A. *Child development and adjustment.* New York: Macmillan, 1962.

Crow, Lester, and Crow, A. *Adolescent development and adjustment.* (2nd ed.) New York: McGraw-Hill, 1965.

Crow, Lester, and Crow, A. *Human development and learning.* New York: Van Nostrand Reinhold, 1965.

Dinkmeyer, Don. *Child development: the emerging self.* Englewood Cliffs, N.J.: Prentice-Hall, 1965.

Douvan, Elizabeth, and Adelson, J. *The adolescent experience.* New York: Wiley, 1966.

English, Horace. *Dynamics of child development.* New York: Holt, Rinehart & Winston, 1961.

Erikson, Erik. *Childhood and society.* (2nd ed.) New York: Norton, 1963, pb.

Ferguson, Lucy. *Personality development.* Belmont, Calif.: Brooks/ Cole, 1970, pb.

Frank, Lawrence. *On the importance of infancy.* New York: Random House, 1966, pb.

Gale, Raymond. *Developmental behavior: a humanistic approach.* New York: Macmillan, 1969.

Gardner, D. *Development in early childhood: the preschool years.* New York: Harper & Row, 1964.

Garrison, Karl. *Psychology of adolescence.*(6th ed.) Englewood Cliffs, N.J.: Prentice-Hall, 1965.

Garrison, Karl et al. *The psychology of childhood: a survey of development and socialization.* New York: Scribner, 1967.

Garrison, Karl, and Jones, F. *The psychology of human development.* Scranton, Pa.: International Textbook, 1969.

Geoghegan, Barbara et al. *Developmental psychology.* Milwaukee: Bruce, 1963.

Ginott, Haim. *Between parent and child.* New York: Macmillan, 1965, pb.

Goethals, George, and Klos, D. (Eds.) *Experiencing youth: first person accounts.* Boston: Little, Brown, 1970, pb.

Gordon, Ira. *Human development: from birth through adolescence.* New York: Harper & Row, 1969.

Gottlieb, David. *The American adolescent.* Homewood, Ill.: Dorsey 1964.

Hadfield, James. *Childhood and adolescence.* Baltimore: Penguin, 1962, pb.

Hawkes, Glen, and Pease, D. *Behavior and development from 5 to 12.* New York: Harper & Row, 1962.

Hoppe, Ronald et al. (Eds.) *Early experiences and the process of socialization.* New York: Academic Press, 1970.

Horrocks, John. *The psychology of adolescence.* (3rd ed.) Boston: Houghton Mifflin, 1969.

Hurlock, Elizabeth. *Child development.* (4th ed.) New York: McGraw-Hill, 1964.

Hurlock, Elizabeth. *Adolescent development.* (3rd ed.) New York: McGraw-Hill, 1967.

Hurlock, Elizabeth. *Developmental psychology.* (3rd ed.) New York: McGraw-Hill, 1968.

Illingworth, Ronald. *Development of the infant and young child.* (2nd ed.) Baltimore: Williams and Wilkins, 1963.

Illingworth, Ronald. *The normal child.* (3rd ed.) Boston: Little, Brown, 1964.

Jenkins, Gladys et al. *These are your children.* Glenview, Ill.: Scott, Foresman, 1966, pb.

Jersild, Arthur. *The psychology of adolescence.* (2nd ed.) New York: Macmillan, 1963.

Jersild, Arthur. *Child psychology.* (6th ed.) Englewood Cliffs, N.J.: Prentice-Hall, 1968.

Johnson, Ronald, and Medinnus, G. *Child psychology: behavior and development.* (2nd ed.) New York: Wiley, 1969.

Kahn, J. *Human growth and the development of personality.* Elmsford, N.Y.: Pergamon, 1965, pb.

Kessler, Jane. *Psychopathology of childhood.* Englewood Cliffs, N.J.: Prentice-Hall, 1966.

Kiell, Norman (Ed.) *The universal experience of adolescence.* New York: International Universities Press, 1964, pb.

Kiell, Norman. *The adolescent through fiction.* New York: International Universities Press, 1965.

Landreth, Catherine. *Early childhood: behavior and learning.* (2nd ed.) New York: Knopf, 1967.

Langer, Jonas. *Theories of development.* New York: Holt, Rinehart & Winston, 1969.

Lewis, M. *Language, thought and personality in infancy and childhood.* New York: Basic Books, 1964.

Loether, Herman. *Problems of aging.* Belmont, Calif.: Dickenson, 1967, pb.

Longstreth, Langdon. *Psychological development of the child.* New York: Ronald, 1968.

McCandless, Boyd. *Children: behavior and development.* (2nd ed.) New York: Holt, Rinehart & Winston, 1967.

McCandless, Boyd. *Adolescents: behavior and development.* Hinsdale, Ill.: Dryden Press, 1970.

McNeil, Elton. *The concept of human development.* Belmont, Calif.: Brooks/Cole, 1966, pb.

McNeil, Elton. *Human socialization.* Belmont, Calif.: Brooks/Cole, 1969.

Maier, Henry. *Three theories of child development: the contributions of Erik H. Erikson, Jean Piaget, and Robert Sears.*(Rev. ed.) New York: Harper & Row, 1969.

Medinnus, Gene, and Johnson, R. *Child and adolescent psychology: behavior and development.* New York: Wiley, 1969.

Meyer, William. *Developmental psychology.* New York: The Center for Applied Research in Education, 1964.

Muller, Philippe. *The tasks of childhood.* New York: McGraw-Hill, 1969, pb.

Munn, Norman. *The evolution and growth of human behavior.*(2nd ed.) Boston: Houghton Mifflin, 1965.

Mussen, Paul. *The psychological development of the child.* Englewood Cliffs, N.J.: Prentice-Hall, 1964, pb.

Mussen, Paul et al. *Child development and personality.* (3rd ed.)New York: Harper & Row, 1969.

Muus, Rolf. *Theories of adolescence.* (2nd ed.) New York: Random House, 1968, pb.

Nash, John. *Developmental psychology: a psychobiological approach.* Englewood Cliffs, N.J.: Prentice-Hall, 1970.

Perkins, Hugh. *Human development and learning.* Belmont, Calif.: Wadsworth, 1969.

Piaget, Jean, and Inhelder, B. *The psychology of the child.* New York: Basic Books, 1969.

Pikunas, Justin. *Fundamental child psychology.*(2nd ed.)Milwaukee: Bruce, 1965.

Pikunas, Justin. *Human development: a science of growth.* New York: McGraw-Hill, 1970.

Pikunas, Justin, and Albrecht, E. *Psychology of human development.* New York: McGraw-Hill, 1961.

Pollard, Marie, and Geoghegan, B. *The growing child in contemporary society.* Milwaukee: Bruce, 1969.

Powell, Marvin. *The psychology of adolescence.* Indianapolis, Ind.: Bobbs-Merrill, 1964.

Reese, Hayne, and Lipsitt, L. (Eds.) *Experimental child psychology.* New York: Academic Press, 1970.

Robinson, Lloyd. *Human growth and development.* Columbus, Ohio: Merrill, 1968, pb.

Rogers, Dorothy. *The psychology of adolescence.* New York: Appleton-Century-Crofts, 1962.

Rogers, Dorothy. *Child psychology.* Belmont, Calif.: Brooks/Cole, 1969.

Sandstrom Carl. *The psychology of childhood and adolescence.* Baltimore: Penguin, 1968, pb.

Scott, John. *Early experience and the organization of behavior.* Belmont, Calif.: Brooks/Cole, 1968, pb.

Scott, Leland. *Child development: an individual longitudinal approach.* New York: Holt, Rinehart & Winston, 1967.

Senn, Milton, and Solnit, A. *Problems in child behavior and development.* Philadelphia: Lea and Febiger, 1968.

Singer, Robert, and Singer, A. *Psychological development in children.* Philadelphia: Saunders, 1969.

Smart, Mollie, and Smart, R. *Children: development and relationship.* New York: Macmillan, 1967.

Smith, Charles. *Child development.* Dubuque, Iowa: Wm C. Brown Company Publishers, 1966, pb.

Smith, Cyril. *Adolescence.* New York: Humanities, 1969.

Spencer, Thomas, and Kass, N. (Eds.) *Perspectives in child psychology: research and review.* New York: McGraw-Hill, 1970.

Staton, Thomas. *Dynamics of adolescent adjustment.* New York: Macmillan, 1963.

Stevenson, Harold (Ed.) *Child psychology: 62nd yearbook of the National Society for the Study of Education.* Chicago: University of Chicago Press, 1963.

Stone, L., and Church, J. *Childhood and adolescence: a psychology of the growing person.* (2nd ed.) New York: Random House, 1968.

Stott, L. *Child development.* New York: Holt, Rinehart & Winston, 1967.

Tanner, James. *Growth at adolescence.* (2nd ed.) Springfield, Ill.: Thomas, 1962.

Thompson, George. *Child psychology: growth trends in psychological adjustment.* (2nd ed.) Boston: Houghton Mifflin, 1962.

Thorpe, Louis, and Johnson, V. *Child psychology and development.* (3rd ed.) New York: Ronald, 1962.

Verville, Elinor. *Behavior problems of children.* Philadelphia: Saunders, 1967.

Vincent, Elizabeth, and Martin, P. *Human psychological development.* New York: Ronald, 1961.

Watson, Robert. *Psychology of the child.* (2nd ed.) New York: Wiley, 1965.

Wenar, Charles. *Personality development: from infancy to maturity.* Boston: Houghton Mifflin, 1970.

Wickes, Frances. *The inner world of childhood.* (Rev. ed.) New York: Appleton-Century-Crofts, 1968, pb.

Readings on Developmental Psychology

Auleta, Michael (Ed.) *Foundations of early childhood education.* New York: Random House, 1969, pb.

Baller, Warren (Ed.) *Readings in the psychology of human growth and development.* (2nd ed.) New York: Holt, Rinehart & Winston, 1969, pb.

Bernard, Harold (Ed.) *Readings in adolescent development.* Scranton, Pa.: International Textbook, 1969, pb.

Bernard, Harold, and Huckins, W. (Eds.) *Readings in human development.* Boston: Allyn and Bacon, 1967, pb.

Bijou, Sidney, and Baer, D. (Eds.) *Child development: readings in experimental analysis.* New York: Appleton-Century Crofts, 1967, pb.

Blain, G., and McArthur, C. (Eds.) *Emotional problems of the student.* New York: Appleton-Century-Crofts, 1961, pb.

Brackbill, Yvonne, and Thompson, G. (Eds.) *Behavior in infancy and early childhood.* New York: Free Press, 1967.

Caplan, Gerald, and Lebovici, S. (Eds.) *Adolescence: psychological perspectives.* New York: Basic Books, 1969.

Chandler, Caroline et al. (Eds.) *Early child care: the new perspectives.* New York: Atherton, 1968.

Clausen, John (Ed.) *Socialization and society.* Boston: Little, Brown, 1968, pb.

Crow, Lester, and Crow, A. (Eds.) *Readings in child and adolescent psychology.* New York: McKay, 1961, pb.

Danzinger, P. (Ed.) *Readings on child socialization.* Elmsford, N.Y.: Pergamon, 1970.

Day, Charles, and Ward, W. (Eds.) *Studies in developmental psychology.* Berkeley: McCutchan, 1968, pb.

Dennis, Wayne (Ed.) *Readings in child psychology.* (2nd ed.) Englewood Cliffs, N.J.: Prentice-Hall, 1963.

Deutsch, Martin et al. (Eds.) *The disadvantaged child.* New York: Basic Books, 1968.

Endler, Norman et al. (Eds.) *Contemporary issues in developmental psychology.* New York: Holt, Rinehart & Winston, 1968.

Erikson, Erik (Ed.) *Youth: change and challenge.* New York: Basic Books, 1963, pb.

Evans, Ellis (Ed.) *Children: readings in behavior and development.* New York: Holt, Rinehart & Winston, 1968.

Evans, Ellis (Ed.) *Adolescents: readings in behavior and development.* Hinsdale, Ill.: Dryden Press, 1970.

Falkner, Frank (Ed.) *Human development.* Philadelphia: Saunders, 1966.

Fitzgerald, Hiram, and McKinney, J. (Eds.) *Developmental psychology.* Homewood, Ill.: Dorsey, 1970.

Frost, Joe (Ed.) *Early childhood education rediscovered.* New York: Holt, Rinehart & Winston, 1968, pb.

Frost, Joe, and Hawkes, G. (Eds.) *The disadvantaged child.* Boston: Houghton Mifflin, 1966, pb.

Gelfand, Donna (Ed.) *Social learning in childhood: readings in theory and application.* Belmont, Calif.: Brooks/Cole, 1969, pb.

Golburgh, Stephen (Ed.) *The experience of adolescence.* Cambridge Mass.: Schenkman, 1965, pb.

Gold, Martin, and Douvan, E. (Eds.) *Adolescent development: readings in research and theory.* Boston: Allyn and Bacon, 1969, pb.

Gordon, Ira (Ed.) *Human development: readings in research.* Glenview, Ill.: Scott, Foresman, 1965, pb.

Grinder, Robert (Ed.) *Studies in adolescence.* (2nd ed.) New York: Macmillan, 1969, pb.

Haimowitz, Morris, and Haimowitz, N. (Eds.) *Human development.* (2nd ed.)New York: Crowell, 1966, pb.

Hamachek, Don (Ed.) *The self in growth, teaching and learning.* Englewood Cliffs, N.J.: Prentice-Hall, 1965.

Hartup, Willard, and Smothergill, N. (Eds.) *The young child: reviews of research.* Washington: National Association for the Education of Young Children, 1967, pb.

Helfer, Ray, and Kempe, C. (Eds.) *The battered child.* Chicago: University of Chicago Press, 1968.

Hoffman, Martin, and Hoffman, L. (Eds.) *Review of child development research.* New York: Russell Sage, 1964, 1966. 2 vols.

Jenkins, Gladys et al. (Eds.) *These are your children.* (3rd ed.) Glenview, Ill.: Scott, Foresman, 1966, pb.

Jones, Mary et al. (Eds.) *The course of human development.* Waltham, Mass.: Blaisdell, 1970.

Kastenbaum, Robert (Ed.) *Contributions to the psychobiology of aging.* New York: Springer, 1965, pb.

Kessen, William (Ed.) *The child.* New York: Wiley, 1965, pb.

Krantz, Kermit, and Semmens, J. (Eds.) *Adolescent social and sexual behavior.* New York: Macmillan, 1970.

Kuhlen, Raymond, and Thompson, G. (Eds.) *Psychological studies of human development.* (3rd ed.) New York: Appleton-Century-Crofts, 1969, pb.

Lorand, Sandor, and Schneer, H. (Eds.) *Adolescents.* New York: Harper & Row, 1961.

Medinnus, Gene, and Johnson, R. (Eds.) *Child and adolescent psychology: behavior and development.* New York: Wiley, 1969, pb.

Meyer, William (Ed.) *Readings in the psychology of childhood and adolescence.* Waltham, Mass.: Blaisdell, 1967, pb.

Mussen, Paul et al. (Eds.) *Readings in child development and personality.* (2nd ed.) New York: Harper & Row, 1969, pb.

Mussen, Paul et al. (Eds.) *Trends and issues in developmental psychology.* New York: Holt, Rinehart & Winston, 1969, pb.

Palermo, David, and Lipsitt, L. (Eds.) *Research readings in child psychology.* New York: Holt, Rinehart & Winston, 1963.

Parke, Ross (Ed.) *Readings in social development.* New York: Holt, Rinehart & Winston, 1969.

Readings in developmental psychology today. Del Mar, Calif.: CRM Books, 1970.

Rebelsky, Freda, and Dorman, L. (Eds.) *Child development and behavior.* New York: Random House, 1970, pb.

Rogers, Dorothy (Ed.) *Issues in adolescent psychology.* New York: Appleton-Century-Crofts, 1969, pb.

Rogers, Dorothy (Ed.) *Issues in child psychology.* Belmont, Calif.: Brooks/Cole, 1969, pb.

Rogers, Dorothy (Ed.) *Readings in child psychology.* Belmont, Calif.: Brooks/Cole, 1969, pb.

Rosenblith, Judy, and Allinsmith, W. (Eds.) *The causes of behavior: readings in child development and educational psychology.* (2nd ed.) Boston: Allyn and Bacon, 1966, pb.

Seidman, Jerome (Ed.) *The adolescent.* (Rev. ed.) New York: Holt, Rinehart & Winston, 1960.

Seidman, Jerome (Ed.) *The child.* (2nd ed.) New York: Holt, Rinehart & Winston, 1969, pb.

Sherif, Muzafer, and Sherif, C. (Eds.) *Problems of youth.* Chicago: Aldine, 1965.

Stendler, Celia (Ed.) *Readings in child behavior and development.* (2nd ed.) New York: Harcourt, Brace and World, 1964.

Stevenson, Harold et al. (Eds.) *Early behavior: comparative and developmental approaches.* New York: Wiley, 1967.

Talbot, Toby (Ed.) *The world of the child.* New York: Doubleday, 1969, pb.

Winder, Alvin and Angus, D. (Eds.) *Adolescence: contemporary studies.* New York: Van Nostrand Reinhold, 1968.

Winter, Gerald, and Nuss, E. (Eds.) *The young adult: identity and awareness.* Glenview, Ill.: Scott, Foresman, 1969, pb.

Exceptional Children

Allen, Robert, and Cortazzo, A. *Psychosocial and educational aspects and problems of mental retardation.* Springfield, Ill.: Thomas, 1970.

Barbe, Walter. *The exceptional child.* New York: The Center for Applied Research in Education, 1963.

Clarke, Ann, and Clarke, A. *Mental deficiency: the changing outlook.* (Rev. ed.) New York: Free Press, 1966.

Cruickshank, William (Ed.) *Psychology of exceptional children and youth.* (2nd ed.) Englewood Cliffs, N.J : Prentice-Hall, 1963.

Everitt, Clarence. *The mentally retarded child.* San Antonio: Naylor, 1968.

Faber, Bernard. *Mental retardation: its social context and social consequences.* Boston: Houghton Mifflin, 1968.

Farber, Nancy. *The retarded child.* New York: Crown, 1968.

Freehill, Maurice. *Gifted children: their psychology and education.* New York: Macmillan, 1961.

Garrison, Karl, and Force, D. *The psychology of exceptional children.* (4th ed.) New York: Ronald, 1965.

Gowan, John, and Demos, G. *The guidance of exceptional children.* New York: McKay, 1965.

Hildreth, Gertrude. *Introduction to the gifted.* New York: McGraw-Hill, 1966.

Hutt, Max, and Gibby, R. *The mentally retarded child: development, education and treatment.* (2nd ed.) Boston: Allyn and Bacon, 1965.

Johnson, Doris, and Myklebust, H. *Learning disabilities: educational principles and practices.* New York: Grune and Stratton, 1967.

Jordan, Thomas. *The exceptional child.* Columbus, Ohio: Merrill, 1962.

Jordan, Thomas. *The mentally retarded.* (2nd ed.) Columbus, Ohio: Merrill, 1966.

Karlin, Isaac et al. *Development and disorders of speech in childhood.* Springfield, Ill.: Thomas, 1965.

Kirk, Samuel et al. *You and your retarded child: a manual for parents of retarded children.* Palo Alto, Calif.: Pacific Books, 1968, pb.

Levine, Edna. *The psychology of deafness.* New York: Columbia University Press, 1960.

Levinson, Abraham. *The mentally retarded child.* (Rev. ed.) New York: John Day, 1965.

Lowenfeld, Berthold. *Our blind children: growing and learning with them.* (2nd ed.) Springfield, Ill.: Thomas, 1964.

Myklebust, Helmer. *The psychology of deafness: sensory deprivation, learning, and adjustment.* New York: Grune and Stratton, 1964.

Myklebust, Helmer. *Your deaf child: a guide for parents.* Springfield, Ill.: Thomas, 1970.

Robinson, Halbert, and Robinson, N. *The mentally retarded child: a psychological approach.* New York: McGraw-Hill, 1964.

Ross, Alan. *The exceptional child in the family.* New York: Grune and Stratton, 1964.

Sarason, Seymour, and Doris, J. *Psychological problems in mental deficiency.* (4th ed.) New York: Harper & Row, 1969.

Spencer, Marietta. *Blind children.* Minneapolis: University of Minnesota Press, 1960.

Telford, Charles, and Sawrey, J. *The exceptional individual.* Englewood Cliffs, N.J.: Prentice-Hall, 1967.

Thomas, George. *Guiding the gifted child.* New York: Random House, 1966.

Thorne, Gareth. *Understanding the mentally retarded.* New York: McGraw-Hill, 1965.

Tredgold, R. et al. (Eds.) *Textbook of mental deficiency.* (10th ed.) Baltimore: Williams and Wilkins, 1963.

Whetnall, E., and Fry, D. *The deaf child.* Washington: The Volta Bureau, 1963.

Willey, R., and Waite, K. *The mentally retarded child.* Springfield, Ill.: Thomas, 1964.

Zahl, Paul. *Blindness.* New York: Harper & Row, 1962.

Readings on Exceptional Children

Barbe, Walter (Ed.) *Psychology and education of the gifted.* New York: Appleton-Century-Crofts, 1965, pb.

Baumeister, Alfred (Ed.) *Mental retardation.* Chicago: Aldine, 1967.

Cleland, Charles, and Swartz, J. (Eds.) *Mental retardation: approaches to institutional change.* New York: Grune and Stratton, 1969.

Dunn, Lloyd (Ed.) *Exceptional children in the schools.* New York: Holt, Rinehart & Winston, 1963.

Dupont, Henry (Ed.) *Educating emotionally disturbed children.* New York: Holt, Rinehart & Winston, 1969.

Faas, Larry (Ed.) *The emotionally disturbed child.* Springfield, Ill.: Thomas, 1970.

Magary, James, and Eichorn, J. (Eds.) *The exceptional child.* (Rev. ed.) New York: Holt, Rinehart & Winston, 1960.

Poser, Charles (Ed.) *Mental retardation: diagnosis and treatment.* New York: Harper & Row, 1969.

Rothstein, Jerome (Ed.) *Mental retardation: readings and resources.* New York: Holt, Rinehart & Winston, 1961.

Stahlecker, L. (Ed.) *Occupational information for the mentally retarded: selected readings.* Springfield, Ill.: Thomas, 1967.

Tarnopol, Lester. (Ed.) *Learning disabilities: introduction to educational and medical management.* Springfield, Ill.: Thomas, 1969.

Trapp, E., and Himelstein, P. (Eds.) *Readings on the exceptional child.* New York: Appleton-Century-Crofts, 1962.

Books Which Describe and Discuss Piaget's Work

Almy, M. *Young children's thinking: studies of some aspects of Piaget's theory.* New York: Teachers College Press, 1966.

Athey, Irene, and Rubadeau, D. (Eds.) *Educational implications of Piaget's theory* Waltham, Mass.: Ginn-Blaisdell, 1970, pb.

Beard, Ruth. *An outline of Piaget's developmental psychology for students and teachers.* New York: Basic Books, 1969.

Boyle, D. *A student's guide to Piaget.* Elmsford, N.Y.: Pergamon, 1969.

Brearley, Molly, and Mitchfield, E. *A guide to reading Piaget.* New York: Schocken, 1966, pb.

Brearley, Molly (Ed.) *The teaching of young children: some applications of Piaget's learning theory.* New York: Schocken, 1970.

Flavell, John. *The developmental psychology of Jean Piaget.* New York: Van Nostrand Reinhold, 1963.

Furth, Hans. *Piaget and knowledge: theoretical foundations.* Englewood Cliffs, N.J.: Prentice-Hall, 1969.

Furth, Hans. *Piaget for teachers.* Englewood Cliffs, N.J.: Prentice-Hall, 1970, pb.

Elkind, David. *Children and adolescents: interpretive essays on Jean Piaget.* New York: Oxford, 1970, pb.

Elkind, David, and Flavell, J. (Eds.) *Studies in cognitive development: essays in honor of Jean Piaget.* New York: Oxford, 1969.

Ginsberg, Herbert, and Opper, S. *Piaget's theory of intellectual development: an introduction.* Englewood Cliffs, N.J.: Prentice-Hall, 1969, pb.

Helmore, G. *Piaget: a practical consideration.* Elmsford, N.Y.: Pergamon, 1969.

Holloway, G. *An introduction to the child's conception of geometry.* New York: Humanities Press, 1967, pb.

Holloway, G. *An introduction to the child's conception of space.* New York: Humanities Press, 1967, pb.

Phillips, John. *The origins of intellect: Piaget's theory.* San Francisco: Freeman, 1969, pb.

Piaget, Jean. *Six psychological studies.* New York: Random House, 1968, pb.

Richmond, P. *An introduction to Piaget.* New York: Basic Books, 1970.

Siegel, Irving et al. *Logical thinking in children.* New York: Holt, Rinehart & Winston, 1968.

Sullivan, Edmund. *Piaget and the school curriculum: a critical appraisal.* Toronto: Publications, Oise, 1967, pb.

Social Psychology

Argyle, Michael. *The psychology of interpersonal behavior.* Baltimore: Penguin, 1967, pb.

Argyle, Michael. *Social interaction.* New York: Atherton, 1970.

Bem, Daryl. *Beliefs, attitudes, and human affairs.* Belmont, Calif.: Brooks/Cole, 1970, pb.

Berkowitz, Leonard. *Aggression.* New York: McGraw-Hill, 1962.

Berscheid, Ellen, and Walster, E. *Interpersonal attraction.* Reading, Mass.: Addison-Wesley, 1969, pb.

Brown, J. *Techniques of persuasion.* Baltimore: Penguin, 1963, pb

Brown, Roger. *Social psychology.* New York: Free Press, 1965.

Buss, Arnold. *The psychology of aggression.* New York: Wiley, 1961.

Cohen, Arthur. *Attitude change and social influence.* New York: Basic Books, 1964.

Collins, Barry. *Social psychology.* Reading, Mass.: Addison-Wesley, 1970.

Cooper, Joseph, and McGaugh, J. *Integrating principles of social psychology.* Cambridge, Mass.: Schenkman, 1963.

Curtis, Jack. *Social psychology.* New York: McGraw-Hill, 1960.

Davis, James. *Group performance.* Reading, Mass.: Addison-Wesley, 1969, pb.

Deutsch, Martin, and Krauss, R. *Theories in social psychology.* New York: Basic Books, 1965.

Dewey, Richard, and Humber, W. *An introduction to social psychology.* New York: Macmillan, 1966.

Doby, John. *Introduction to social psychology.* New York: Appleton-Century-Crofts, 1966.

Dubin, R. et al. *Leadership and productivity.* San Francisco: Chandler, 1965, pb.

Frank, Jerome. *Sanity and survival: psychological aspects of war and peace.* New York: Random House, 1967, pb.

Freedman, Jonathan et al. *Social psychology.* Englewood Cliffs, N.J.: Prentice-Hall, 1970.

Gergen, Kenneth. *The psychology of behavior exchange.* Reading, Mass.: Addison-Wesley, 1969, pb.

Gergen, Kenneth, and Marlowe, D. *Personality and social behavior.* Reading, Mass.: Addison-Wesley, 1970.

Grossack, Martin, and Gardner, H. *Man and men: social psychology as social science.* Scranton, Pa.: International Textbook, 1970, pb.

Hastorf, Albert et al. *Person perception.* Reading, Mass.: Addison Wesley, 1970, pb.

Hennessy, Bernard. *Public opinion.* Belmont, Calif.: Wadsworth, 1965.

Hollander, Edwin. *Principles and methods of social psychology.* New York: Oxford, 1967.

Homans, George. *Social behavior: its elementary forms.* New York: Harcourt, Brace and World, 1961.

Insko, Chester. *Theories of attitude change.* New York: Appleton-Century-Crofts, 1967.

Jones, Edward, and Gerard, H. *Foundations of social psychology.* New York: Wiley, 1967.

Karlins, Marvin, and Abelson, H. *Persuasion: how opinions and attitudes are changed.* New York: Springer, 1970, pb.

Kaufmann, Harry. *Aggression and altruism.* New York: Holt, Rinehart & Winston, 1970, pb.

Katz, Daniel, and Kahn, R. *The social psychology of organizations.* New York: Wiley, 1966.

Kiesler, Charles et al. *Attitude change: a critical analysis of theoretical approaches.* New York: Wiley, 1969.

Kiesler, Charles, and Kiesler, S. *Conformity.* Reading, Mass.: Addison-Wesley, 1969, pb.

Krech, David et al. *Individual in society.* New York: McGraw-Hill, 1962.

Lambert, William, and Lambert, W. *Social psychology.* Englewood Cliffs, N.J.: Prentice-Hall, 1964, pb.

Lana, Robert. *Assumptions of social psychology.* New York: Appleton-Century-Crofts, 1969, pb.

Lindesmith, Alfred, and Strauss, A. *Social psychology.* (3rd ed.) New York: Holt, Rinehart & Winston, 1968.

Lindgren, Henry. *An introduction to social psychology.* New York: Wiley, 1967.

McDavid, John, and Harari, H. *Social psychology: individuals, groups, societies.* New York: Harper & Row, 1968.

McGinnies, Elliott. *Social behavior: a functional analysis.* Boston: Houghton Mifflin, 1970.

McGrath, Joseph. *Social psychology.* New York: Holt, Rinehart & Winston, 1964, pb.

Mann, L. *Social psychology.* New York: John Wiley and Sons, Inc., 1970, pb.

Mills, Judson (Ed.) *Experimental social psychology.* New York: Macmillan, 1969.

Newcomb, Theodore et al. *Social psychology: the study of human interaction.* New York: Holt, Rinehart & Winston, 1965.

Pepitone, Albert. *Attraction and hostility.* New York: Atherton, 1964.

Sargent, S., and Williamson, R. *Social psychology*. (3rd ed.) New York: Ronald, 1966.

Scheibe, Karl. *Beliefs and values*. New York: Holt, Rinehart & Winston, 1970, pb.

Schellenberg, James. *An introduction to social psychology*. New York: Random House, 1969.

Secord, Paul, and Backman, C. *Social psychology*. New York: McGraw-Hill, 1964.

Shaw, Marvin, *Group dynamics* New York: McGraw-Hill 1970.

Shaw, Marvin, and Costanzo, P. *Theories of social psychology*. New York: McGraw-Hill, 1970.

Sherif, Muzafer, and Sherif, C. *Social psychology*. New York: Harper & Row, 1969.

Shibutani, Tamotsu. *Society and personality: an interactionist approach to social psychology*. Englewood Cliffs, N.J.: Prentice-Hall, 1961.

Smelser, Neil. *Theory of collective behavior*. New York: Macmillan, 1962.

Sprott, Walter. *Social psychology*. New York: Barnes and Noble, 1966, pb.

Stagner, Ross. *Psychological aspects of international conflict*. Belmont, Calif.: Brooks/Cole, 1968, pb.

Suedfeld, Peter. *Social processes*. Dubuque, Iowa: Wm. C. Brown Company Publishers, 1966, pb.

Swingle, Paul (Ed.) *Experiments in social psychology*. New York: Academic Press, 1968.

Toch, Hans. *The social psychology of social movements*. Indianapolis: Bobbs-Merrill, 1965, pb.

Walker, Edward, and Heyns, R. *An anatomy for conformity*. Belmont, Calif.: Brooks/Cole, 1967, pb.

Ward, Charles. *Laboratory manual in experimental social psychology*. New York: Holt, Rinehart & Winston, 1969.

Watson, Goodwin. *Social psychology: issues and insights*. Philadelphia: Lippincott, 1966.

Weick, Karl. *The social psychology of organizing*. Reading, Mass.: Addison-Wesley, 1969, pb.

Wheeler, Ladd. *Interpersonal influence*. Boston: Allyn and Bacon, 1970, pb.

Zajonc, Robert. *Social psychology: an experimental approach.* Belmont, Calif.: Brooks/Cole, 1966, pb.

Zimbardo, Philip, and Ebbesen, E. *Influencing attitudes and changing behavior.* Reading, Mass.: Addison-Wesley, 1969, pb.

Readings on Social Psychology

Allen, Vernon (Ed.) *Psychological factors in poverty.* Chicago: Markham, 1970.

Backman, Carl, and Secord, P. (Eds.) *Problems in social psychology.* New York: McGraw-Hill, 1966, pb.

Barnlund, Dean (Ed.) *Interpersonal communication: survey and studies.* Boston: Houghton Mifflin, 1968.

Bennis, Warren et al. (Eds.) *Interpersonal dynamics: essays and readings on human interaction.* (Rev. ed.) Homewood, Ill.: Dorsey, 1968.

Bennis, Warren et al. (Eds.) *The planning of change.* (2nd ed.)New York: Holt, Rinehart & Winston, 1969.

Berelson, Bernard, and Janowitz, M (Eds.) *Reader in public opinion and communication.* (2nd ed.)New York: Free Press, 1965.

Berg, I., and Bass, B. (Eds.) *Conformity and deviation.* New York: Harper & Row, 1961.

Berkowitz, Leonard (Ed.) *Roots of aggression.* New York: Atherton, 1969, pb.

Biddle, Bruce, and Thomas, E. (Eds.) *Role theory.* New York: Wiley, 1966.

Borgatta, Edgar (Ed.) *Social psychology.* Chicago: Rand McNally, 1969, pb.

Bradford, L. et al. (Eds.) *T-group theory and laboratory methods.* New York: Wiley, 1964.

Burton, Arthur (Ed.) *Encounter: theory and practice of encounter groups.* San Francisco: Jossey-Bass, 1970.

Cartwright, Dorwin, and Zander, A. (Eds.) *Group dynamics.* (3rd ed.) New York: Harper & Row, 1968.

Charters, W., and Gage, N. (Eds.) *Readings in the social psychology of education.* Boston: Allyn and Bacon, 1963, pb.

Dean, Dwight (Ed.) *Dynamic issues in social psychology.* New York: Random House, 1969, pb.

Deutsch, Martin et al. (Eds.) *Social class, race and psychological development.* New York: Holt, Rinehart & Winston, 1968.

Elms, Alan (Ed.) *Role playing, reward and attitude change.* New York: Van Nostrand Reinhold, 1969, pb.

Evans, Richard, and Rozelle, R. (Eds.) *Social psychology in life.* Boston: Allyn and Bacon, 1970, pb.

Evans, Robert (Ed.) *Readings in collective behavior.* Chicago: Rand McNally, 1969, pb.

Fishbein, Martin (Ed.) *Readings in attitude theory and measurement.* New York: Wiley, 1967.

Garn, Stanley (Ed.) *Readings on race.* (2nd ed.) Springfield, Ill.: Thomas, 1968.

Gibb, C. (Ed.) *Leadership.* Baltimore: Penguin, 1969, pb.

Golembiewski, Robert, and Blumberg, A. (Eds.) *Sensitivity training and the laboratory method.* Itasca, Ill.: Peacock, 1970.

Gordon, Chad, and Gergen, K. (Eds.) *The self in social interaction: Volume I: classics and contemporary perspectives.* New York: Wiley, 1968.

Graham, Hugh, and Gurr, T. (Eds.) *The history of violence in America.* New York: Bantam, 1970, pb.

Greenwald, Anthony et al. (Eds.) *Psychological foundations of attitudes.* New York: Academic Press, 1968.

Hare, Paul et al. (Eds.) *Small groups: studies in social interaction.* (Rev. ed.) New York: Knopf, 1965.

Hollander, Edwin, and Hunt, R. (Eds.) *Current perspectives in social psychology.* (2nd ed.) New York: Oxford, 1967, pb.

Hyman, Herbert, and Singer, E. (Eds.) *Readings in reference group theory and research.* New York: Free Press, 1968.

Jahoda, Marie, and Warren, N. (Eds.) *Attitudes.* Baltimore: Penguin, 1966, pb.

Kelman, Herbert (Ed.) *International behavior.* New York: Holt, Rinehart & Winston, 1965.

Lindesmith, Alfred, and Strauss, A. (Eds.) *Readings in social psychology.* New York: Holt, Rinehart & Winston, 1969, pb.

Lindgren, Henry (Ed.) *Contemporary research in social psychology.* New York: Wiley, 1969, pb.

Macaulay, Jacqueline, and Berkowitz, L. (Eds.) *Altruism and helping behavior.* New York: Academic Press, 1970.

Maccoby, Eleanor et al. (Eds.) *Readings in social psychology.* (3rd ed.) New York: Holt, Rinehart & Winston, 1958.

McNeil, Elton (Ed.) *The nature of human conflict.* Englewood Cliffs, N.J.: Prentice-Hall, 1965.

McGinnies, Elliott, and Ferster, C. (Eds.) *The reinforcement of social behavior.* Boston: Houghton Mifflin, 1970, pb.

McLaughlin, Barry (Ed.) *Studies in social movements.* New York: Free Press, 1969.

Manis, Jerome, and Meltzer, B. (Eds.) *Symbolic interaction.* Boston: Allyn and Bacon, 1967.

Megargee, Edwin, and Hokanson, J. (Eds.) *The dynamics of aggression.* New York: Harper & Row, 1970, pb.

Montagu, M. (Ed.) *Man and aggression.* New York: Oxford, 1968, pb.

Petrullo, Luigi, and Bass, B. (Eds.) *Leadership and interpersonal behavior.* New York: Holt, Rinehart & Winston, 1961.

Proshansky, Harold, and Seidenberg, B. (Eds.) *Basic studies in social psychology.* New York: Holt, Rinehart & Winston, 1965.

Readings in social psychology today. Del Mar, Calif.: CRM Books, 1970.

Rose, Arnold (Ed.) *Human behavior and social processes: an interactionist approach.* Boston: Houghton Mifflin, 1967.

Rosnow, Ralph, and Robinson, E. (Eds.) *Experiments in persuasion.* New York: Academic Press, 1967.

Sampson, Edward (Ed.) *Approaches, contexts, and problems of social psychology.* Englewood Cliffs, N.J.: Prentice-Hall, 1964.

Schein, E., and Bennis, W. (Eds.) *Personal and organizational change through group methods: the laboratory method.* New York: Wiley, 1965.

Sherif, Muzafer. *Social interaction: process and products.* Chicago: Aldine, 1967.

Shubik, Martin (Ed.) *Game theory and related approaches to social behavior.* New York: Wiley, 1964.

Smith, Alfred (Ed.) *Communication and culture.* New York: Holt, Rinehart & Winston, 1966.

Snider, James, and Osgood, C. (Eds.) *Semantic differential technique.* Chicago: Aldine, 1969.

Stein, Maurice et al. (Eds.) *Identity and anxiety: survival of the person in mass society.* New York: Free Press, 1960, pb.

Steiner, Ivan, and Fishbein, M. (Eds.) *Current studies in social psychology.* New York: Holt, Rinehart & Winston, 1965.

Stone, Gregory, and Farberman, H. (Eds.) *Social psychology through symbolic interaction.* Waltham, Mass.: Blaisdell, 1970.

Stoodley, Bartlett (Ed.) *Society and self: a reader in social psychology.* New York: Free Press, 1962, pb.

Toch, Hans (Ed.) *Legal and criminal psychology.* New York: Holt, Rinehart & Winston, 1961.

Toch, Hans, and Smith, H. (Eds.) *Social perception.* New York: Van Nostrand Reinhold, 1968, pb.

Vinacke, W. et al. (Eds.) *Dimensions of social psychology: a book of readings.* Glenview, Ill.: Scott, Foresman, 1964, pb.

Wagner, Richard, and Sherwood, J. (Eds.) *The study of attitude change.* Belmont, Calif.: Brooks/Cole, 1969, pb.

Wrightsman, Lawrence (Ed.) *Contemporary issues in social psychology.* Belmont, Calif.: Brooks/Cole, 1968, pb.

Zajonc, Robert (Ed.) *Animal social psychology: a reader of experimental studies.* New York: Wiley, 1969.

Zimbardo, Philip (Ed.) *The cognitive control of motivation: the consequences of choice and dissonance.* Glenview, Ill.: Scott, Foresman, 1969.

Industrial and Organizational Psychology

Bass, Bernard. *Organizational psychology.* Boston: Allyn and Bacon, 1965.

Bass, Bernard, and Vaughan, J. *Training in industry.* Belmont, Calif.: Wadsworth, 1966, pb.

Berrien, F. *Industrial psychology.* Dubuque, Iowa: Wm. C. Brown Company Publishers, 1967, pb.

Blum, Milton, and Naylor, J. *Industrial psychology: its theoretical and social foundations.* New York: Harper & Row, 1968.

Chapanis, Alphonse. *Man-machine engineering.* Belmont, Calif.: Wadsworth, 1965, pb.

Davis, Keith. *Human relations at work.* New York: McGraw-Hill, 1967.

Dunnette, Marvin. *Personnel selection and placement.* Belmont, Calif.: Wadsworth, 1966, pb.

Dunnette, Marvin, and Kirchner, W. *Psychology applied to industry.* New York: Appleton-Century-Crofts, 1965, pb.

Engel, James et al. *Consumer behavior.* New York: Holt, Rinehart & Winston, 1968.

Fraser, John. *Industrial psychology.* Long Island City, N.Y.: Pergamon, 1962, pb.

Kelly, Joseph. *Organizational behavior.* Homewood, Ill.: Dorsey, 1969.

Leavitt, Harold. *Managerial psychology.* (2nd ed.) Chicago: University of Chicago Press, 1964, pb.

Maier, Norman. *Psychology in industry.* (3rd ed.) Boston: Houghton Mifflin, 1965.

Sayles, Leonard, and Strauss, G. *Human behavior in organizations.* Englewood Cliffs, N.J.: Prentice-Hall, 1966.

Schein, Edgar. *Organizational psychology.* Englewood Cliffs, N.J.: Prentice-Hall, 1965, pb.

Segel, Laurence. *Industrial psychology.* (Rev. ed.) Homewood, Ill.: Dorsey, 1962.

Smith, Henry. *Psychology of industrial behavior.* (2nd ed.) New York: McGraw-Hill, 1964.

Stagner, Ross, and Rosen, H. *Psychology of union-management relations.* Belmont, Calif.: Wadsworth, 1965, pb.

Tannenbaum, Arnold. *Social psychology of the work organization.* Belmont, Calif.: Wadsworth, 1966, pb.

Von Haller Gilmer, Beverly. *Industrial psychology.* (2nd ed.) New York: McGraw-Hill, 1966.

Vroom, Victor. *Work and motivation.* New York: Wiley, 1964.

Whyte, William. *Organizational behavior: theory and application.* Homewood, Ill.: Dorsey, 1969.

Readings on Industrial and Organizational Psychology

Bennis, Warren et al. (Eds.) *The planning of change.* (2nd ed.) New York: Holt, Rinehart & Winston, 1969.

Cummings, Larry (Ed.) *Readings in organizational behavior and human performance.* Homewood, Ill.: Dorsey, 1969, pb.

Davis, Keith, and Scott, W. (Eds.) *Readings in human relations.* (2nd ed.) New York: McGraw-Hill, 1964.

Engel, James et al. (Eds.) *Cases in consumer behavior.* New York: Holt, Rinehart & Winston, 1969.

Fleishman, Edwin (Ed.) *Studies in personnel and industrial psychology.* Homewood, Ill.: Dorsey, 1967.

Howell, William, and Goldstein, I. (Eds.) *Engineering psychology.* New York: Appleton-Century-Crofts, 1970.

Karn, Harry, and Von Haller Gilmer, B. (Eds.) *Readings in industrial and business psychology.* (2nd ed.) New York: McGraw-Hill, 1962, pb.

Kassarjian, Harold, and Robertson, T. (Eds.) *Perspectives in consumer behavior.* Glenview, Ill.: Scott, Foresman, 1968, pb.

Kollat, David et al. (Eds.) *Research in consumer behavior.* New York: Holt, Rinehart & Winston, 1970.

Leavitt, Harold, and Pondy, L. (Eds.) *Readings in managerial psychology.* Chicago: University of Chicago Press, 1964, pb.

Ronan, William and Prien, E. (Eds.) *Perspectives on the measurement of human performance.* New York: Appleton-Century-Crofts, 1970, pb.

Rubenstein, Albert, and Haberstroh, C. (Eds.) *Some theories of organization.* (Rev. ed.) Homewood, Ill.: Dorsey, 1966.

Schultz, Duane (Ed.) *Psychology and industry.* New York: Macmillan, 1970, pb.

Tannenbaum, Robert et al. (Eds.) *Leadership and organization.* New York: McGraw Hill, 1961.

Wolf, William (Eds.) *Management: readings toward a general theory.* Belmont, Calif.: Wadsworth, 1964, pb.

Applied Psychology

Anastasi, Anne. *Fields of applied psychology.* New York: McGraw-Hill, 1964.

Brown, J. et al. *Applied psychology.* New York: Macmillan, 1966.

Crane, George et al. *Psychology applied.* Chicago: Hopkins Syndicate, 1969.

Henderson, Robert et al. (Eds.) *Helping yourself with applied psychology.* Englewood Cliffs, N J : Prentice-Hall, 1967.

Hepner, Harry. *Psychology applied to life and work.* (4th ed.) Englewood Cliffs, N.J.: Prentice-Hall, 1966.

Von Haller Gilmer, Beverly. *Applied psychology.* New York: McGraw-Hill, 1967.

Educational Psychology

Ausubel, David. *Educational psychology: a cognitive view.* New York: Holt, Rinehart & Winston, 1968.

Ausubel, David, and Robinson, F. *School learning: an introduction to educational psychology.* New York: Holt, Rinehart & Winston, 1969.

Backman, Carl, and Secord, P. *A social psychological view of education.* New York: Harcourt, Brace and World, 1968, pb.

Bernard, Harold. *Psychology of learning and teaching.* (2nd ed.) New York: McGraw-Hill, 1966.

Bigge, Morris. *Learning theories for teachers.* New York: Harper & Row, 1964, pb.

Bigge, Morris, and Hunt, M. *Psychological foundations of education.* (2nd ed.) New York: Harper & Row, 1968.

Blair, Glenn et al. *Educational psychology.* (3rd ed.) New York: Macmillan, 1968.

Bugelski, Bergen. *The psychology of learning applied to teaching.* New York: Bobbs-Merrill, 1964.

Campanelle, Thomas. *Psychology of education.* Philadelphia: Chilton, 1960.

Carpenter, Finlay, and Haddan, E. *Systematic application of psychology to education.* New York: Macmillan, 1964, pb.

Clayton, Thomas. *Teaching and learning: a psychological perspective.* Englewood Cliffs, N.J.: Prentice-Hall, 1965.

Craig, Robert. *The psychology of learning in the classroom.* New York: Macmillan, 1966, pb.

Cronbach, Lee. *Educational psychology.* (2nd ed.) New York: Harcourt, Brace and World, 1963

Crow, Lester, and Crow, A. *Educational psychology.* New York: Van Nostrand Reinhold, 1963.

Davitz, Joel, and Ball, S. *Psychology of the educational process.* New York: McGraw-Hill, 1970.

De Cecco, John. *The psychology of learning and instruction: educational psychology.* Englewood Cliffs, N.J.: Prentice-Hall, 1968.

Di Vesta, Francis, and Thompson, G. *Educational psychology.* (2nd ed.) New York: Appleton-Century-Crofts, 1970.

Dreikurs, Rudolf. *Psychology in the classroom.* (2nd ed.) New York: Harper & Row, 1968.

Edwards, Allen, and Scannell, D. *Educational psychology: the teaching-learning process.* Scranton, Pa.: International Textbook, 1968.

Eson, Morris. *Psychological foundations of education.* New York: Holt, Rinehart & Winston, 1964.

Evans, E. *Modern educational psychology.* New York: Humanities Press, 1969, pb.

Flanders, Ned. *Analyzing teacher behavior.* Reading, Mass.: Addison-Wesley, 1970.

Fleming, C. *Teaching: a psychological analysis.* London: Menthuen, 1968.

Frandsen, Arden. *Educational psychology.* (2nd ed.) New York: McGraw-Hill, 1967.

Gagné, Robert. *Conditions of learning.* (2nd ed.) New York: Holt, Rinehart & Winston, 1970.

Garrison, Karl et al. *Educational psychology.* (2nd ed.) New York: Appleton-Century-Crofts, 1964.

Garry, Ralph. *The psychology of learning.* New York: The Center for Applied Research in Education, 1963.

Garry, Ralph, and Kingsley H. *The nature and conditions of learning.* (3rd ed.) Englewood Cliffs, N.J.: Prentice-Hall, 1970.

Guskin, Alan, and Guskin, S. *A social psychology of education.* Reading, Mass.: Addison-Wesley, 1970.

Jayaswal, Sita. *Foundations of educational psychology.* New York: Allied Publication, 1964.

Kelly, Francis, and Cody, J. *Educational psychology: a behavioral science view.* Columbus, Ohio: Merrill, 1969.

Kelly, William *Educational psychology.* (Rev. ed.) Milwaukee: Bruce, 1965.

Klausmeier, Herbert, and Goodwin, W. *Learning and human abilities: educational psychology.* (2nd ed.) New York: Harper & Row, 1966.

Kolesnik, Walter. *Educational psychology.* (2nd ed.) New York: McGraw-Hill, 1970.

Kuethe, James. *The teaching-learning process.* Glenview, Ill.: Scott, Foresman, 1968, pb.

Lembo, John. *The psychology of effective classroom instruction.* Columbus, Ohio: Merrill, 1969.

Lindgren, Henry. *Educational psychology in the classroom.* (3rd ed.) New York: Wiley, 1967.

Loree, M. *Psychology of education.* (2nd ed.) New York: Ronald 1970.

McDonald, Frederick. *Educational psychology.* (2nd ed.) Belmont, Calif.: Wadsworth, 1965.

McFarland, Henry. *Psychology and teaching.* (2nd ed.) Mystic, Conn.: Verry, 1965.

Mathis, B. et al. *Psychological foundations of education.* New York: Academic Press, 1970.

Meacham, Merle, and Wiesen, A. *Changing classroom behavior: a manual for precision teaching.* Scranton, Pa.: International Textbook, 1969, pb.

Morse, William, and Wingo, G. *Psychology and teaching.* (3rd ed.) Glenview, Ill.: Scott, Foresman, 1969.

Mouly, George. *Psychology for effective teaching.* (2nd ed.) New York: Holt, Rinehart & Winston, 1968.

Murray, John. *Educational psychology.* (2nd ed.) New York: St. John's University Press, 1968.

Peel, Edwin. *The psychological basis of education.* New York: Philosophical Library, 1967.

Pintner, Rudolf. *Educational psychology.* (6th ed.) New York: Barnes and Noble, 1968, pb.

Richardson, Elizabeth. *The environment of learning.* New York: Weybright and Talley, 1968.

Sawrey, James, and Telford, C. *Educational psychology.* (3rd ed.) Boston: Allyn and Bacon, 1968.

Seagoe, May. *The learning process and school practice.* Scranton, Pa.: International Textbook, 1970, pb.

Skinner, B. *The technology of teaching.* New York: Appleton-Century-Crofts, 1968, pb.

Smith, Henry. *Psychology in teaching.* Englewood Cliffs, N.J.: Prentice-Hall, 1962.

Smith, Louis, and Hudgins, B. *Educational psychology: an application of social and behavioral theory.* New York: Knopf, 1964.

Sorenson, Herbert. *Psychology in education.* (4th ed.) New York: McGraw-Hill, 1964.

Stephens, John. *The psychology of classroom learning.* New York: Holt, Rinehart & Winston, 1965.

Stones, E. *An introduction to educational psychology.* New York: Barnes and Noble, 1966, pb.

Strom, Robert. *Psychology for the classroom.* Englewood Cliffs, N.J.: Prentice-Hall, 1969.

Thyne, James. *The psychology of learning and techniques of teaching.* New York: Philosophical Library, 1964.

Townsend, Edward, and Burke, P. *Learning for teachers.* New York: Macmillan, 1962.

Travers, John. *Learning: analysis and application.* New York: McKay, 1965, pb.

Travers, John. *Fundamentals of educational psychology.* Scranton, Pa : International Textbook, 1970.

Travers, Robert. *Essentials of learning: an overview for students of education.* (2nd ed.) New York: Macmillan, 1967.

Trow, William. *Psychology in teaching and learning.* Boston: Houghton Mifflin, 1960.

Weiss, Thomas et al. *Psychological foundations of education.* Dubuque, Iowa: Wm. C. Brown Company Publishers, 1963.

White, William, *Psychosocial principles applied to classroom teaching.* New York: McGraw-Hill, 1969.

Wilson, John et al. *Psychological foundations of learning and teaching.* New York: McGraw-Hill, 1969.

Readings on Educational Psychology

Anderson, Richard, and Ausubel, D. (Eds.) *Readings in the psychology of cognition.* New York: Holt, Rinehart & Winston, 1965.

Anderson, Richard et al. (Eds.) *Current research on instruction.* Englewood Cliffs, N.J.: Prentice-Hall, 1969.

Atkinson, R., and Wilson, H. (Eds.) *Computer-assisted instruction.* New York: Academic Press, 1969, pb.

Ausubel, David (Ed.) *Readings in school learning.* New York: Holt, Rinehart & Winston, 1969, pb.

Barbe, Walter (Ed.) *Psychology and education of the gifted.* New York: Appleton-Century-Crofts, 1965.

Bernard, Harold, and Huckins, W. (Eds.) *Readings in educational psychology.* Scranton, Pa.: International Textbook, 1967, pb.

Bower, Eli, and Hollister, W. (Eds.) *Behavioral science frontiers in education.* New York: Wiley, 1967.

Clarizio, Harvey et al. (Eds.) *Contemporary issues in educational psychology.* Boston: Allyn and Bacon, 1970, pb.

Clark, Donald (Ed.) *The psychology of education.* New York: Macmillan, 1967, pb.

Crow, Lester, and Crow, A. (Eds.) *Readings in human learning.* New York: McKay, 1963.

Cruickshank, William and Johnson, G. (Eds.) *Education of exceptional children and youth.* Englewood Cliffs, N.J.: Prentice-Hall, 1967.

De Cecco, John (Ed.) *Human learning in the school.* New York: Holt, Rinehart & Winston, 1963, pb.

Dupont, Henry (Ed.) *Educating emotionally disturbed children.* New York: Holt, Rinehart & Winston, 1969.

Edwards, Allen (Ed.) *Educational psychology: the teaching-learning process.* Scranton, Pa.: International Textbook, 1968.

Feather, Bryant, and Olson, W. (Eds.) *Children, psychology and the schools.* Glenview, Ill.: Scott, Foresman, 1969, pb.

Frey, Sherman, and Haugen, E. (Eds.) *Readings in classroom learning.* New York: Van Nostrand Reinhold, 1969.

Frierson, Edward, and Barbe, W. (Eds.) *Educating children with learning disabilities.* New York: Appleton-Century-Crofts, 1967.

Frost, Joe, and Hawkes, G. (Eds.) *The disadvantaged child.* New York: Houghton Mifflin, 1966, pb.

Fullagar, William et al. (Eds.) *Readings for educational psychology.* New York: Crowell, 1964, pb.

Hamachek, Don (Ed.) *Human dynamics in psychology and education.* Boston: Allyn and Bacon, 1968.

Harris, T., and Schwahn, W. (Eds.) *Selected readings on the learning process.* New York: Oxford, 1961, pb.

Hess, Robert et al. (Eds.) *Early education.* Chicago: Aldine, 1968.

Jones, Richard (Ed.) *Contemporary educational psychology.* New York: Harper & Row, 1967, pb.

Komisar, Bolek (Ed.) *Psychological concepts in education.* Chicago: Rand McNally, 1967.

Kuhlen, Raymond (Ed.) *Studies in educational psychology.* Waltham, Mass.: Blaisdell, 1968, pb.

Lindgren, Henry (Ed.) *Readings in educational psychology.* New York: Wiley, 1968.

MacGinitie, Walter, and Ball, S. (Eds.) *Readings in psychological foundations of education.* New York: McGraw-Hill, 1968.

Miles, Matthew, and Charters, W. (Eds.) *Learning in social settings: new readings in the social psychology of education.* Boston: Allyn and Bacon, 1970.

Miller, Harry (Ed.) *Education for the disadvantaged.* New York: Macmillan, 1967, pb.

Morse, William, and Wingo, G. (Eds.) *Classroom psychology: readings in educational psychology.* Glenview, Ill.: Scott, Foresman, 1970, pb.

Mosher, Ralph (Ed.) *Readings for educational psychology.* New York: Harcourt, Brace and World, 1965.

Murray, John (Ed.) *Readings in educational psychology.* Jamaica, N.Y.: St. Johns, 1968.

Noll, Victor, and Noll, R. (Eds.) *Readings in educational psychology.* (2nd ed.) New York: Macmillan, 1968, pb.

Page, Ellis, and Cronbach, L. (Eds.) *Readings for educational psychology.* New York: Harcourt, Brace and World, 1967, pb.

Parker, Ronald (Ed.) *Readings in educational psychology.* Boston: Allyn and Bacon, 1968, pb.

Readings in educational psychology today. Del Mar, Calif.: CRM Books, 1970.

Ripple, Richard (Ed.) *Readings in learning and human abilities.* New York: Harper & Row, 1964, pb.

Rosenblith, Judy, and Allinsmith, W. (Eds.) *The causes of behavior: readings in child development and educational psychology.* Boston: Allyn and Bacon, 1966, pb.

Seidman, Jerome (Ed.) *Readings in educational psychology.* (2nd ed.) Boston: Houghton Mifflin, 1965, pb.

Smith, Louis, and Hudgins, B. (Eds.) *Educational psychology: an application of social and behavioral theory.* New York: Knopf, 1964.

Sprinthall, Richard, and Sprinthall, N. (Eds.) *Educational psychology.* New York: Van Nostrand Reinhold, 1969, pb.

Starr, B. (Ed.) *The psychology of school adjustment.* New York: Random House, 1970, pb.

Torrance, E., and White, W. (Eds.) *Issues and advances in educational psychology.* Itasca, Ill.: Peacock, 1969, pb.

Trapp, E., and Himelstein, P. (Eds.) *Readings on the exceptional child.* New York: Appleton-Century-Crofts, 1962.

Adjustment and Mental Hygiene

Arkoff, Abe. *Adjustment and mental health.* New York: McGraw-Hill, 1968.

Bonney, Merl. *The normal personality.* Berkeley, Calif.: McCutchan, 1969, pb.

Carroll, Herbert. *Mental hygiene: the dynamics of adjustment.* Englewood Cliffs, N.J.: Prentice-Hall, 1969.

Coleman, James. *Psychology and effective behavior.* Glenview, Ill.: Scott, Foresman, 1969.

Crow, Lester. *Psychology of human adjustment.* New York: Knopf, 1967.

Gordon, Jesse. *Personality and behavior.* New York: Macmillan 1963.

Haas, Kurt. *Understanding adjustment and behavior.* (2nd ed.) Englewood Cliffs, N.J.: Prentice-Hall, 1970.

Heidenreich, Charles. *Personality and social adjustment.* Dubuque, Iowa: Wm. C. Brown Company Publishers, 1967, pb.

Jourard, Sidney. *Personal adjustment.* (2nd ed.) New York: Macmillan, 1963.

Kaplan, Louis. *Foundations of human behavior.* New York: Harper & Row, 1965.

Keezer, William. *Mental health and human behavior.* (3rd ed.) Dubuque, Iowa: Wm. C. Brown Company Publishers, 1971, pb.

Lazarus, Richard. *Personality and adjustment.* Englewood Cliffs, N.J.: Prentice-Hall, 1963, pb.

Lazarus, Richard. *Patterns of adjustment and human effectiveness.* New York: McGraw-Hill, 1969.

Lehner, George, and Kube, E. *Dynamics of personal adjustment.* (2nd ed.) Englewood Cliffs, N.J.: Prentice-Hall, 1964.

Leuba, Clarence. *Personality: interpersonal relations and self-understanding.* Columbus, Ohio: Merrill, 1962, pb.

Levine, Louis. *Personal and social development: the psychology of effective behavior.* New York: Holt, Rinehart & Winston, 1963.

Lindgren, Henry. *Psychology of personal development.* (2nd ed.) New York: Van Nostrand Reinhold, 1969.

McKinney, Fred. *Psychology of personal adjustment.* New York: Wiley, 1960.

Munn, Norman. *Psychology: the fundamentals of human adjustment.* (5th ed.) Boston: Houghton Mifflin, 1966.

Roberts, Guy. *Personal growth and adjustment.* Boston: Holbrook Press, 1968.

Sawrey, James, and Telford, C. *Psychology of adjustment.* (2nd ed.) Boston: Allyn and Bacon, 1967.

Schneiders, Alexander. *Personality dynamics and mental health.* (Rev. ed.) New York: Holt, Rinehart & Winston, 1965.

Sechrest, Lee, and Wallace, J. *Psychology and human problems.* Columbus, Ohio: Merrill, 1967.

Smith, Henry. *Personality development.* New York: McGraw-Hill, 1968.

Tallent, Norman. *Psychological perspectives on the person.* New York: Van Nostrand Reinhold, 1967, pb.

Thorpe, Louis. *The psychology of mental health.* (2nd ed.) New York: Ronald, 1960.

Tucker, Irving. *Adjustment: models and mechanisms.* New York: Academic Press, 1970.

Readings on Adjustment and Mental Hygiene

Gorlow, Leon, and Katkovsky, W. (Eds.) *Readings in the psychology of adjustment.* (2nd ed.) New York: McGraw-Hill, 1967, pb.

Grebstein, Lawrence (Ed.) *Toward self-understanding.* Glenview, Ill.: Scott, Foresman, 1969, pb.

Hountras, Peter (Ed.) *Mental hygiene.* Columbus, Ohio: Merrill, 1961.

Lindgren, Henry (Ed.) *Readings in personal development.* New York: Van Nostrand Reinhold, 1969.

Seidman, Jerome (Ed.) *Educating for mental health.* New York: Crowell, 1963, pb.

Wrenn, Robert, and Ruiz, R. (Eds.) *The normal personality: issues to insights.* Belmont, Calif.: Brooks/Cole, 1970, pb.

Abnormal Psychology

Axline, Virginia. *Dibs in search of self.* Boston: Houghton Mifflin, 1964, pb.

Beech, H. *Changing man's behavior.* Baltimore: Penguin, 1969, pb.

Blum, Gerald. *Psychodynamics: the science of unconscious mental forces.* Belmont, Calif.: Brooks/Cole, 1966, pb.

Brammer, Lawrence, and Shostrom E. *Therapeutic psychology.* (2nd ed.) Englewood Cliffs, N.J.: Prentice-Hall, 1968.

Buss, Arnold. *Psychopathology.* New York: Wiley, 1966.

Cameron, Norman. *Personality development and psychopathology.* Boston: Houghton Mifflin, 1963.

Cleckley, Hervey. *The mask of sanity.* (4th ed.) St. Louis: Mosby, 1964, pb.

Cole, Lawrence. *Understanding abnormal behavior.* San Francisco: Chandler, 1970.

Coleman, James, and Broen, W. *Abnormal psychology and modern life.* (4th ed.) Chicago: Scott, Foresman, 1971.

Coleman, James. *Abnormal behavior.* Dubuque, Iowa: Wm. C. Brown Company Publishers, 1966, pb.

Coville, Walter et al. *Abnormal psychology.* New York: Barnes and Noble, 1960, pb.

Davis, Russell. *Introduction to psychopathology.* (2nd ed.) New York: Oxford, 1966, pb.

Eysenck, Hans, and Rachman, S. *Causes and cures of neurosis.* San Diego: Knapp, 1965.

Fisher, William. *Theories of anxiety.* New York: Harper & Row, 1970.

Ford, Donald, and Urban, H. *Systems of psychotherapy: a comparative study.* New York: Wiley, 1963.

Frank, Jerome. *Persuasion and healing.* Baltimore: Johns Hopkins Press, 1961.

Frazier, Shervert, and Carr, A. *Introduction to psychopathology.* New York: Macmillan, 1964.

Goffman, Erving. *Asylums.* Chicago: Aldine, 1961, pb.

Goldstein, Michael, and Palmer, J. *The experience of anxiety: a casebook.* New York: Oxford, 1963, pb.

Green, Hannah. *I never promised you a rose garden.* New York: Holt, Rinehart & Winston, Inc., 1964, pb.

Hare, Robert. *Psychotherapy: theory and research.* New York: John Wiley & Sons, Inc., 1970, pb.

Heine, Ralph. *Psychotherapy.* Englewood Cliffs, N.J.: Prentice-Hall, 1969, pb.

Holland, Glen. *Fundamentals of psychotherapy.* New York: Holt, Rinehart & Winston, 1965.

Inglis, James. *The scientific study of abnormal behavior: experimental and clinical research.* Chicago: Aldine, 1966.

Kaplan, Bert (Ed.) *The inner world of mental illness.* New York: Harper & Row, 1964, pb.

Kisker, George. *The disorganized personality.* New York: McGraw-Hill, 1964.

Landis, Carney, and Mettler, Fred. *Varieties of psychopathological experience.* New York: Holt, Rinehart & Winston, 1964.

Levitt, Eugene. *The psychology of anxiety.* Indianapolis, Ind.: Bobbs-Merrill, 1967, pb.

London, Perry, and Rosehan, D. (Eds.) *Foundations of abnormal psychology.* New York: Holt, Rinehart & Winston, 1968.

Luchins, A. *Group therapy*. New York: Random House, 1964, pb.

Lundin, Robert. *Principles of psychopathology*. Columbus, Ohio: Merrill, 1965.

McCall, Raymond. *Abnormal psychology: a descriptive approach*. New York: Van Nostrand Reinhold, 1970.

McNeil, Elton. *The quiet furies*. Englewood Cliffs, N.J.: Prentice-Hall, 1969, pb.

McNeil, Elton. *Neuroses and personality disorder*. Englewood Cliffs, N.J.: Prentice-Hall, 1970, pb.

McNeil, Elton. *The psychoses*. Englewood Cliffs, N.J.: Prentice-Hall, 1970, pb.

Maher, Brendan. *Principles of psychopathology: an experimental approach*. New York: McGraw-Hill, 1966.

Masserman, Jules. *Therapy of personality disorders*. Dubuque, Iowa: Wm. C. Brown Company Publishers, 1966, pb.

Mehrabian, Albert. *Changing behavior: tactics of social influence*. Englewood Cliffs, N.J.: Prentice-Hall, 1970, pb.

Mendels, Joseph. *Concepts of depression*. New York: John Wiley & Sons, Inc., 1970, pb.

Menninger, Karl et al. *The vital balance*. New York: Viking, 1963, pb.

Mensh, Ivan. *Clinical psychology*. New York: Macmillan, 1966, pb.

Millon, Theodore. *Modern psychopathology*. Philadelphia: Saunders, 1969.

Mowrer, O. *Abnormal reactions or actions?* Dubuque, Iowa: Wm. C. Brown Company Publishers, 1966, pb.

Nemiah, John. *Foundations of psychopathology*. New York: Oxford, 1966, pb.

Parker, Beulah. *My language is me: psychotherapy with a disturbed adolescent*. New York: Basic Books, 1962.

Pronko, Nicholas. *Textbook of abnormal psychology*. Baltimore: Williams and Wilkins, 1967.

Rosen, Ephraim, and Gregory, I. *Abnormal psychology*. Philadelphia: Saunders, 1965.

Rotter, Julian. *Clinical psychology*. Englewood Cliffs, N.J.: Prentice-Hall, 1964, pb.

Schofield, William. *The purchase of friendship*. Englewood Cliffs, N.J.: Prentice-Hall, 1964, pb.

Schulz, Clarence, and Kilgalen, R. *Case studies in schizophrenia.* New York: Basic Books, 1969.

Stern, Paul. *The abnormal person and his world: an introduction to abnormal psychopathology.* New York: Van Nostrand Reinhold, 1964.

Strange, Jack. *Abnormal psychology: understanding behavior disorders.* New York: McGraw-Hill, 1965.

Suinn, Richard. *Fundamentals of behavior pathology.* New York: Wiley, 1970.

Szasz, Thomas. *The myth of mental illness.* New York: Hoeber-Harper, 1961, pb.

Thorpe, Louis et al. *The psychology of abnormal behavior: a dynamic approach.* (2nd ed.) New York: Ronald, 1961.

Ullmann, Leonard, and Krasner, L. *A psychological approach to abnormal behavior.* Englewood Cliffs, N.J.: Prentice-Hall, 1969.

Wenrich, W. *A primer of behavior modification.* Belmont, Calif.: Brooks/Cole, 1970, pb.

White, Robert. *The abnormal personality.* (3rd ed.) New York: Ronald, 1964.

Yates, Aubrey. *Frustration and conflict.* New York: Wiley, 1962.

Yates, Aubrey. *Behavior therapy.* New York: John Wiley & Sons, Inc., 1970.

Zax, Melvin, and Stricker, G. *Patterns of psychopathology.* New York: Macmillan, 1963, pb.

Readings on Abnormal and Clinical Psychology

Ard, Ben (Ed.) *Counseling and psychotherapy: classics on theories and issues.* Palo Alto, Calif.: Science and Behavior Books, 1966.

Berenson, Bernard, and Carkhuff, R. (Eds.) *Sources of gains in counseling and psychotherapy: readings and commentary.* New York: Holt, Rinehart & Winston, 1967.

Berger, Louis (Ed.) *Clinical cognitive psychology.* Englewood Cliffs, N.J.: Prentice-Hall, 1969.

Braun, John (Ed.) *Clinical psychology in transition.* (Rev. ed.) Cleveland: World, 1966.

Buss, Arnold, and Buss, E. (Eds.) *Theories of schizophrenia.* New York: Atherton, 1969, pb.

Carter, Jerry (Ed.) *Research contributions from psychology to community mental health.* New York: Behavioral Publications, 1968, pb.

Cook, Patrick (Ed.) *Introductory readings in community psychology and community mental health.* San Francisco: Holden-Day, 1970.

Eysenck, Hans (Ed.) *Experiments in behavior therapy.* Long Island City, N.J.: Pergamon, 1964.

Eysenck, Hans (Ed.) *Behavior therapy and the neuroses.* Long Island City, N.Y.: Pergamon, 1960.

Faas, Larry (Ed.) *The emotionally disturbed child.* Springfield, Ill.: Thomas, 1970.

Fagan, Joen, and Shepherd, I. (Eds.) *Gestalt therapy now.* Palo Alto, Calif.: Science and Behavior Books, 1969.

Fliess, Robert (Ed.) *The psychoanalytic reader.* New York: International Universities Press, 1969.

Franks, Cyril (Ed.) *Conditioning techniques in clinical practice and research.* New York: Springer, 1964.

Franks, Cyril (Ed.) *Behavior therapy.* New York: McGraw-Hill, 1969.

Gazda, George (Ed.) *Basic approaches to group psychotherapy and group counseling.* Springfield, Ill.: Thomas, 1970.

Gazda, George (Ed.) *Innovations to group therapy.* Springfield, Ill.: Thomas, 1970.

Goldstein, Arnold, and Dean, S. (Eds.) *The investigation of psychotherapy.* New York: Wiley, 1966.

Guerney, Bernard (Ed.) *Psychotherapeutic agents: new roles for nonprofessionals, parents, and teachers.* New York: Holt, Rinehart & Winston, 1967.

Guiora, Alexander, and Brandwin, M. (Eds.) *Perspectives in clinical psychology.* New York: Van Nostrand Reinhold, 1968, pb.

Hamilton, Max (Ed.) *Abnormal psychology.* Baltimore: Penguin, 1967, pb.

Harms, Ernst, and Brody, C. (Eds.) *Readings in clinical psychology.* New York: McKay, 1968, pb.

Hart, Joseph, and Tomlinson, T. (Eds.) *New directions in client-centered therapy.* Boston: Houghton Mifflin, 1970.

Holmes, David (Ed.) *Reviews of research in behavior pathology.* New York: Wiley, 1968, pb.

Jackson, Don (Ed.) *The etiology of schizophrenia.* New York: Basic Books, 1960.

Krasner, Leonard, and Ullmann, L. (Eds.) *Research in behavior modification: new developments and applications.* New York: Holt, Rinehart & Winston, 1965.

Lubin, Bernard and Levitt, E. (Eds.) *The clinical psychologist.* Chicago: Aldine, 1967.

Mahrer, Alvin (Ed.) *The goals of psychotherapy.* New York: Appleton-Century-Crofts, 1967.

Megargee, Edwin (Ed.) *Research in clinical assessment.* New York: Harper & Row, 1966.

Millon, Theodore (Ed.) *Theories of psychopathology: essays and critiques.* Philadelphia: Saunders, 1967, pb.

Milton, Ohmer, and Wahler, R. (Eds.) *Behavior disorders: perspectives and trends.* (2nd ed.) Philadelphia: Lippincott, 1969, pb.

Mowrer, O. (Ed.) *Morality and mental health.* Chicago: Rand McNally, 1967.

Neuringer, Charles, and Michael, J. (Eds.) *Behavior modification in clinical psychology.* New York: Appleton-Century-Crofts, 1970.

Nunokawa, Walter (Ed.) *Human values and abnormal behavior.* Glenview, Ill.: Scott, Foresman, 1965, pb.

Page, James (Ed.) *Approaches to psychopathology.* New York: Columbia University Press, 1966.

Palmer, James, and Goldstein, M. (Eds.) *Perspectives in psychopathology.* New York: Oxford, 1965, pb.

Plog, Stanley, and Edgerton, R. (Eds.) *Changing perspectives in mental illness.* New York: Holt, Rinehart & Winston, 1969.

Quay, Herbert (Ed.) *Readings in psychopathology.* New York: Van Nostrand Reinhold, 1963, pb.

Quay, Herbert (Ed.) *Children's behavior disorders.* New York: Van Nostrand Reinhold, 1968, pb.

Rabkin, Leslie (Ed.) *Psychopathology and literature.* San Francisco: Chandler, 1966, pb.

Rabkin, Leslie, and Carr, J. (Eds.) *Sourcebook in abnormal psychology.* Boston: Houghton Mifflin, 1967, pb.

Readings in clinical psychology today. Del Mar, Calif.: CRM Books, 1970.

Roff, Merrill et al. (Eds.) *Developmental abnormal psychology: a casebook.* New York: Holt, Rinehart & Winston, 1966, pb.

Rosenbaum, Max, and Berger, M. (Eds.) *Group psychotherapy and group function.* New York: Basic Books, 1963.

Rosenhan, David, and London, P. (Eds.) *Theory and research in abnormal psychology.* New York: Holt, Rinehart & Winston, 1969, pb.

Sahakian, William (Ed.) *Psychotherapy and counseling: studies in techniques.* Chicago: Rand McNally, 1969.

Sahakian, William (Ed.) *Psychopathology today: experimentation, theory, and research.* Itasca, Ill.: Peacock, 1970, pb.

Sarason, Irwin (Ed.) *Psychoanalysis and the study of behavior.* New York: Van Nostrand Reinhold, 1965, pb.

Sarason, Irwin (Ed.) *Science and theory in psychoanalysis.* New York: Van Nostrand Reinhold 1965, pb.

Sarbin, Theodore (Ed.) *Studies in behavior pathology.* New York: Holt, Rinehart & Winston, 1961.

Savage, R. (Ed.) *Readings in clinical psychology.* New York: Pergamon, 1966.

Scheff, Thomas (Ed.) *Mental illness and social processes.* New York: Harper & Row, 1967.

Southwell, Eugene, and Feldman, H. (Eds.) *Abnormal psychology: readings in theory and research.* Belmont, Calif.: Brooks/Cole, 1969, pb.

Stollak, Gary et al. (Eds.) *Psychotherapy research.* Chicago: Rand McNally, 1966.

Stone, Alan, and Stone, S. (Eds.) *The abnormal personality through literature.* Englewood Cliffs, N.J.: Prentice-Hall, 1966, pb.

Sutherland, Robert, and Smith, B. (Eds.) *Understanding mental health.* New York: Van Nostrand Reinhold, 1965, pb.

Ullmann, Leonard, and Krasner, L. (Eds.) *Case studies in behavior modification.* New York: Holt, Rinehart & Winston, 1965.

Vetter, Harold (Ed.) *Language behavior in schizophrenia.* Springfield, Ill.: Thomas, 1968.

Weinberg, S. (Ed.) *The sociology of mental illness.* Chicago: Aldine, 1967.

Zax, Melvin, and Stricker, G. (Eds.) *The study of abnormal behavior.* (2nd ed.) New York: Macmillan, 1969, pb.

Counseling and Guidance

Adams, James. *Problems in counseling: a case study approach.* New York: Macmillan, 1962, pb.

Arbuckle, Dugald. *Pupil personnel services in the modern school.* Boston: Allyn and Bacon, 1966.

Arbuckle, Dugald. *Counseling: philosophy, theory and practice.* (2nd ed.) Boston: Allyn and Bacon, 1970.

Benjamin, Alfred. *The helping interview.* Boston: Houghton Mifflin, 1969, pb.

Bennett, Margaret. *Guidance and counseling in groups.* (2nd ed.) New York: McGraw-Hill, 1967.

Bernard, Harold, and Fullmer, D. *Principles of guidance.* Scranton, Pa.: International Textbook, 1969.

Blanchard, H., and Flaum L. *Guidance: a longitudinal approach.* Minneapolis, Minn.: Burgess, 1962.

Blocher, David. *Developmental counseling.* New York: Ronald, 1966.

Bordin, Edward. *Psychological counseling.* (2nd ed.) New York: Appleton-Century-Crofts, 1968.

Byrne, Richard. *The school counselor.* Boston: Houghton Mifflin, 1963.

Crow, Lester, and Crow, A. *An introduction to guidance.* New York: Van Nostrand Reinhold, 1960.

Dimick, Kenneth. *Child counseling.* Dubuque, Iowa: Wm. C. Brown Company Publishers, 1970.

Fullmer, Daniel, and Bernard, H. *Counseling: content and process.* Chicago: Science Research Associates, 1964.

Glanz, Edward. *Foundations and principles of guidance.* Boston: Allyn and Bacon, 1964.

Glennen, Robert. *Guidance: an orientation for the undergraduate.* Boulder, Colorado: Pruett Press, 1966.

Herr, Edwin, and Cramer, S. *Guidance of the college-bound.* New York: Appleton-Century-Crofts, 1969, pb.

Holland, John. *The psychology of vocational choice.* Waltham, Mass.: Blaisdell, 1966, pb.

Hutson, Percival. *The guidance function in education.* (2nd ed.) New York: Appleton-Century-Crofts, 1968.

Jones, Arthur. *Principles of guidance.* (5th ed.) New York: McGraw-Hill, 1963.

Langford, Louise. *Guidance of the young child.* New York: Wiley, 1960.

Lee, James, and Pallone, N. *Guidance and counseling in schools: foundations and principles.* New York: McGraw-Hill, 1966.

Lewis, Edwin. *The psychology of counseling.* New York: Holt, Rinehart & Winston, 1970.

McKinney, Fred. *Understanding personality: cases in counseling.* Boston: Houghton Mifflin, 1965.

Miller, C. *Guidance services.* New York: Harper & Row, 1965.

Miller, Frank. *Guidance principles and services.* (2nd ed.) Columbus, Ohio: Merrill, 1968.

Mortensen, D., and Schmuller, A. *Guidance in today's schools.* (2nd ed.) New York: Wiley, 1966.

Moser, Leslie, and Moser, R. *Counseling and guidance: an exploration.* Englewood Cliffs, N J.: Prentice-Hall, 1963.

Nordberg, Robert. *Guidance: a systematic introduction.* New York: Random House, 1970.

Ohlsen, Merle. *Guidance services in the modern school.* New York: Holt, Rinehart & Winston, 1964.

Ohlsen, Merle. *Group counseling.* New York: Holt, Rinehart & Winston, 1970.

Osipow, Samuel. *Theories of career development.* New York: Appleton-Century-Crofts, 1968.

Patterson, Cecil. *Counseling and guidance in schools: a first course.* New York: Harper & Row, 1962.

Patterson, Cecil. *Theories of counseling and psychotherapy.* New York: Harper & Row, 1966.

Peters, Herman, and Farwell, G. *Guidance: a developmental approach.* Chicago: Rand McNally, 1967.

Roeber, Edward et al. *A strategy for guidance.* New York: Macmillan, 1969.

Sachs, Benjamin. *The student, the interview and the curriculum: dynamics of counseling in the schools.* Boston: Houghton Mifflin, 1966.

Shertzer, Bruce, and Stone, S. *Fundamentals of guidance.* Boston: Houghton Mifflin, 1966.

Stefflre, Buford (Ed.) *Theories of counseling.* New York: McGraw-Hill, 1965.

Stone, Shelley, and Shertzer, B. (Eds.) *Guidance monograph series.* Boston: Houghton Mifflin, 1968, 28 separate paperbacks.

Thoroman, E. *The vocational counseling of adults and young adults.* Boston: Houghton Mifflin, 1968.

Traxler, Arthur, and North, R. *Techniques of guidance.* (3rd ed.) New York: Harper & Row, 1966.

Tyler, Leona. *The work of the counselor.* (3rd ed.) New York: Appleton-Century-Crofts, 1969.

Warters, Jane. *Group guidance.* New York: McGraw-Hill, 1960.

Warters, Jane. *Techniques of counseling.* (2nd ed.) New York: McGraw-Hill, 1964.

Weitz, Henry. *Behavior change through guidance.* New York: Wiley, 1964.

Zeran, Franklin et al. *Guidance.* New York: Van Nostrand Reinhold, 1964.

Readings on Counseling and Guidance

Adams, James (Ed.) *Counseling and guidance: a summary view.* New York: Macmillan, 1965, pb.

Arbuckle, Dugald (Ed.) *Counseling and psychotherapy: an overview.* New York: McGraw-Hill, 1967.

Bentley, Joseph (Ed.) *The counselor's role.* Boston: Houghton Mifflin, 1968, pb.

Borow, Henry (Ed.) *Man in a world at work.* Boston: Houghton Mifflin, 1964.

Clarizio, Harvey (Ed.) *Mental health and the educative process.* Chicago: Rand McNally, 1969.

Crow, Lester, and Crow, A. (Eds.) *Readings in guidance.* New York: McKay, 1962, pb.

Demos, George, and Grant, B. (Eds.) *Vocational guidance readings.* Springfield, Ill.: Thomas, 1965.

Diedrich, Richard, and Dye, H. (Eds.) *Group counseling.* Boston: Houghton Mifflin, 1970, pb.

Dinkmeyer, Don (Ed.) *Guidance and counseling in the elementary school.* New York: Holt, Rinehart & Winston, 1968, pb.

Gazda, George (Ed.) *Theories and methods of group counseling in the schools.* Springfield, Ill.: Thomas, 1969.

Gowan, John, and Demos, G. (Eds.) *The guidance of exceptional children.* New York: McKay, 1965.

Hansen, Donald (Ed.) *Explorations in sociology and counseling.* Boston: Houghton Mifflin, 1969.

Hopson, B., and Hayes, J. (Eds.) *The theory and practice of vocational guidance.* Long Island City, N.Y.: Pergamon, 1968.

Kemp, C. (Ed.) *Perspectives on the group process.* Boston: Houghton Mifflin, 1964.

Koplitz, Eugene (Ed.) *Guidance in the elementary school.* Dubuque, Iowa: Wm. C. Brown Company Publishers, 1968, pb.

Krumboltz, John, and Thoresen, C. (Eds.) *Behavioral counseling.* New York: Holt, Rinehart & Winston, 1969.

Lee, James, and Pallone, N. (Eds.) *Readings in guidance and counseling.* New York: Sheed and Ward, 1966.

Lloyd-Jones, Esther, and Rosenau, N. (Eds.) *Social and cultural foundations of guidance.* New York: Holt, Rinehart & Winston, 1968.

Lofquist, Lloyd, and England, W. (Eds.) *Problems in vocational counseling.* Dubuque, Iowa: Wm. C. Brown Company Publishers, 1961.

McGowan, John, and Schmidt, L. (Eds.) *Counseling.* New York: Holt, Rinehart & Winston, 1962.

Miller, Carroll, and Weigel, G. *Today's guidance.* Boston: Allyn and Bacon, 1970, pb.

Miller, Frank (Ed.) *Guidance principles and services.* (2nd ed.) Columbus, Ohio: Merrill, 1968.

Muro, James (Ed.) *Readings in group counseling.* Scranton, Pa.: International Textbook, 1968.

Osipow, Samuel, and Walsh, W. (Eds.) *Behavior change in counseling.* New York: Appleton-Century-Crofts, 1970, pb.

Patterson, Cecil (Ed.) *The counselor in the school.* New York: McGraw-Hill, 1967, pb.

Peters, Herman et al. (Eds.) *Counseling.* Columbus, Ohio: Merrill, 1962.

Peters, Herman et al. (Eds.) *Guidance in the elementary school.* New York: Macmillan, 1963.

Peters, Herman, and Hansen, J. (Eds.) *Vocational guidance and career development.* New York: Macmillan, 1966, pb.

Roth, Robert et al. (Eds.) *The psychology of vocational development.* Boston: Allyn and Bacon, 1970.

Shertzer, Bruce, and Stone, S. (Eds.) *Introduction to guidance.* Boston: Houghton Mifflin, 1970, pb.

Smith, C., and Mink, O. (Eds.) *Foundations of guidance and counseling.* Philadelphia: Lippincott, 1969, pb.

Van Hoose, William, and Pietrofesa, J. (Eds.) *Guidance and counseling in the twentieth century.* Boston: Houghton Mifflin, 1969.

Zytowski, Donald (Ed.) *Vocational behavior.* New York: Holt, Rinehart & Winston, 1968.

Personality

Allport, Gordon. *Patterns and growth in personality.* New York: Holt, Rinehart & Winston, 1961.

Allport, Gordon (Ed.) *Letters from Jenny.* New York: Harcourt, Brace and World, 1965, pb.

Babladelis, Georgia, and Adams, S. *The shaping of personality: text and readings for a social learning view.* Englewood Cliffs, N.J.: Prentice-Hall, 1967, pb.

Bales, Robert. *Personality and interpersonal behavior.* New York: Holt, Rinehart & Winston, 1970.

Baughman, E., and Welsh, G. *Personality: a behavioral science.* Englewood Cliffs, N.J.: Prentice-Hall, 1962.

Bischof, Ledford. *Interpreting personality theories.* (2nd ed.) New York: Harper & Row, 1970.

Bonner, Hubert. *Psychology of personality.* New York: Ronald, 1961.

Byrne, Donn. *An introduction to personality: a research approach.* Englewood Cliffs, N.J.: Prentice-Hall, 1966.

Carson, Robert. *Interaction concepts of personality.* Chicago: Aldine, 1970.

Cattell, Raymond. *The scientific analysis of personality.* Baltimore: Penguin, 1965, pb.

Cohen, Yehudi. *Social structure and personality: a casebook.* New York: Holt, Rinehart & Winston, 1961.

Dalton, Robert. *Personality and social interaction.* Boston: Heath, 1961.

Dreger, Ralph. *Fundamentals of personality.* Philadelphia: Lippincott, 1962.

Endleman, Robert. *Personality and social life: text and readings.* New York: Random House, 1967.

Eysenck, H. *The structure of human personality.* (3rd ed.) London: Methuen, 1970, pb.

Geiwitz, P. *Non-Freudian personality theories.* Belmont, Calif.: Brooks/Cole, 1969, pb.

Gilbert, G. *Personality dynamics: a biosocial approach.* New York: Harper & Row, 1970.

Hall, Calvin, and Lindzey, G. *Theories of personality.* (2nd ed.) New York: Wiley, 1970.

Janis, Irving et al. *Personality: dynamics, development, and assessment.* New York: Harcourt, Brace and World, 1969.

Lazarus, Richard. *Personality and adjustment.* Englewood Cliffs, N.J.: Prentice-Hall, 1963, pb.

Leuba, Clarence. *Personality: interpersonal relations and self-understanding.* Columbus, Ohio: Merrill, 1962, pb.

Levy, Leon. *Conceptions of personality: theories and research.* New York: Random House, 1970.

Liebert, Robert, and Spielger, M. *Personality: an introduction to theory and research.* Homewood, Ill.: Dorsey, 1970.

Lundin, Robert. *Personality.* Dubuque, Iowa: Wm. C. Brown Company Publishers, 1966, pb.

Lundin, Robert. *Personality: a behavioral analysis.* (2nd ed.) New York: Macmillan, 1969.

McCurdy, H. *The personal world: an introduction to the study of personality.* New York: Harcourt, Brace and World, 1961.

Maddi, Salvatore. *Personality theories: a comparative analysis.* Homewood, Ill.: Dorsey, 1968.

Maslow, Abraham. *Toward a psychology of being.* (2nd ed.) New York: Van Nostrand Reinhold, 1968, pb.

Mehrabian, Albert. *An analysis of personality theories.* Englewood Cliffs, N.J.: Prentice-Hall, 1968.

Mischel, W. *Personality and assessment.* New York: Wiley, 1968.

Pervin, Lawrence. *Personality: theory, assessment, research.* New York: Wiley, 1970.

Ruitenbeek, Hendrik (Ed.) *Varieties of personality theory.* New York: Dutton, 1964, pb.

Sanford, Nevitt. *Self and society.* New York: Atherton, 1966.

Sanford, Nevitt. *Issues in personality theory.* San Francisco: Jossey-Bass, 1970.

Sarason, Irwin. *Personality.* New York: Wiley, 1966.

Sarnoff, Irving. *Personality dynamics and development.* New York: Wiley, 1962.

Smith, Barry, and Vetter, H. *Theoretical approaches to personality.* New York: Appleton-Century-Crofts, 1970.

Stagner, Ross. *Psychology of personality.* (3rd ed.) New York: McGraw-Hill, 1961.

Wessman, Alden, and Ricks, D. *Mood and personality.* New York: Holt, Rinehart & Winston, 1966, pb.

White, Robert. *Lives in progress: a study of the natural growth of personality.* (2nd ed.) New York: Holt, Rinehart & Winston, 1966, pb.

Readings on Personality

Bryne, Donn, and Hamilton, M. (Eds.) *Personality research.* Englewood Cliffs, N.J.: Prentice-Hall, 1966, pb.

Chiang, Hung-Min, and Maslow, A. (Eds.) *The healthy personality.* New York: Van Nostrand Reinhold, 1969, pb.

Lazarus, Richard, and Opton, E. (Eds.) *Personality.* Baltimore: Penguin, 1967, pb.

Lindzey, Gardner, and Hall, C. (Eds.) *Theories of personality: primary sources and research.* New York: Wiley, 1965.

Mancuso, James (Ed.) *Readings for a cognitive theory of personality.* New York: Holt, Rinehart & Winston, 1970, pb.

Mednick, Martha, and Mednick, S. (Eds.) *Research in personality.* New York: Holt, Rinehart & Winston, 1963.

Millon, Theodore (Ed.) *Approaches to personality.* New York: Pitman, 1968.

Norbeck, Edward et al. (Eds.) *The study of personality: an interdisciplinary appraisal.* New York: Holt, Rinehart & Winston, 1968.

Sahakian, William (Ed.) *Psychology of personality: readings in theory.* Chicago: Rand McNally, 1965.

Sarason, Irwin (Ed.) *Contemporary research in personality.* (2nd ed.) New York: Van Nostrand Reinhold, 1969, pb.

Semeonoff, Boris (Ed.) *Personality assessment.* Baltimore: Penguin, 1966, pb.

Smelser, Neil, and Smelser, W. (Eds.) *Personality and social systems.* (2nd ed.) New York: Wiley, 1970.

Southwell, Eugene, and Merbaum M. (Eds.) *Personality: readings in theory and research.* Belmont, Calif.: Wadsworth, 1964, pb.

Vetter, Harold, and Smith, B. (Eds.) *Personality theory: a sourcebook.* New York: Appleton-Century-Crofts, 1970.

Wepman, Joseph, and Heine, R. (Eds.) *Concepts of personality.* Chicago: Aldine, 1963.

White, Robert (Ed.) *The study of lives.* New York: Atherton, 1966, pb.

Worchel, Philip, and Bryne, D. (Eds.) *Personality change.* New York: Wiley, 1964.

Tests and Measurements

Adams, Georgia, and Torgerson, T. *Measurement and evaluation in education, psychology, and guidance.* New York: Holt, Rinehart & Winston, 1964.

Ahmann, J., and Glock, M. *Evaluating pupil growth: principles of tests and measurements.* (3rd ed.) Boston: Allyn and Bacon, 1967.

Albright, L. et al. *The use of psychological tests in industry.* Cleveland: Howard Allen, 1963.

Allen, Robert. *Guide to psychological tests and measurements.* (3rd ed.) Coral Gables, Florida: University of Miami Press, 1960.

Allison, Joel et al. *The interpretation of psychological tests.* New York: Harper & Row, 1968.

Anastasi, Anne. *Psychological testing.* (3rd ed.) New York: Macmillan, 1968.

Brown, Frederick. *Principles of education and psychological testing.* Hinsdale, Ill.: Dryden Press, 1970.

Coombs, Clyde. *A theory of data.* New York: Wiley, 1964.

Cronbach, Lee. *Essentials of psychological testing.* (3rd ed.) New York: Harper & Row, 1970.

Downie, N. *Fundamentals of measurement.* New York: Oxford, 1967.

Edwards, Allen. *The measurement of personality traits by scales and inventories.* New York: Holt, Rinehart & Winston, 1970.

Freeman, Frank. *Theory and practice of psychological testing.* (3rd ed.) New York: Holt, Rinehart & Winston, 1962.

Gathercole, C. *Assessment in clinical psychology.* Baltimore: Penguin, 1968, pb.

Gekoski, Norman. *Psychological testing: theory, interpretation and practices.* Springfield, Ill.: Thomas, 1964.

Ghiselli, Edwin. *Theory of psychological measurements.* New York: McGraw-Hill, 1964.

Goldman, Leo. *Using tests in counseling.* New York: Appleton-Century-Crofts, 1961.

Goude, G. *On fundamental measurement in psychology.* New York: Humanities Press, 1962, pb.

Guion, Robert. *Personnel testing.* New York: McGraw-Hill, 1965.

Gulliksen, Harold, and Messick, S. (Eds.) *Psychological scaling.* New York: Wiley, 1960.

Harrower, Mary. *Appraising personality: an introduction to projective techniques.* New York: Watts, 1964.

Helmstadter, G. *Principles of psychological measurement.* New York: Appleton-Century-Crofts, 1964.

Horowitz, Leonard. *Measurement.* Dubuque, Iowa: Wm. C. Brown Company Publishers, 1966, pb.

Horrocks, John. *Assessment of behavior.* Columbus, Ohio: Merrill, 1964.

Horst, Paul. *Psychological measurement and prediction.* Belmont, Calif.: Brooks/Cole, 1966.

Horst, Paul. *Personality: measurement of dimensions.* San Francisco: Jossey-Bass, 1968.

Kagan, Jerome, and Lesser, G. *Contemporary issues in thematic apperceptive methods.* Springfield, Ill.: Thomas, 1961.

Kelly, E. *Assessment of human characteristics.* Belmont, Calif.: Brooks/Cole, 1967, pb.

Kleinmuntz, Benjamin. *Personality measurement: an introduction.* Homewood, Ill.: Dorsey, 1967.

Lawshe, Charles, and Balma, M. *Principles of personnel testing.* (2nd ed.) New York: McGraw-Hill, 1966.

Lord, Frederic, and Novick, M. *Statistical theories of mental test scores.* Reading, Mass.: Addison-Wesley, 1968.

Lyman, Howard. *Test scores and what they mean.* (2nd ed.) Englewood Cliffs, N.J.: Prentice-Hall, 1970.

Magnusson, David. *Test theory.* Reading, Mass.: Addison-Wesley, 1967.

Messick, Samuel, and Ross, J. *Measurement in personality and cognition.* New York: Wiley, 1962.

Nunnally, Jim. *Psychometric theory.* New York: McGraw-Hill, 1967.

Nunnally, Jim. *Introduction to psychological measurement.* (2nd ed.) New York: McGraw-Hill, 1970.

Oppenheim, A. *Questionnaire design and attitude measurement.* New York: Basic Books, 1966.

Palmer, James. *The psychological assessment of children.* New York: Wiley, 1970.

Payne, David. *The specification and measurement of learning outcomes.* Waltham, Mass.: Ginn-Blaisdell, 1967, pb.

Rabin, A. (Ed.) *Projective techniques in personality assessment: a modern introduction.* New York: Springer, 1968.

Remmers, Hermann et al. *A practical introduction to measurement and evaluation.* New York: Harper & Row, 1965.

Rozeboom, William. *Foundations of the theory of prediction.* Homewood, Ill.: Dorsey, 1966.

Savage, R. *Psychometric assessment of the individual child.* Baltimore: Penguin, 1969, pb.

Shaw, Marvin, and Wright, J. *Scales for the measurement of attitudes.* New York: McGraw-Hill, 1967.

Super, Donald, and Crites, J. *Appraising vocation fitness by means of psychological tests.* (Rev. ed.)New York: Harper & Row, 1962.

Thorndike, Robert, and Hagen, E. *Measurement and evaluation in psychology and education.* (3rd ed.) New York: Wiley, 1969.

Tyler, Leona. *Tests and measurements.* Englewood Cliffs, N J.: Prentice-Hall, 1963, pb.

Wood, Dorothy. *Test construction.* Columbus, Ohio: Merrill, 1960.

Readings on Tests and Measurements

Barnette, W. (Ed.) *Readings in psychological tests and measurements.* (Rev. ed.) Homewood, Ill.: Dorsey, 1968, pb.

Chase, Clinton, and Ludlow H. (Eds.) *Readings in educational and psychological measurement.* Boston: Houghton Mifflin, 1966, pb.

Flynn, John, and Garber, H. (Eds.) *Assessing behavior: readings in educational and psychological measurement.* Reading, Mass.: Addison-Wesley, 1967, pb.

Gronland, Norman (Ed.) *Readings in measurement and evaluation: education and psychology.* New York: Macmillan, 1968.

Hirt, Michael (Ed.) *Rorschach science: readings in theory and method.* New York: Free Press, 1962.

Jackson, Douglas, and Messick, S. (Eds.) *Problems in human assessment.* New York: McGraw-Hill, 1967.

Mehrens, William, and Ebel, R. (Eds.) *Principles of educational and psychological measurement.* Chicago: Rand McNally, 1967, pb.

Mittler, Peter (Ed.) *The psychological assessment of mental and physical handicaps.* London: Methuen, 1970.

Payne, David, and McMorris, R. (Eds.) *Educational and psychological measurement: contributions to theory and practice.* Waltham, Mass.: Blaisdell, 1967, pb.

Ronan, William, and Prien, E. (Eds.) *Perspectives on the measurement of human performance.* New York: Appleton-Century-Crofts, 1970.

Semenoff, Boris (Ed.) *Personality assessment.* Baltimore: Penguin, 1966, pb.

Sherman, Murray (Ed.) *A Rorschach reader.* New York: International Universities Press, 1961.

Comparative and Animal Psychology*

Altman, Joseph. *Organic foundations of animal behavior.* New York: Holt, Rinehart & Winston, 1966.

Barnett, S. *The rat: a study in behaviour.* Chicago: Aldine, 1963, pb.

Breland, Keller, and Breland, M. *Animal behavior.* New York: Macmillan, 1966, pb.

Broadhurst, Peter. *The science of animal behaviour.* Baltimore: Penguin, 1963, pb.

Chauvin, R. *Animal societies: from the bee to the gorilla.* New York: Hill and Wang, 1968.

Cloudsley-Thompson, J. *Animal behaviour.* New York: Macmillan, 1961.

Denny, M., and Ratner, Stanley. *Comparative psychology.*(Rev. ed.) Homewood, Ill.: Dorsey, 1970.

Dethier, V., and Stellar, E. *Animal behavior.* (3rd ed.) Englewood Cliffs, N.J.: Prentice-Hall, 1969, pb.

DeVore, Irven (Ed.) *Primate behavior.* New York: Holt, Rinehart & Winston, 1965.

Etkin, William (Ed.) *Social behavior and organization among vertebrates.* Chicago: University of Chicago Press, 1964.

Fox, M. (Ed.) *Abnormal behavior in animals.* Philadelphia: Saunders, 1968. This is a book of readings (rdgs).

Gray, Philip. *The comparative analysis of behavior.* Dubuque, Iowa: Wm. C. Brown Company Publishers, 1966, pb.

Hanson, Earl. *Animal diversity.* (3rd ed.) Englewood Cliffs, N.J.: Prentice-Hall, 1969.

---

*Advanced graduate books also included.

Hafez, E. (Ed.) *The behaviour of domestic animals.* (2nd ed.)Baltimore: Williams and Wilkins, 1962.

Hinde, Robert. *Animal behaviour: a synthesis of ethology and comparative psychology.* New York: McGraw-Hill, 1966.

Klopfer, Peter, and Hailman, J. *An introduction to animal behavior: ethology's first century.* Englewood Cliffs, N.J.: Prentice-Hall, 1967.

McGill, Thomas (Ed.) *Readings in animal behavior.* New York: Holt, Rinehart & Winston, 1965, rdgs.

Maier, Norman, and Schneirla, T. *Principles of animal psychology.* (Rev. ed.) New York: Dover, 1964, pb.

Maier, Richard, and Maier, B. *Comparative animal behavior.* Belmont, Calif.: Brooks/Cole, 1970.

Manning, Aubrey. *An introduction to animal behavior.* Reading, Mass.: Addison-Wesley, 1967, pb.

Marler, Peter, and Hamilton, W. *Mechanisms of animal behavior.* New York: Wiley, 1966.

Morris, Desmond (Ed.) *Primate ethology.* Chicago: Aldine, 1967.

Morris, Desmond, and Morris, R. *Men and apes.* New York: McGraw-Hill, 1966.

Portmann, Adolph. *Animals as social beings.* New York: Viking Press, 1961.

Schrier, Allan et al. (Eds.) *Behavior of nonhuman primates.* New York: Academic Press, 1965. 2 vols.

Sebeok, Thomas (Ed.) *Animal communication: techniques of study and results of research.* Bloomington, Ind.: Indiana University Press, 1968.

Sluckin, Wladyslaw. *Imprinting and early learning.* Chicago: Aldine, 1965, pb.

Smythe, Reginald. *Animal psychology.* Springfield, Ill.: Thomas, 1962.

Southwick, Charles (Ed.) *Primate social behavior.* New York: Van Nostrand Reinhold, 1963, pb, rdgs.

Tavolga, William. *Principles of animal behavior.* New York: Harper & Row, 1969, pb.

Thorpe, W., and Zangwill, O. (Eds.) *Current problems in animal behaviour.* London: Cambridge, 1961.

Tompkins, Travis et al. (Eds.) *Readings in behavioral pharmacology.* New York: Appleton-Century-Crofts, 1970, rdgs.

Waters, Rolland et al. (Eds.) *Principles of comparative psychology.* New York: McGraw-Hill, 1960.

Wynne-Edwards, V. *Animal dispersion in relation to social behaviour.* London: Oliver and Boyd, 1962.

Experimental Psychology**

Andreas, Burton. *Experimental psychology.* New York: Wiley, 1960.

Baker, Lawrence. *General experimental psychology.* New York: Oxford, 1960.

Beauchamp, Kenneth et al. (Eds.) *Current topics in experimental psychology.* New York: Holt, Rinehart & Winston, 1970, pb, rdgs.

Candland, Douglas. *Psychology: the experimental approach.* New York: McGraw-Hill, 1968.

Corso, John. *Experimental psychology of sensory behavior.* New York: Holt, Rinehart & Winston, 1967.

D'Amato, M. *Experimental psychology: methodology, psychophysics and learning.* New York: McGraw-Hill, 1970.

Harrower, Mary. *The psychologist at work: an introduction to experimental psychology.* (1937 ed.) Freeport, N.Y.: Books for Libraries, 1969.

Kling, J., and Riggs, L. (Eds.) *Woodworth/Schlosberg's experimental psychology.* (3rd ed.) New York: Holt, Rinehart & Winston, 1971.

Lyons, Joseph. *A primer of experimental psychology.* New York: Harper & Row, 1965, pb.

McGuigan, F. *Experimental psychology: a methodological approach.* (2nd ed.) Englewood Cliffs, N.J.: Prentice-Hall, 1968.

Matheson, Douglas et al. *Introduction to experimental psychology.* New York: Holt, Rinehart & Winston, 1970.

Osgood, Charles. *Method and theory in experimental psychology.* New York: Oxford, 1953.

Piaget, Jean et al. *Experimental psychology.* New York: Basic Books, 1968-1970. 9 vols.

** Advanced graduate books included plus sources published prior to 1960.

Plutchik, Robert. *Foundations of experimental research.* New York: Harper & Row, 1968, pb.

Postman, Leo, and Egan, J. *Experimental psychology: an introduction.* New York: Harper & Row, 1949.

Readings in experimental psychology today. Del Mar, Calif.: CRM Books, 1970, rdgs.

Restle, Frank, and Greeno, J. *Introduction to mathematical psychology.* Reading, Mass.: Addison-Wesley, 1970.

Sidowski, Joseph (Ed.) *Experimental methods and instrumentation in psychology.* New York: McGraw-Hill, 1966. Appendix lists instrument manufacturers and animal suppliers.

Siwek, Paul. *Experimental psychology.* New York: Wagner, 1959.

Stevens, S. (Ed.) *Handbook of experimental psychology.* New York: Wiley, 1951.

Underwood, Benton. *Experimental psychology.* (2nd ed.) New York: Appleton-Century-Crofts, 1966.

Woodworth, Robert, and Schlosberg, H. *Experimental psychology.* (Rev. ed.) New York: Holt, Rinehart & Winston, 1954.

Zimny, George. *Method in experimental psychology.* New York: Ronald, 1961.

Methods of Research*

Al-Issa, Ihsan, and Dennis, W. *Cross-cultural studies of behavior.* New York: Holt, Rinehart & Winston, 1970.

Badia, Pietro et al. (Eds.) *Research problems in psychology.* Reading, Mass.: Addison-Wesley, 1970, pb, rdgs.

Bakan, David. *On method: toward a reconstruction of psychological investigations.* San Francisco: Jossey-Bass, 1967.

Barker, Roger. *Ecological psychology: concepts and methods for studying the environment of human behavior.* Stanford, Calif.: Stanford University Press, 1968.

Best, John. *Research in education.* Englewood Cliffs, N.J.: Prentice-Hall, 1970.

Bolsly, Morris. *Guide to gathering information in face-to-face interviews.* Ramsey, N.J.: Ramsey-Wallace Corp., 1967.

---

*Advanced graduate books also included.

Borg, Walter. *Educational research.* New York: McKay, 1963.

Borgatta, Edgar, and Crowther, B. *A workbook for the study of social interaction processes.* Chicago: Rand McNally, 1965, pb.

Bross, Irwin. *Design for decision.* New York: Macmillan, 1965, pb.

Brown, Clinton (Ed.) *Methods in psychophysiology.* Baltimore: Williams and Wilkins, 1967.

Budd, Richard et al. *Content analysis of communications.* New York: Macmillan, 1967.

Campbell, Donald, and Stanley, J. *Experimental and quasi-experimental designs for research.* Chicago: Rand McNally, 1966, pb.

Chassan, J. *Research design in clinical psychology and psychiatry.* New York: Appleton-Century-Crofts, 1967.

Cochran, William. *Sampling techniques.* (2nd ed.)New York: Wiley, 1963.

Colby, Kenneth. *An introduction to psychoanalytic research.* New York: Basic Books, 1960.

Cook, David. *A guide to educational research.* Boston: Allyn and Bacon, 1965.

Cornsweet, Tom *The design of electric circuits in the behavioral sciences.* New York: Wiley, 1963.

Davidson, Park, and Costello, C. *N=1: experimental studies of single cases.* New York: Van Nostrand Reinhold, 1969, pb.

Edwards, Allen. *Experimental design in psychological research.* (3rd ed.)New York: Holt, Rinehart & Winston, 1968.

Fairweather, George. *Methods for experimental social innovation.* New York: Wiley, 1967.

Fenlason, Anne et al. *Essentials in interviewing.* New York: Harper & Row, 1962.

Finney, David. *An introduction to the theory of experimental design.* Chicago: University of Chicago Press, 1960, pb.

Fisher, Ronald. *The design of experiments.*(7th ed.)New York: Hafner, 1960.

Fox, David. *The research process in education.* New York: Holt, Rinehart & Winston, 1969.

Friedman, Neil. *The social nature of psychological research: the psychology experiment as a social interaction.* New York: Basic Books, 1967.

Galfo, Armand, and Miller, E. *Interpreting educational research.* Dubuque, Iowa: Wm. C. Brown Company Publishers, 1970.

Gephart, William and Ingle, R. (Eds.) *Educational research: selected readings.* Columbus, Ohio: Merrill, 1969, rdgs.

Giorgi, Amedeo. *Psychology as a human science: a phenomenologically based approach.* New York: Harper & Row, 1970, pb.

Glock, Charles (Ed.) *Survey research in the social sciences.* New York: Russell Sage, 1967.

Good, Carter. *Essentials of educational research.* New York: Appleton-Century-Crofts, 1966.

Gordon, Ira. *Studying the child in school.* New York: Wiley, 1966, pb.

Gordon, Raymond. *Interviewing.* Homewood, Ill.: Dorsey, 1969.

Gottschalk, Louis, and Auerback, A. (Eds.) *Methods of research in psychotherapy.* New York: Appleton-Century-Crofts, 1966, rdgs.

Hall, Calvin, and Van De Castle, R. *The content analysis of dreams.* New York: Appleton-Century-Crofts, 1966.

Handy, Rollo. *Methodology of the behavioral sciences.* Springfield, Ill.: Thomas, 1964.

Hayman, John. *Research in education.* Columbus, Ohio: Merrill, 1968, pb.

Helmstadter, Gerald. *Research concepts in human behavior.* New York: Appleton-Century-Crofts, 1970.

Hillway, Tyrus. *Introduction to research.* New York: Macmillan, 1964.

Holsti, Ole. *Content analysis for the social sciences and humanities.* Reading, Mass.: Addison-Wesley, 1969, pb.

Holt, Robert, and Turner, J. (Eds.) *The methodology of comparative research.* New York: Free Press, 1970.

Instrumentation in psychology. *American Psychologist,* 1969, 24, 187-397.

Kaplan, Abraham *The conduct of inquiry.* San Francisco: Chandler, 1964, pb.

Kelman, Herbert. *A time to speak—on human values and social research.* San Francisco: Jossey-Bass, 1967.

Kerlinger, Frederick. *Foundations of behavioral research: educational and psychological inquiry.* New York: Holt, Rinehart & Winston, 1964.

Kirk, Roger. *Experimental design: procedures for the behavioral sciences.* Belmont, Calif.: Brooks/Cole, 1968.

Kish, Leslie. *Survey sampling.* New York: Wiley, 1965.

Klopfer, Walter. *The psychological report: use and communication of psychological findings.* New York: Grune and Stratton, 1960.

Kurtz, K. *Foundations of psychological research.* Boston: Allyn and Bacon, 1965.

Lathrop, Richard. *Introduction to psychological research.* New York: Harper & Row, 1969.

Levitt, Eugene. *Clinical research design and analysis in the behavioral sciences.* Springfield, Ill.: Thomas, 1961.

Lindzey, Gardner. *Projective techniques and cross-cultural research.* New York: Appleton-Century-Crofts, 1961.

Luce, Duncan et al. (Eds.) *Readings in mathematical psychology.* New York: 1963, 1965. 2 vols., rdgs.

McAshan, Hildreth. *Elements of educational research.* New York: McGraw-Hill, 1963, pb.

McGrath, J. *Research methods and designs for education.* Scranton, Pa.: International Textbook, 1970.

Maher, Brendan. *Introduction to research in psychotherapy.* New York: McGraw-Hill, 1970, pb.

Maslow, Abraham. *The psychology of science: a reconnaissance.* New York: Harper & Row, 1966.

Mouly, George. *The science of educational research.* New York: American Book, 1963.

Murstein, Bernard. *Theory and research in projective techniques (emphasizing the TAT).* New York: Wiley, 1963.

Myers, Jerome. *Fundamentals of experimental design.* Boston: Allyn and Bacon, 1966.

O'Neil, W. *An introduction to method in psychology.* (3rd ed.) New York: Cambridge University Press, 1963.

Oppenheim, A. *Questionnaire design and attitude measurement.* New York: Basic Books, 1966.

Palmer, J. *Psychological assessment of children.* New York: Wiley, 1970.

Pascal, Gerald, and Jenkins, W. *Systematic observation of gross human behavior.* New York: Grune and Stratton, 1961.

Pittenger, Robert et al. *The first five minutes.* Ithaca, N.Y.: Paul Martineau, 1960.

Rabin, Albert, and Haworth, M. (Eds.) *Projective techniques with children.* New York: Grune and Stratton, 1960.

Ray, William. *An introduction to experimental design.* New York: Macmillan, 1960.

Rich, John. *Interviewing children and adolescents.* New York: St. Martain's Press, 1968.

Richardson, Stephen et al. *Interviewing.* New York: Basic Books, 1965.

Rosenthal, Robert. *Experimenter effects in behavioral research.* New York: Appleton-Century-Crofts, 1966.

Rosenthal, Robert, and Rosnow, R. (Eds.) *Artifact in behavioral research.* New York: Academic Press, 1969, rdgs.

Rothney, John. *Methods of studying the individual child: the psychological case study.* Waltham, Mass.: Blaisdell, 1968, pb.

Rummel, J. *An introduction to research procedures in education.* (2nd ed.) New York: Harper & Row, 1964.

Sax, Gilbert. *Empirical foundations of education research.* Englewood Cliffs, N.J.: Prentice-Hall, 1968.

Schultz, Duane. *The science of psychology: critical reflections.* New York: Appleton-Century-Crofts, 1970, pb., rdgs.

Scott, William, and Wertheimer, M. *Introduction to psychological research.* New York: Wiley, 1962.

Selltiz, Claire et al. *Research methods in social relations.* (Rev. ed.) New York: Holt, Rinehart & Winston, 1961.

Shontz, Franklin. *Research methods in personality.* New York: Appleton-Century-Crofts, 1965.

Shouksmith George. *Assessment through interviewing.* Long Island City, N.Y.: Pergamon, 1968.

Sidman, Murray. *Tactics of scientific research: evaluating experimental data in psychology.* New York: Basic Books, 1960, pb.

Sidney, E., and Brown, M. *The skills of interviewing.* New York: Humanities Press, 1961.

Simkins, Lawrence. *The basis of psychology as a behavioral science.* Waltham, Mass.: Blaisdell, 1970, pb.

Simon, Julian. *Basic research methods in social science.* New York: Random House, 1968.

Slonim, M. *Sampling in a nutshell.* New York: Simon and Schuster, 1960.

Stanley, Julian (Ed.) *Improving experimental design and statistical analysis.* Chicago: Rand McNally, 1967.

Summers, Gene. *Attitude measurement.* Chicago: Rand McNally, 1970, pb., rdgs.

Travers, Robert. *An introduction to educational research.* (3rd ed.) New York: Macmillan, 1969.

Van Dalen, Deobold, and Meyer, W. *Understanding educational research.* New York: McGraw-Hill, 1962.

Varma, M. *An introduction to educational and psychological research.* New York: Taplinger, 1966.

Venables, Paul, and Martin, I. (Eds.) *A manual of psychophysiological methods.* New York: Wiley, 1967.

Wandt, Edwin (Ed.) *A cross-section of educational research.* New York: McKay 1965, pb, rdgs.

Watson, Robert. *The clinical method in psychology.* New York: Wiley, 1963.

Webb, Eugene et al. *Unobtrusive measurements: nonreactive research in the social sciences.* Chicago: Rand McNally, 1966, pb.

Whiting, John et al. *Field guide for a study of socialization.* New York: Wiley, 1966.

Wiersma, William. *Research methods in education.* Philadelphia: Lippincott, 1969.

Willems, Edwin, and Raush, H. (Eds.) *Naturalistic viewpoint in psychological research.* New York: Holt, Rinehart & Winston, 1969.

Wise, John et al. *Methods of research in education.* Boston: Heath, 1967.

Wright, Herbert. *Recording and analyzing child behavior.* New York: Harper & Row, 1967, pb.

Zucker, Mitchell. *Electronic circuits for the behavioral and biomedical sciences: a reference book of useful solid-state circuits.* San Francisco: Freeman, 1969.

Statistics*

Adkins, Dorothy. *Statistics: an introduction for students in the behavioral sciences.* Columbus, Ohio: Merrill, 1964, pb.

Adler, Henry, and Roessler, E. *Introduction to probability and statistics.* (4th ed.) San Francisco: Freeman, 1968.

Armore, Sidney. *Introduction to statistical analysis and inference.* New York: Wiley, 1966.

Baggaley, Andrew. *Intermediate correlational methods.* New York: Wiley, 1964.

Bashaw, W. *Mathematics for statistics.* New York: Wiley, 1969, pb.

Bloomers, Paul, and Lindquist, E. *Elementary statistical methods in psychology and education.* Boston: Houghton Mifflin, 1960.

Bogdanoff, E. *Introduction to descriptive statistics.* Belmont, Calif.: Dickenson, 1970, pb.

Bradley, James. *Distribution-free statistical tests.* Englewood Cliffs, N.J.: Prentice-Hall, 1968.

Chase, Clinton. *Elementary statistical procedures.* New York: McGraw-Hill, 1967.

Clarke, Robert et al. *Statistical reasoning and procedures.* Columbus, Ohio: Merrill, 1965.

Cohen, Jacob. *Statistical power analysis for the behavioral sciences.* New York: Academic Press, 1969.

Cotton, John. *Elementary statistical theory for behavioral scientists.* Reading, Mass.: Addison-Wesley, 1967, pb.

Courts, Frederick. *Psychological statistics: an introduction.* Homewood, Ill.: Dorsey, 1966.

Dixon, Wilfrid, and Massey, F. *Introduction to statistical analysis.* (3rd ed.) New York: McGraw-Hill, 1969.

---

*Advanced graduate books also included.

Downie, N., and Heath, R. *Basic statistical methods.* (3rd ed.) New York: Harper & Row, 1970.

DuBois, Philip. *An introduction to psychological statistics.* New York: Harper & Row, 1965.

Edgington, Eugene. *Statistical inference: the distribution-free approach.* New York: McGraw-Hill, 1969.

Edwards, Allen. *Statistical methods.* (2nd ed.) New York: Holt, Rinehart & Winston, 1967.

Edwards, Allen. *Statistical analysis.* (3rd ed.) New York: Holt, Rinehart & Winston, 1969.

Elzey, Freeman. *A first reader in statistics.* Belmont, Calif.: Wadsworth, 1967.

Ericksen, Gerald. *Scientific inquiry in the behavioral sciences.* Glenview, Ill.: Scott, Foresman and Company, 1970.

Ferguson, George. *Statistical analysis in psychology and education.* (2nd ed.) New York: McGraw-Hill, 1966.

Freeman, Linton. *Elementary applied statistics.* New York: Wiley, 1965.

Fried, Robert. *Introduction to statistics: selected procedures for the behavioral sciences.* New York: Oxford, 1969.

Games, Paul, and Klare, G. *Elementary statistics: data analysis for the behavioral sciences.* New York: McGraw-Hill, 1967.

Garrett, Henry. *Elementary statistics.* (2nd ed.) New York: McKay, 1962.

Garrett, Henry. *Statistics in psychology and education.* New York: McKay, 1966.

Gelbaum, Bernard, and March, J. *Mathematics for the social and behavioral sciences: probability, calculus, and statistics.* Philadelphia: Saunders, 1969. 2 vols.

Glass, Gene, and Stanley, J. *Statistical methods in education and psychology.* Englewood Cliffs, N.J.: Prentice-Hall, 1970.

Gourevitch, Vivian. *Statistical methods: a problem-solving approach.* Boston: Allyn and Bacon, 1965.

Guenther, William. *Concepts of statistical inference.* New York: McGraw-Hill, 1965.

Guilford, Joy. *Fundamental statistics in psychology and education.* (4th ed.) New York: McGraw-Hill, 1965.

Haber, Audrey, and Runyon, R. *General statistics.* Reading, Mass.: Addison-Wesley, 1969.

Hammond, Kenneth et al. *Introduction to the statistical method.* (2nd ed.)New York: Knopf, 1970.

Hardyck, Curtis, and Petrinovich, L. *Introduction to statistics for the behavioral sciences.* Philadelphia: Saunders, 1969.

Harman, Harry. *Modern factor analysis.* (Rev. ed.)Chicago: University of Chicago Press, 1967.

Harnett, Donald. *Introduction to statistical methods.* Reading, Mass.: Addison-Wesley, 1970.

Hays, William. *Statistics.* New York: Holt, Rinehart & Winston, 1963.

Hays, William. *Basic statistics.* Belmont, Calif.: Brooks/Cole, 1967, pb.

Heath, Helen. *Elementary statistics.* Springfield, Ill.: Thomas, 1968.

Henderson, Norman. *Statistical research methods in education and psychology.* New York: Oxford, 1964, pb.

Hoel, Paul. *Elementary statistics.* (2nd ed.)New York: Wiley, 1966.

Hultquist, Robert. *Introduction to statistics.* New York: Holt, Rinehart & Winston, 1969.

Huntsberger, David. *Elements of statistical inference.* (2nd ed.) Boston: Allyn and Bacon, 1967.

Klugh, Henry. *Statistics: the essentials for research.* New York: Wiley, 1970.

Kolstoe, Ralph. *Introduction to statistics for the behavioral sciences.* Homewood, Ill.: Dorsey, 1969.

Kozelka, Robert. *Elements of statistical inference.* Reading, Mass.: Addison-Wesley, 1961.

Levy, Sheldon. *Inferential statistics in the behavioral sciences.* New York: Holt, Rinehart & Winston, 1968.

Li, C. *Introduction to experimental statistics.* New York: McGraw-Hill, 1964.

Lindgren, B. *Statistical theory.* New York: Macmillan, 1962.

Lindgren, B, and McElrath, G. *Introduction to probability and statistics.* New York: Macmillan, 1966.

Lordahl, Daniel. *Modern statistics for behavioral sciences.* New York: Ronald, 1967.

McCall, Robert. *Fundamental statistics for psychology.* New York: Harcourt, Brace and World, 1970.

McGee, Victor. *Principles of statistics: traditional and bayesian.* New York: Appleton-Century-Crofts, 1970.

McNemar, Quinn. *Psychological statistics.* (4th ed.)New York: Wiley, 1969.

Mendenhall, William. *Introduction to probability and statistics.* (2nd ed.)Belmont, Calif.: Wadsworth, 1967.

Meredith, William. *Basic mathematical and statistical tables for psychology and education.* New York: McGraw-Hill, 1967.

Minium, Edward. *Statistical reasoning in psychology and education.* New York: Wiley, 1970.

Mood, Alexander, and Graybill, F. *Introduction to the theory of statistics.* New York: McGraw-Hill, 1963.

Morrison, Donald. *Multivariate statistical methods.* New York: McGraw-Hill, 1967.

Mosteller, Frederick et al. *Probability with statistical applications.* (2nd ed.)Reading, Mass.: Addison-Wesley, 1970.

Pierce, A. *Fundamentals of nonparametric statistics.* Belmont, Calif.: Dickenson, 1970.

Ray, William. *Statistics in psychological research.* New York: Macmillan, 1962.

Ray, William. *Basic statistics.* New York: Appleton-Century-Crofts, 1968, pb.

Roscoe, John. *Fundamental research statistics for the behavioral sciences.* New York: Holt, Rinehart & Winston, 1969.

Runyon, Richard and Haber, A. *Fundamentals of behavioral statistics.* Reading, Mass.: Addison-Wesley, 1967.

Savage, I. *Statistics: uncertainty and behavior.* Boston: Houghton Mifflin, 1968.

Smith, Milton. *A simplified guide to statistics for education and psychology.* (4th ed.) New York: Holt, Rinehart & Winston, 1970, pb.

Spence, Janet et al. *Elementary statistics.* (2nd ed.) New York: Appleton-Century-Crofts, 1968.

Stilson, Donald. *Probability and statistics in psychological research and theory.* San Francisco: Holden-Day, 1966.

Tate, Merle. *Statistics in education and psychology: a first course.* New York: Macmillan, 1965.

Turney, Billy, and Robb, G. *Simplified statistics for education and psychology: a work-text with feedback.* Scranton, Pa.: International Textbook, 1968, pb.

Wallis, W., and Roberts, H. *The nature of statistics.* New York: Crowell-Collier, 1962, pb.

Weinberg, George, and Schumaker, J. *Statistics: an intuitive approach.* (2nd ed.) Belmont, Calif.: Brooks/Cole, 1969.

Winer, Benjamin. *Statistical principles in experimental design.* New York: McGraw-Hill, 1962.

Yamane, Taro. *Statistics: an introductory analysis.* (2nd ed.) New York: Harper & Row, 1967.

Yeomans, K. *Introducing statistics: statistics for the social scientist. Vol. 1.* Baltimore: Penguin, 1968, pb.

Yeomans, K. *Applied statistics: statistics for the social scientist. Vol 2.* Baltimore: Penguin, 1968, pb.

Young, Hugh. *Statistical treatment of experimental data.* New York: McGraw-Hill, 1962.

Young, Robert, and Veldman, D. *Introductory statistics for the behavioral sciences.* New York: Holt, Rinehart & Winston, 1965.

Readings on Statistics

Haber, Audrey et al. (Eds.) *Readings in statistics.* Reading, Mass.: Addison-Wesley, 1970, pb.

Heermann, Emil, and Braskamp, L. (Eds.) *Readings in statistics for the behavioral sciences.* Englewood Cliffs, N.J.: Prentice-Hall, 1970.

Lieberman, Bernhardt (Ed.) *Contemporary problems in statistics.* New York: Oxford, 1970.

Messick, David (Ed.) *Mathematical thinking in behavioral sciences: readings from Scientific American.* San Francisco: Freeman, 1968, pb.

Morrison, Denton and Henkel, R. (Eds.) *The significance test controversy.* Chicago: Aldine, 1970.

Steger, Joseph (Ed.) *Readings in statistics for the behavioral scientist.* New York: Holt, Rinehart & Winston, 1970, pb.

Learning

Adams, Jack. *Human memory.* New York: McGraw-Hill, 1967.

Annett, John. *Feedback and human behaviour.* Baltimore: Penguin, 1969, pb.

Atkinson, Richard et al. *An introduction to mathematical learning theory.* New York: Wiley, 1965.

Bandura, Albert. *Principles of behavior modification.* New York: Holt, Rinehart & Winston, 1969.

Bartz, Wayne. *Memory.* Dubuque, Iowa: Wm. C. Brown Company Publishers, 1968, pb.

Beecroft, Robert. *Classical conditioning.* Goleta, Calif.: Psychonomic Press, 1966.

Bilodeau, E. (Ed.) *Principles of skill acquisition.* New York: Academic Press, 1970, pb.

Borger, Robert, and Seaborne, A. *The psychology of learning.* Baltimore: Penguin, 1966, pb.

Bourne, Lyle. *Human conceptual behavior.* Boston: Allyn and Bacon, 1966.

Brown, Roger. *Psycholinguistics.* New York: Free Press, 1970.

Church, Joseph. *Language and the discovery of reality.* New York: Random House, 1961, pb.

Deese, James. *Psycholinguistics.* Boston: Allyn and Bacon, 1970, pb.

Deese, James, and Hulse, S. *The psychology of learning.* (3rd ed.) New York: McGraw-Hill, 1967.

Dinsmoor, James. *Operant conditioning: an experimental analysis of behavior.* Dubuque, Iowa: Wm. C. Brown Company Publishers, 1969, pb.

Dolinsky, Richard. *Human learning.* Dubuque, Iowa: Wm. C. Brown Company Publishers, 1966, pb.

Ellis, Henry. *Transfer of learning.* New York: Macmillan, 1965, pb.

Filloux, J-C. *Memory and forgetting.* New York: Walker, 1963.

Fitts, Paul, and Posner, M. *Human performance.* Belmont, Calif.: Wadsworth, 1967, pb.

Gagné, Robert. *The conditions of learning.* New York: Holt, Rinehart & Winston, 1965.

Yates, Frances. *The art of memory.* Chicago: University of Chicago Press, 1966.

Readings on Learning

Anderson, Richard, and Ausubel, D. (Eds.) *Readings in the psychology of cognition.* New York: Holt, Rinehart & Winston, 1965.

Anderson, Wallace, and Stageberg, N. (Eds.) *Introductory readings on language.* New York: Holt, Rinehart & Winston, 1966, pb.

Birney, Robert, and Teevan, R. (Eds.) *Instinct.* New York: Van Nostrand Reinhold, 1961, pb.

Birney, Robert, and Teevan, R. (Eds.) *Reinforcement.* New York: Van Nostrand Reinhold, 1961, pb.

Boe, Erling, and Church, R. (Eds.) *Punishment: issues and experiments.* New York: Appleton-Century-Crofts, 1968, pb.

Braun, John (Ed.) *Contemporary research in learning.* New York: Van Nostrand Reinhold, 1963, pb.

Bryne, William (Ed.) *Molecular approaches to learning and memory.* New York: Academic Press, 1970.

Catania, Charles (Ed.) *Contemporary research in operant behavior.* Glenview, Ill.: Scott, Foresman and Company, 1968, pb.

DeCecco, John (Ed.) *Educational technology: readings in programmed instruction.* New York: Holt, Rinehart & Winston, 1964, pb.

DeCecco, John (Ed.) *The psychology of language, thought, and instruction.* New York: Holt, Rinehart & Winston, 1967.

Gagné, Robert (Ed.) *Learning and individual differences.* Columbus, Ohio: Merrill, 1967.

Goldstein, Henry et al. (Eds.) *Controversial issues in learning.* New York: Appleton-Century-Crofts, 1965, pb.

Grose, Robert, and Birney, R. (Eds.) *Transfer of learning.* New York: Van Nostrand Reinhold, 1963, pb.

Hall, John (Ed.) *Readings in the psychology of learning.* Philadelphia: Lippincott, 1967, pb.

Harper, Robert et al. (Eds.) *The cognitive processes.* Englewood Cliffs, N.J.: Prentice-Hall, 1964.

Harris, Theodore, and Schwahn, W. (Eds.) *Selected readings on the learning/process.* New York: Oxford, 1961, pb.

Hildum, Donald (Ed.) *Language and thought.* New York: Van Nostrand Reinhold, 1967, pb.

Honig, Werner (Ed.) *Operant behavior: areas of research and application.* New York: Appleton-Century-Crofts, 1966.

Jakobovitz, Leon, and Miron, M. (Eds.) *Readings in the psychology of language.* Englewood Cliffs, N.J.: Prentice-Hall, 1967.

Kausler, Donald (Ed.) *Readings in verbal learning.* New York: Wiley, 1966.

Kimble, Gregory (Ed.) *Foundations of conditioning and learning.* New York: Appleton-Century-Crofts, 1967.

Markel, Norman (Ed.) *Psycholinguistics.* Homewood, Ill.: Dorsey, 1969, pb.

Milner, Peter, and Glickman, S. (Eds.) *Cognitive processes and the brain.* New York: Van Nostrand Reinhold, 1965, pb.

Norman, Donald (Ed.) *Models of human memory.* New York: Academic Press, 1970.

Oldfield, R., and Marshall, J. (Eds.) *Language.* Baltimore: Penguin, 1968, pb.

Osgood, Charles, and Sebeok, T. (Eds.) *Psycholinguistics.* Bloomington, Ind.: Indiana University Press, 1965, pb.

Pribram, Karl (Ed.) *On the biology of learning.* New York: Harcourt, Brace and World, 1969, pb.

Pribram, Karl, and Broadbent, D. (Eds.) *Biology of memory.* New York: Academic Press, 1970.

Richter, Derek (Ed.) *Aspects of learning and memory.* New York: Basic Books, 1966.

Riopelle, A. (Ed.) *Animal problem solving.* Baltimore: Penguin, 1967, pb.

Rosenberg, Sheldon (Ed.) *Directions in psycholinguistics.* New York: Macmillan, 1965.

Sahakian, William (Ed.) *The psychology of learning.* Chicago: Markham, 1970.

Saporta, Sol (Ed.) *Psycholinguistics.* New York: Holt, Rinehart & Winston, 1961.

Salzinger, Kurt, and Feldman, R. (Eds.) *A quantitative approach to verbal behavior.* Long Island City, N.Y.: Pergamon, 1970.

Slamecka, Norman (Ed.) *Human learning and memory.* New York: Oxford, 1967, pb.

Smith, Alfred (Ed.) *Communication and culture: readings in the codes of human interaction.* New York: Holt, Rinehart & Winston, 1967.

Staats, Arthur (Ed.) *Human learning: studies extending conditioning principles to complex behavior.* New York: Holt, Rinehart & Winston, 1964.

Ulrich, Roger et al. (Eds.) *Control of human behavior.* Glenview, Ill.: Scott, Foresman and Company, 1966, 1970. 2 vols.

Verhave, Thom (Ed.) *The experimental analysis of behavior.* New York: Appleton-Century-Crofts, 1966, pb.

Wike, Edward (Ed.) *Secondary reinforcement.* New York: Harper & Row, 1966.

Wilson, Graham (Ed.) *A linguistic reader.* New York: Harper & Row, 1964.

Williams, Frederick (Ed.) *Language and poverty.* Chicago: Markham, 1970.

Thinking, Intelligence and Creativity

Barron, Frank. *Creative person and creative process.* New York: Holt, Rinehart & Winston, 1969.

Butcher, H. *Human intelligence: its nature and assessment.* London: Methuen, 1968, pb.

Carroll, John. *Language and thought.* Englewood Cliffs, N.J.: Prentice-Hall, 1964, pb.

Eisner, E. *Think with me about creativity.* Dansville, N.Y.: Owen, 1963, pb.

Glucksberg, Sam. *Symbolic processes.* Dubuque, Iowa: Wm. C. Brown Company Publishers, 1966, pb.

Gordon, W. *Synectics.* New York: Harper & Row, 1961, pb.

Guilford, Joy. *The nature of human intelligence.* New York: McGraw-Hill, 1967.

Guilford, Joy. *Intelligence, creativity, and their educational implications.* San Diego: Educational and Industrial Testing Service, 1969, pb.

Hunt, J. *Intelligence and experience.* New York: Ronald, 1961.

Jensen, Arthur et al. *Environment, heredity and intelligence.* Cambridge, Mass.: Harvard Educational Review, Reprint Series, No. 2, 1969, pb.

⋅Kneller, G. *The art and science of creativity.* New York: Holt, Rinehart & Winston, 1965, pb.

⋅ Manis, Melvin. *Cognitive processes.* Belmont, Calif.: Brooks/Cole, 1966, pb.

⋅ Osborn, A. *Applied imagination.* New York: Scribner, 1963, pb.

⋅ Parnes, Sidney. *Creative behavior guidebook.* New York: Scribner, 1967, pb.

⋅ Ray, Wilbert. *The experimental psychology of original thinking.* New York: Macmillan, 1967, pb.

Vernon, Philip. *Intelligence and cultural environment.* London: Methuen, 1969

Readings on Thinking, Intelligence and Creativity

Anderson, H. (Ed.) *Creativity in childhood and adolescence.* New York: Science and Behavior Books, 1965.

Aschner, H., and Bish, C. (Eds.) *Productive thinking in education.* Washington: National Education Association, 1965.

Duncan, Carl (Ed.) *Thinking: current experimental studies.* Philadelphia: Lippincott, 1967, pb.

Feigenbaum, Edward, and Feldman, J. (Eds.) *Computers and thought.* New York: McGraw-Hill, 1963.

Jenkins, James, and Paterson, D. (Eds.) *Studies in individual differences: the search for intelligence.* New York: Appleton-Century-Crofts, 1961.

McGuigan, F. (Ed.) *Thinking: studies of covert language processes.* New York: Appleton-Century-Crofts, 1966, pb.

Mandler, Jean, and Mandler, G. (Eds.) *Thinking: from association to Gestalt.* New York: Wiley, 1964, pb.

Mooney, Ross, and Razik, T. (Eds.) *Explorations in creativity.* New York: Harper & Row, 1967.

Parnes, Sidney, and Harding, H. (Eds.) *A source book for creative thinking.* New York: Scribner, 1962, pb.

Taylor, C. (Ed.) *Creativity: progress and potential.* New York: McGraw-Hill, 1964.

Tyler, Leona (Ed.) *Intelligence: some recurring issues.* New York: Van Nostrand Reinhold, 1969, pb.

Watson, P., and Johnson-Laird, P. (Eds.) *Thinking and reasoning.* Baltimore: Penguin, 1968, pb.

Wiseman, Stephen (Ed.) *Intelligence and ability.* Baltimore: Penguin, 1967, pb.

Motivation and Emotion

Atkinson, John. *An introduction to motivation.* New York: Van Nostrand Reinhold, 1964.

Bartoshuk, A. *Motivation.* Dubuque, Iowa: Wm. C. Brown Company Publishers, 1966, pb.

Bindra, Dalbir. *Motivation: a systematic reinterpretation.* New York: Ronald, 1959.

Birch, David, and Veroff, J. *Motivation: a study of action.* Belmont, Calif.: Brooks/Cole, 1966, pb.

Bolles, Robert. *Theory of motivation.* New York: Harper & Row, 1967.

Brown, Judson. *The motivation of human behavior.* New York: McGraw-Hill, 1961.

Cofer, C., and Appley, M. *Motivation: theory and research.* New York: Wiley, 1964.

Delgado, Jose. *Emotions.* Dubuque, Iowa: Wm. C. Brown Company Publishers, 1966, pb.

Duffy, Elizabeth. *Activation and behavior.* New York: Wiley, 1962.

Fabun, Don. *On motivation.* New York: Macmillan, 1970, pb.

Fiske, Donald, and Maddi, S. *Functions of varied experience.* Homewood, Ill.: Dorsey, 1961, pb.

Fowler, Harry. *Curiosity and exploratory behavior.* New York: Macmillan, 1965, pb.

Fuller, John *Motivation: a biological perspective.* New York: Random House, 1962, pb.

Hall, John. *Psychology of motivation.* Philadelphia: Lippincott, 1961.

Jacobsen, E. *Biology of emotions.* Springfield, Ill: Thomas, 1967.

Lawson, Reed. *Frustration: the development of a scientific concept.* New York: Macmillan, 1965, pb.

Lazarus, Richard. *Psychological stress and the copying process.* New York: McGraw-Hill, 1966.

Levitt, Eugene. *The psychology of anxiety.* Indianapolis, Ind.: Bobbs-Merrill, 1967, pb.

Madsen, K. *Theories of motivation: a comparative study of modern theories of motivation.* (4th ed.)Kent, Ohio: Kent State University Press, 1968.

Marx, Melvin, and Tombaugh, T. *Motivation: psychological principles and educational implications.* San Francisco: Chandler, 1967, pb.

Maslow, Abraham. *Motivation and personality.*(2nd ed.)New York: Harper & Row, 1970, pb.

Murray, Edward. *Motivation and emotion.* Englewood Cliffs, N.J.: Prentice-Hall, 1964, pb.   *BF 683   M 8*

Plutchik, Robert. *The emotions: facts, theories and a new model.* New York: Random House, 1962.

Rethlingshafer, Dorothy. *Motivation as related to personality.* New York: McGraw-Hill, 1963.

Sawrey, James. *Frustration and conflict.* Dubuque, Iowa: Wm. C. Brown Company Publishers, 1969, pb.

Toman, W. *An introduction to psychoanalytic theory of motivation.* New York: Pergamon, 1960.

Troland, Leonard. *The fundamentals of human motivation.* New York: Hafner, 1967.

Vernon, M. *Human motivation.* New York: Cambridge University Press, 1969, pb.

Young, Paul. *Motivation and emotion: a survey of determinants of human and animal activity.* New York: Wiley, 1961.

Readings on Motivation and Emotion

Arnold, Magda (Ed.) *The nature of emotion.* Baltimore: Penguin, 1969, pb.

Bindra, Dalbir, and Stewart, J. (Eds.) *Motivation.* Baltimore: Penguin, 1966, pb.

Birney, Robert, and Teevan, R. (Eds.) *Measuring human motivation.* New York: Van Nostrand Reinhold, 1962, pb.

Candland, Douglas (Ed.) *Emotion: bodily change.* New York: Van Nostrand Reinhold, 1962, pb.

Cicala, George (Ed.) *Animal drives.* New York: Van Nostrand Reinhold, 1965, pb.

Davitz, Joel (Ed.) *The communication of emotional meaning.* New York: McGraw-Hill, 1964.

Eysenck, Hans (Ed.) *Experiments in motivation.* New York: Macmillan, 1964.

Gellhorn, Ernest (Ed.) *Biological foundations of emotion: research and commentary.* Glenview, Ill.: Scott, Foresman, 1968, pb.

Haber, Ralph (Ed.) *Current research in motivation.* New York: Holt, Rinehart & Winston, 1966.

Lester, David (Ed.) *Explorations in exploration: stimulation seeking.* New York: Van Nostrand Reinhold, 1969, pb.

Levine, Jacob (Ed.) *Motivation in humor.* New York: Atherton, 1969, pb.

Russell, Wallace (Ed.) *Milestones in motivation.* New York: Appleton-Century-Crofts, 1970.

Stacey, Chalmers, and DeMartino, M. (Eds.) *Understanding human motivation.* (Rev. ed.) Cleveland: Allen, 1963.

Teevan, Richard, and Birney, R. (Eds.) *Theories of motivation in learning.* New York: Van Nostrand Reinhold, 1963, pb.

Teevan, Richard, and Birney, R. (Eds.) *Theories of motivation in personality and social psychology.* New York: Van Nostrand Reinhold, 1964, pb.

Whalen, Richard (Ed.) *Hormones and behavior.* New York: Van Nostrand Reinhold, 1967, pb.

Yates, Aubrey (Ed.) *Frustration and conflict.* New York: Van Nostrand Reinhold, 1965, pb.

Sensation and Perception

Alpern, Mathew et al. *Sensory processes.* Belmont, Calif.: Brooks/Cole, 1967, pb.

Bartley, S. *Principles of perception.* (2nd ed.) New York: Harper & Row, 1969.

Bedichek, R. *The sense of smell.* Garden City, N.Y.: Doubleday, 1960.

Brownfield, Charles. *Isolation: clinical and experimental approaches.* New York: Random House, 1965, pb.

Burnham, R. et al. *Color: a guide to basic facts and concepts.* New York: Wiley, 1963.

Cornsweet, Tom. *Visual percpetion.* New York: Academic Press, 1970.

Corso, John. *The experimental psychology of sensory behavior.* New York: Holt, Rinehart & Winston, 1967.

Day, R. *Perception.* Dubuque, Iowa: Wm. C. Brown Company Publishers, 1966, pb.

Day, R. *Human perception.* New York: John Wiley & Sons, Inc., 1969.

Dember, William *The psychology of perception.* New York: Holt, Rinehart & Winston, 1960.

Dröscher, Vitus. *The magic of the senses: new discoveries in animal perception.* New York: Dutton, 1969.

Epstein, William. *Varieties of perceptual learning.* New York: McGraw-Hill, 1967.

Forgus, Ronald. *Perception: the basic process in cognitive development.* New York: McGraw-Hill, 1966.

Gibson, Eleanor. *Principles of perceptual learning and development.* New York: Appleton-Century-Crofts, 1969.

Gibson, James. *The senses considered as perceptual systems.* Boston: Houghton Mifflin, 1966.

Green, David, and Swets, J. *Signal detection theory and psychophysics.* New York: Wiley, 1966.

Gregory, Richard. *Eye and brain: the psychology of seeing.* New York: McGraw-Hill, 1966, pb.

Hochberg, Julian. *Perception.* Englewood Cliffs, N.J.: Prentice-Hall, 1964, pb.

Hurvich, Leo, and Jameson, D. *The perception of brightness and darkness.* Boston: Allyn and Bacon, 1966, pb.

Klein, George. *Perception, motives and personality.* New York: Random House, 1970.

Le Grand, Yves. *Light, color and vision.* (2nd ed.) London: Chapman and Hall, 1968.

Leibowitz, Herschel. *Visual perception.* New York: Macmillan, 1965, pb.

Lowenstein, Otto. *The senses.* Baltimore: Penguin, 1966, pb.

Mueller, Conrad. *Sensory psychology.* Englewood Cliffs, N.J.: Prentice-Hall, 1965, pb.

Neisser, Ulric. *Cognitive psychology.* New York: Appleton-Century-Crofts, 1967.

Pirenne, M. *Vision and the eye.* (2nd ed.) New York: Barnes and Noble, 1967.

Van Bergeijk, W. et al. *Waves and the ear.* New York: Doubleday Anchor, 1960, pb.

Vernon, Jack. *Inside the black room: studies of sensory deprivation.* New York: Clarkson Potter, 1964, pb.

Vernon, M. *The psychology of perception.* Baltimore: Penguin, 1962, pb.

Von Fieandt, Kai. *The world of perception.* Homewood, Ill.: Dorsey, 1966.

Weintraub, Daniel, and Walker, E. *Perception.* Belmont, Calif.: Brooks/Cole, 1966, pb.

Wilentz, Joan. *The senses of man.* New York: Crowell, 1968.

Wright, R. *The science of smell.* New York: Basic Books, 1964.

Readings on Sensation and Perception

Dember, William (Ed.) *Visual perception: the nineteenth century.* New York: Wiley, 1964, pb.

Graham, Clarence (Ed.) *Vision and visual perception.* New York: Wiley, 1965.

Haber, Ralph (Ed.) *Contemporary theory and research in visual perception.* New York: Holt, Rinehart & Winston, 1966.

Haber, Ralph (Ed.) *Information processing approaches to visual perception.* New York: Holt, Rinehart & Winston, 1969.

Harris, J. (Ed.) *Forty germinal papers in human hearing.* Groton, Conn.: The Journal of Auditory Research, 1969.

Kidd, Aline, and Rivoire, J. (Eds.) *Perceptual development in children.* New York: International Universities Press, 1966, pb.

McCleary, Robert (Ed.). *Genetic and experimental factors in perception.* Glenview, Ill.: Scott, Foresman, 1970, pb.

Spigel, Irwin (Ed.) *Readings in the study of visually perceived movement.* New York: Harper & Row, 1965.

Swets, John (Ed.) *Signal detection and recognition by human observers.* New York: Wiley, 1964.

Teevan, Richard, and Birney, R. (Eds.) *Color vision.* New York: Van Nostrand Reinhold, 1961, pb.

Tibbetts, Paul (Ed.) *Perception: selected readings in science and phenomenology.* Chicago: Quadrangle, 1969, pb.

Uhr, Leonard (Ed.) *Pattern recognition.* New York: Wiley, 1966, pb.

Vernon, M. (Ed.) *Experiments in visual perception: selected readings.* Baltimore: Penguin, 1966, pb.

Physiological Psychology

Armington, John. *Physiological basis of psychology.* Dubuque, Iowa: Wm. C. Brown Company Publishers, 1966, pb.

Asimov, I. *The human brain.* New York: New American Library, 1965, pb.

Brazier, Mary. *The electrical activity of the nervous system: a textbook for students.* (3rd ed.)New York: Macmillan, 1968.

Butter, Charles. *Neuropsychology.* Belmont, Calif.: Brooks/Cole, 1968, pb.

Deutsch, J., and Deutsch, D. *Physiological psychology.* Homewood, Ill.: Dorsey, 1966.

Galambos, R. *Nerves and muscles.* Garden City, N.Y.: Doubleday, 1962, pb.

Gardner, Ernest. *Fundamentals of neurology.* (5th ed.)Philadelphia: Saunders, 1968.

Groch, J. *You and your brain.* New York: Harper & Row, 1963.

Grossman, Sebastian. *A textbook of physiological psychology.* New York: Wiley, 1967.

Hirsch, Jerry. *Behavioral genetics.* Dubuque, Iowa: Wm. C. Brown Company Publishers, 1966, pb.

Hokanson, Jack. *The physiological basis of motivation.* New York: Wiley, 1969, pb.

Isaacson, Robert et al. *A primer of physiological psychology.* New York: Harper & Row, 1970.

Lachman, Sheldon. *History and methods of physiological psychology.* Detroit: Hamilton Press, 1963.

Leukel, Francis. *Introduction to physiological psychology.* St. Louis: Mosby, 1968.

McCleary, Robert, and Moore, R. *Subcortical mechanisms of behavior.* New York: Basic Books, 1965.

Magoun, H. *The waking brain.* (2nd ed.) Springfield, Ill.: Thomas, 1963.

Milner, Peter. *Physiological psychology.* (2nd ed.) New York: Holt, Rinehart & Winston, 1970.

Morgan, Clifford. *Physiological psychology.* (3rd ed.) New York: McGraw-Hill, 1965.

Ochs, Sidney. *Elements of neurophysiology.* New York: Wiley, 1965.

Pfeiffer, John. *The human brain.* New York: Pyramid, 1962, pb.

Sternbach, Richard. *Principles of psychophysiology: an introductory text and readings.* New York: Academic Press, 1966.

Stevens, Charles. *Neurophysiology: a primer.* New York: Wiley, 1966.

Teitelbaum, Philip. *Physiological psychology.* Englewood Cliffs, N.J.: Prentice-Hall, 1967, pb.

Thompson, Richard. *Foundations of physiological psychology.* New York: Harper & Row, 1967.

Walter, W. *The living brain.* New York: Norton, 1963, pb.

Woodburne, Lloyd. *The neural basis of behavior.* Columbus, Ohio: Merrill, 1967.

Wooldridge, Dean. *The machinery of the brain.* New York: McGraw-Hill, 1963, pb.

Readings on Physiological Psychology

Bakan, Paul (Ed.) *Attention.* New York: Van Nostrand Reinhold, 1966, pb.

Barnes, C., and Kircher, C. (Eds.) *Readings in neurophysiology.* New York: Wiley, 1968.

Gellhorn, Ernest (Ed.) *Biological foundations of emotion: research and commentary.* Glenview, Ill.: Scott, Foresman, 1968, pb.

Glaser, Gilbert. *EEG and behavior.* New York: Basic Books, 1962.

Glickman, Stephen, and Milner, P. (Eds.) *The neurological basis for motivation.* New York: Van Nostrand Reinhold, 1969, pb.

Gross, Charles, and Zeigler, H. (Eds.) *Readings in physiological psychology: learning and motivation.* New York: Harper & Row, 1969, pb.

Gross, Charles, and Zeigler, H. (Eds.) *Readings in physiological psychology: motivation.* New York: Harper & Row, 1969, pb.

Gross, Charles, and Zeigler, H. (Eds.) *Readings in physiological psychology: neurophysiology/sensory processes.* New York: Harper & Row, 1969, pb.

Harvey, John (Ed.) *Behavioral analysis of drug action.* Glenview, Ill.: Scott, Foresman and Company, 1970, pb.

Isaacson, Robert (Ed.) *Basic readings in neuropsychology.* New York: Harper & Row 1964, pb.

Landauer, Thomas (Ed.) *Readings in physiological psychology.* New York: McGraw-Hill, 1967, pb.

Louttit, Richard (Ed.) *Research in physiological psychology.* Belmont, Calif.: Brooks/Cole, 1969, pb.

McCleary, Robert (Ed.) *Genetic and experimental factors in perception: research and commentary.* Glenview Ill.: Scott, Foresman, 1970, pb.

McGaugh, James et al. (Eds.) *Psychobiology: the biological basis of behavior.* San Francisco: Freeman, 1966, pb.

Milner, Peter, and Glickman, S. (Eds.) *Cognitive processes and the brain.* New York: Van Nostrand Reinhold, 1965, pb.

Mostofsky, David (Ed.) *Attention: contemporary theory and analysis.* New York: Appleton-Century-Crofts, 1970.

Pribram Karl (Ed.) *Brain and behavior. 1: mood, states and mind.* Baltimore: Penguin, 1969, pb.

Pribram, Karl (Ed.) *Brain and behavior. 2: perception and action.* Baltimore: Penguin, 1969, pb.

Pribram, Karl (Ed.) *Brain and behavior. 3: memory mechanisms.* Baltimore: Penguin, 1969, pb.

Pribram, Karl (Ed.) *Brain and behavior. 4: adaptation.* Baltimore: Penguin, 1969, pb.

Russell, Roger (Ed.) *Frontiers in physiological psychology.* New York: Academic Press, 1967.

Strange, Jack, and Foster, R. (Eds.) *Readings in physiological psychology.* Belmont, Calif.: Brooks/Cole, 1966, pb.

Whalen, Richard (Ed.) *Hormones and behavior.* New York: Van Nostrand Reinhold, 1967, pb.

History of Psychology**

Adams, Grace. *Psychology: science or superstition?* New York: Van Rees, 1931.

Alexander, Franz et al. (Eds.) *Psychoanalytic pioneers.* New York: Basic Books, 1966.

Appley, Mortimer, and Rickwood, J. *Psychology in Canada.* Ottawa: Science Secretariat; Privy Council Office, 1967.

Baldwin, James. *History of psychology.* New York: Putnam, 1913. 2 vols.

Boring, Edwin. *Sensation and perception in the history of experimental psychology.* New York: Appleton-Century-Crofts, 1942.

Boring, Edwin. *A history of experimental psychology.*(2nd ed.)New York: Appleton-Century-Crofts, 1950.

Boring, Edwin. *History, psychology and science: selected papers.* (Edited by R. Watson and D. Campbell) New York: Wiley, 1963.

Brennan, R. *History of psychology from the standpoint of a Thomist.* New York: Macmillan, 1945.

Brett, George. *A history of psychology.* London: Allen and Unwin, 1912-1921. 3 vols.

Brett, George. *Psychology, ancient and modern.* New York: Longmans, Green, 1928.

Bromberg, Walter. *The mind of man: a history of psychotherapy and psychoanalysis.* New York: Harper & Row, 1959, pb.

Brooks, C., and Cranefield, P. *The historical development of physiological thought.* New York: Hafner, 1959.

Capretta, Patrick. *A history of psychology in outline.* New York: Dell, 1967, pb.

Cattell, James. *Psychology in America.* New York: Science, 1929.

Dessoir, Max. *Outlines of the history of psychology.* New York: Macmillan, 1912.

Deutsch, A. *The history of mental hygiene.* New York: Columbia University Press, 1944.

** Advanced graduate books included plus sources published prior to 1960.

DuBois, Philip. *A history of psychological testing.* Boston: Allyn and Bacon, 1970.

Esper, Erwin. *A history of psychology.* Philadelphia: Saunders, 1964.

Fay, Jay. *American psychology before William James.* New Brunswick, N.J.: Rutgers University Press, 1939, pb.

Fearing, Franklin. *Reflex action: a study in the history of physiological psychology.* Baltimore: Williams and Wilkins, 1930.

Flugel, John, and West, Donald. *A hundred years of psychology: 1833-1933 with additional part V: 1933-1963.* New York: Basic Books, 1964.

Foucault, M. *Madness and civilization: a history of insanity in the age of reason.* New York: Pantheon, 1965.

Freeman, L., and Small, M. *Story of psychoanalysis.* New York: Pocket Books, 1960.

Gauld, Alan. *The founders of psychical research.* New York: Schocken, 1968.

Grinder, Robert. *A history of genetic psychology: the first science of human development.* New York: Wiley, 1967.

Hall, G. *Founders of modern psychology.* New York: Appleton-Century-Crofts, 1912.

Havemann, Ernest. *Age of psychology.* New York: Simon and Schuster, 1957.

Hearnshaw, L. *A short history of British psychology: 1840-1940.* New York: Barnes and Noble, 1964.

Hulin, Wilbur. *A short history of psychology.* New York: Holt, 1934.

Kanner, Leo. *A history of the care and study of the mentally retarded.* Springfield, Ill.: Thomas, 1967.

Kantor, Jacob. *The scientific evolution of psychology.* Granville, Ohio: Principia Press, 1963, 1969. 2 vols.

Klein, D. *A history of scientific psychology.* New York: Basic Books, 1969.

Klemm, Otto. *History of psychology.* New York: Scribner, 1914.

Lachman, S. *History and methods of physiological psychology: a brief overview.* Detroit: Hamilton, 1963.

Levine, Murray, and Levine, A. *A social history of the helping services: clinic, court, school and community.* New York: Appleton-Century-Crofts, 1970.

Mercier, D. *The origins of contemporary psychology.* New York: Kenedy and Sons, 1918.

Meyer, D. *Positive thinkers.* New York: Doubleday, 1965, pb.

Miller, George. *Psychology: the science of mental life.* New York: Harper & Row, 1962.

Misiak, Henryk. *The philosophical roots of scientific psychology.* New York: Fordham University Press, 1961.

Misiak, Henryk, and Sexton, V. *History of psychology: an overview.* New York: Grune and Stratton, 1966.

Moore, J. *The foundations of psychology.* Princeton, N.J.: Princeton University Press, 1933.

Muller-Freienfels, Richard. *The evolution of modern psychology.* New Haven, Conn.: Yale University Press, 1935.

Murphy, Gardner. *Historical introduction to modern psychology.* (Rev. ed.) New York: Harcourt, Brace and World, 1949.

Murphy, Gardner. *Psychological thought from Pythagoras to Freud: an informal introduction.* New York: Harcourt, Brace and World, 1968, pb.

Oberndorf, Clarence. *A history of psychoanalysis in America.* New York: Harper & Row, 1964, pb.

O'Neil, W. *The beginnings of modern psychology.* Baltimore: Penguin, 1968, pb.

Peters, R. (Ed.) *Brett's history of psychology.* Abridged. (2nd rev. ed.) Cambridge, Mass.: The M.I.T. Press, 1965, pb.

Peterson, Joseph. *Early conceptions and tests of intelligence.* Yonkers, N.Y.: World Book, 1925.

Pillsbury, W. *The history of psychology.* New York: Norton, 1929.

Progoff, Ira. *The death and rebirth of psychology.* New York: Julian Press, 1956.

Ray, M. *Doctors of the mind.* Indianapolis: Bobbs-Merrill, 1963.

Reeves, J. *Body and mind in western thought: an introduction to some origins of modern psychology.* Harmondsworth, Middlesex: Penguin Books, 1958.

Reeves, Joan. *Thinking about thinking.* New York: Braziller, 1966.

Reisman, John. *The development of clinical psychology.* New York: Appleton-Century-Crofts, 1966, pb.

Ridenour, N. *Mental health in the United States: a fifty-year history.* Cambridge, Mass.: Harvard University Press, 1961.

Roback, Abraham. *History of psychology and psychiatry.* New York: Philosophical Library, 1961.

Roback, Abraham. *A history of American psychology.* (Rev. ed.) New York: Collier, 1964, pb.

Roback, Abraham (Ed.) *Present-day psychology.* New York: Greenwood, 1968.

Roback, Abraham, and Kiernan, T. *Pictorial history of psychology and psychiatry.* New York: Philosophical Library, 1970.

Sargent, Stansfeld, and Stafford, K. *Basic teachings of the great psychologists.* New York: Blakiston, 1944, pb.

Schultz, Duane. *A history of modern psychology.* New York: Academic Press, 1969.

Shakow, David, and Rapaport, D. *Influences of Freud on American psychology.* New York: International Universities Press, 1964, pb.

Spearman, C. *Psychology down the ages.* London: Macmillan, 1937. 2 vols.

Thompson, Robert. *Pelican history of psychology.* Baltimore: Penguin, 1968, pb.

Thoules, Robert. *Psychical research, past and present.* London: Society for Psychical Research, 1952.

Van den Berg, J. *The changing nature of man: introduction to historical psychology.* New York: Dell, 1964, pb.

Walker, Nigel. *A short history of psychotherapy.* London: Routledge and Kegan Paul, 1957.

Wangh, M. (Ed.) *Fruition of an idea: fifty years of psychoanalysis in New York.* New York: International Universities Press, 1962.

Warren, Howard. *A history of association psychology from Hartley to Lewes.* New York: Scribner, 1921.

Watson, Robert. *The great psychologists from Aristotle to Freud.* (2nd ed.) Philadelphia: Lippincott, 1968.

Watson, Robert. *A brief history of educational psychology.* Granville, Ohio: Psychological Record, 1963, pb.

Wertheimer, Michael. *A brief history of psychology.* New York: Holt, Rinehart & Winston, 1970, pb.

Williams, R., and Bellows, R. *Background of contemporary psychology.* Columbus, Ohio: Hedrick, 1935.

Wolman, Benjamin (Ed.) *Historical roots of contemporary psychology.* New York: Harper & Row, 1968.

Zilboorg, Gregory, and Henry, G. *A history of medical psychology.* New York: Norton, 1941.

Readings on the History of Psychology**

Blumenthal, Arthur (Ed.) *Language and psychology: historical aspects of psycholinguistics.* New York: John Wiley & Sons, Inc., 1970, pb.

Brozek, Josef (Ed.) *Fifty years of Soviet psychology.* White Plains: International Arts and Sciences Press, 1969.

Crafts, L. (Ed.) *Recent experiments in psychology.* New York: McGraw-Hill, 1938.

Dennis, Wayne (Ed.) *Readings in the history of psychology.* New York: Appleton-Century-Crofts, 1948.

Drever, James (Ed.) *Sourcebook in psychology.* New York: Philosophical Library, 1960.

Ehrenwald, J. (Ed.) *From medicine man to Freud: an anthology.* New York: Dell, 1956.

Ellis, Willis (Ed.) *A sourcebook of Gestalt psychology.* New York: Harcourt, Brace and World, 1938.

Garrett, Henry (Ed.) *Great experiments in psychology.* (3rd ed.) New York: Appleton-Century-Crofts, 1951.

Goshen, Charles (Ed.) *Documentary history of psychiatry: a sourcebook on historical principles.* New York: Philosophical Library, 1967.

Henle, Mary (Ed.) *Documents of Gestalt psychology.* Berkeley, Calif.: University of California Press, 1961.

Herrnstein, Richard, and Boring, E. (Eds.) *A sourcebook in the history of psychology.* Cambridge, Mass.: Harvard University Press, 1965.

Mandler, Jean, and Mandler, G. (Eds.) *Thinking: from association to Gestalt.* New York: Wiley, 1964, pb.

Marks, Robert (Ed.) *Great ideas in psychology.* New York: Bantam 1966, pb.

**Advanced graduate books included plus sources published prior to 1960.

Murphy, Gardner, and Murphy, L. (Eds.) *Asian psychology.* New York: Basic Books, 1968.

Murphy, Gardner, and Murphy, L. (Eds.) *Western psychology: from the Greeks to William James.* New York: Basic Books, 1969.

Postman, Leo (Ed.) *Psychology in the making: histories of selected research problems.* New York: Knopf, 1962.

Rand, Benjamin. *The classical psychologists.* Boston: Houghton Mifflin, 1912.

Sahakian, William (Ed.) *History of psychology: a sourcebook in systematic psychology.* Itasca, Ill.: Peacock, 1968. Includes "Landmarks in the History of Psychology" and "Bibliography of Works in English Relating to the History of Psychology."

Shipley, Thorne (Ed.) *Classics in psychology.* New York: Philosophical Library, 1961.

Venderplas, James (Ed.) *Controversial issues in psychology.* Boston: Houghton Mifflin, 1966.

Wann, T. (Ed.) *Behaviorism and phenomenology.* Chicago: University of Chicago Press, 1964, pb.

Systems and Theories**

Brunswik, Egon. *The conceptual framework of psychology.* Chicago: University of Chicago Press, 1952.

Chaplin, James, and Krawiec, T. *Systems and theories of psychology.*(2nd ed.)New York: Holt, Rinehart & Winston, 1968.

Dennis, Wayne et al. *Current trends in psychological theory.* Pittsburg: University of Pittsburg Press, 1951.

Dennis, Wayne et al. *Current trends in psychological theory.* Pittsburg: University of Pittsburg Press, 1961.

Feigl, Herbert, and Scriven, M. (Eds.) *The foundations of science and the concepts of psychology and psychoanalysis.* Minneapolis: University of Minnesota Press, 1956.

Gilgen, Albert (Ed.) *Contemporary scientific psychology.* New York: Academic Press, Inc., 1970.

Heidbreder, Edna. *Seven psychologies.* New York: Appleton-Century-Crofts, 1933, pb.

Helson, Harry (Ed.) *Theoretical foundations of psychology.* New York: Van Nostrand Reinhold, 1950.

**Advanced graduate books included plus sources published prior to 1960.

Helson, Harry, and Bevan, W. (Eds.) *Contemporary approaches to psychology.* New York: Van Nostrand Reinhold, 1967.

Keller, Fred. *The definition of psychology: an introduction to psychological systems.* New York: Appleton-Century-Crofts, 1937, pb.

Krantz, David (Ed.) *Schools of psychology.* New York: Appleton-Century-Crofts, 1969, pb.

Levine, A. *Current psychologies.* Cambridge, Mass.: Sci-Art, 1940.

Mandler, George, and Kessen, W. *The language of psychology.* New York: Wiley, 1959, pb.

Marx, Melvin (Ed.) *Psychological theory: a sourcebook.* New York: Macmillan, 1951.

Marx, Melvin (Ed.) *Theories in contemporary psychology.* New York: Macmillan, 1963.

Marx, Melvin, and Hillix, W. *Systems and theories in psychology.* New York: McGraw-Hill, 1963.

Murchison, C. (Ed.) *Psychologies of 1925.* Worcester, Mass.: Clark University Press, 1926.

Murchison, C. (Ed.) *Psychologies of 1930.* Worcester, Mass.: Clark University Press, 1930.

Neel, Ann. *Theories of psychology: a handbook.* Boston: Schenkman, 1968, pb.

Turner, Merle. *Philosophy and the science of behavior.* New York: Appleton-Century-Crofts, 1967.

Wolman, Benjamin. *Contemporary theories and systems in psychology.* New York: Harper & Row, 1960.

Wolman, Benjamin (Ed.) *Scientific psychology: principles and approaches.* New York: Basic Books, 1965.

Woodworth, Robert, and Sheehan, M. *Contemporary schools of psychology.* (3rd ed.) New York: Ronald, 1964.

Laboratory Manuals

Baker, Lawrence et al. *Laboratory experiments in general psychology.* New York: Oxford, 1960, pb.

Bilodeau, Edward. *Laboratory outlines for experimental psychology.* Glenview, Ill.: Scott, Foresman and Company, 1962, pb.

DeBold, Richard. *Manual of contemporary experiments in psychology.* Englewood Cliffs, N.J.: Prentice-Hall, 1968, pb.

Fernald, L. *Experiments and studies in general psychology.* Boston: Houghton Mifflin, 1965, pb.

Hart, Benjamin. *Experimental neuropsychology: a laboratory manual.* San Francisco: Freeman, 1969.

Heckman, Barbara, and Fried, R. *A manual of laboratory studies in psychology.* New York: Oxford, 1965, pb.

Hergenhahn, B. *A self-directing introduction to psychological experimentation.* Belmont, Calif.: Brooks/Cole, 1970.

Homme, Lloyd, and Klaus, D. *Laboratory studies in the analysis of behavior.* (3rd ed.)Hyattsville, Md.: Westinghouse Learning Corporation, 1970, pb.

Humphrey, George (Ed.) *Psychology through experiment.* London: Menthuen, 1963.

Jung, John, and Bailey, J. *Contemporary psychology experiments: adaptations for laboratory.* New York: Wiley, 1966, pb.

Lane, Harlan, and Bem, D. *A laboratory manual for the control and analysis of behavior.* Belmont, Calif.: Wadsworth, 1965, pb.

McConnell, James (Ed.) *A manual of psychological experimentation on planarians.* Ann Arbor, Mich.: The Worm Runner Digest, 1965.

Michael, Jack. *Laboratory studies in operant behavior.* New York: McGraw-Hill, 1963.

Notterman, Joseph. *Laboratory manual for experiments in behavior.* New York: Random House, 1971, pb.

Ost, John et al. *A laboratory introduction to psychology.* New York: Academic Press, 1969.

Reese, Ellen. *Experiments in operant behavior.* New York: Appleton-Century-Crofts, 1964, pb.

Roach, James et al. *Experiments in general psychology.* New York: Harper & Row, 1965.

Sachs, Herbert. *Student projects in child psychology.* Dubuque, Iowa: Wm. C. Brown Company Publishers, 1967.

Shafer, James. *Laboratory experiences in psychology.* New York: Holt, Rinehart & Winston, 1965.

Smith, Bernard. *Laboratory experience in psychology: a first tear's work.* Long Island City, New York: Pergamon, 1965, pb.

Snellgrove, Louis. *Psychological experiments and demonstrations.* New York: McGraw-Hill, 1967, pb.

Spatz, K. *Laboratory manual for experimental psychology.* New York: Appleton-Century-Crofts, 1970, pb.

Stevens, Joseph et al. *Laboratory experiments in psychology.* New York: Holt, Rinehart & Winston, 1965.

Stoker, Allen (Ed.) *Animal behavior in laboratory and field.* San Francisco: Freeman, 1968.

Tinker, Miles, and Russell, W. *Introduction to methods in experimental psychology.* (3rd ed.) New York: Appleton-Century-Crofts, 1958, pb.

Ward, Charles. *Laboratory manual in experimental social psychology.* New York: Holt, Rinehart & Winston, 1970, pb.

Appendix I

Introductions to the Library

Cook, Margaret. *The new library key.* (2nd ed.) New York: Wilson, 1963, pb.

Gates, Jean. *Guide to the use of books and libraries.* (2nd ed.) New York: McGraw-Hill, 1969, pb.

Knight, Hattie. *The 1-2-3 guide to libraries.* (4th ed.) Dubuque, Iowa: Wm. C. Brown Company Publishers, 1970, pb.

Style Manuals

Campbell, William. *Form and style in thesis writing.* (3rd ed.) Boston: Houghton Mifflin, 1969.

Editorial staff of the University of Chicago Press. *A manual of style.* (12th ed.) Chicago: University of Chicago Press, 1969.

Hodges, J., and Whitten, M. *Harbrace college handbook.* (6th ed.) New York: Harcourt, Brace and World, 1967.

Publication manual of the American Psychological Association. Washington: American Psychological Association, 1967, pb.

Strunk, W., and White, E. *The elements of style.* New York: Macmillan, 1963, pb.

Swingle, Paul. (Ed.) *Experiments in social psychology.* New York: Academy Press, 1968.

Turabian, Kate. *Student's guide for writing college papers.* (2nd ed.) Chicago: University of Chicago, 1970, pb.

Study Guides

Anderson, Bert. *Introduction to college.* New York: Holt, Rinehart & Winston, 1969, pb.

Cattell, Nancy, and Sharp, S. *College and career: adjusting college and selecting an occupation.* New York: Appleton-Century-Crofts, 1970, pb.

Collins, Charles. *College orientation: education for relevance.* Boston: Holbrook, 1969, pb.

Kalish, Richard. *Making the most of college.* (2nd ed.) Belmont, Calif.: Brooks/Cole, 1969.

Lindgren, Henry. *The psychology of college success.* New York: Wiley, 1968, pb.

Morgan, Clifford and Deese, J. *How to study.* (2nd ed.) New York: McGraw-Hill, 1970, pb.

Resnick, William and Heller, D. (Eds.) *On your own in college.* (2nd ed.) Columbus, Ohio: Merrill, 1969, pb.

Robinson, Francis. *Effective study.* (4th ed.) New York: Harper & Row, 1970, pb.

Voeks, Virginia. *On becoming an educated person.* (3rd ed.) Philadelphia: Saunders, 1970, pb.

General Career Information

Calvert, Robert, and Steele, J. *Planning your career.* New York: McGraw-Hill, 1963.

Hopke, William (Ed.) *The encyclopedia of careers and vocational guidance.* Garden City, N.Y.: Doubleday, 1967. 2 vols.

Peterson, Clarence. *Careers for college graduates.* New York: Barnes and Noble, 1968.

Ury, Claude. Career-related guidance for youth. *Wilson Library Bulletin,* 1970, 44, 621-631.

Watermulder, Georgia. *Careers for college woman: a bibliography of vocational materials.* Ann Arbor, Mich.: University of Michigan, 1968, pb.

Career Information on Psychology

American Psychological Association. 1200 Seventeenth Street, N.W., Washington, 20036. Single copies of the pamphlets listed below may be obtained free from the APA.

A career in industrial psychology.

A career in psychology.

Psychologists are scientists too.

Angel, Juvenal. *Careers and opportunities in psychology.* New York: World Trade Academy Press, 1960. (Modern Vocational Trends Career Monographs)

Angel, Juvenal. *Careers in guidance and student-personnel services.* (2nd ed.) New York: World Trade Academy Press, 1960. (Modern Vocational Trends Career Monographs)

Clark, Kenneth. *America's psychologists: a survey of a growing profession.* Washington: American Psychological Association, 1957.

Davidson, Henry. *Opportunities in a psychiatry career.* New York: Vocational Guidance Manuals, 1964.

Finger, Frank. "Professional problems": preparation for a career in college teaching. *American Psychologist,* 1969, 24, 1044-1049.

Hirt, Michael. *A career as a psychologist.* Cambridge, Mass.: Bellman, 1962. (Vocational and Professional Monographs, No. 107)

Hoffman-La Roche, Inc. *Careers in psychiatry.* New York: Macmillan, 1968, pb.

Loughary, John (Ed.) *Counseling: a growing profession.* Washington: American Personnel and Guidance Association, 1965.

Manpower, and psychology. *American Psychologist,* 1968, 23. Entire May issue.

National Association for Retarded Children. *Careers in the field of mental retardation.* New York: National Association for Retarded Children, 1968, pb.

Ogg, Elizabeth. *Psychologists in action.* Pamphlet 229. New York: Public Affairs Committee, Inc., 1955, pb.

Ogg, Elizabeth. *Jobs and futures in mental health.* New York: Public Affairs Committee, Inc., 1960, pb.

Smith, Noel. A career guide for psychology majors. *Improving College and University Teaching,* Spring 1970, 18(2), 112-114.

Super, Donald. *Opportunities in psychology careers.* New York: Educational Books Division of Universal Publication and Distribution Corporation, 1968. (Vocational Guidance Manual)

United States Health, Education and Welfare Department. *Career opportunities in service to the disadvantaged and handicapped.* Washington: Government Printing Office, 1969, pb.

United States Health, Education and Welfare Department. *Career opportunities in the field of mental retardation.* Washington: Government Printing Office, 1969, pb.

Watson, Robert. *Psychology as a profession.* Garden City, N.Y.: Doubleday, 1954, pb.

Webb, Wilse (Ed.) *The profession of psychology.* New York: Holt, Rinehart & Winston, 1962.

Graduate School Entrance Examinations

Brownstein, Samuel, and Weiner, M. *How to prepare for the graduate record examination.* New York: Barrons Educational Series, 1967, pb.

1400 analogy questions (Miller Analogies Test). New York: Arco, 1967, pb.

How to pass graduate record examination advanced tests: psychology. New York: Cowles Educational Corporation, 1968, pb.

How to pass graduate record examination: advanced test: psychology. New York: College Publishing Co., 1967.

How to pass high on the graduate record examination. New York: Arco, 1967, pb.

How to pass Miller analogies test. New York: Cowles Educational Corporation, 1965, pb.

Millman, Susan, and Nisbett, R. *GRE psychology advanced test.* New York: Arco, 1967.

Graduate Education

Anderson, Holger, and Koeppel, J. *A directory of graduate programs in psychology.* Memphis, Tenn.: Green Light, 1965.

Annual guide to graduate study [year]. Princeton, N.J.: Peterson's Guides, 1970. 12 vols.

Berelson, Bernard. *Graduate education in the United States.* New York: McGraw-Hill, 1960.

Braun, John (Ed.) *Clinical psychology in transition.* (Rev. ed.)Cleveland: World, 1966, rdgs.

Carmichael, Oliver. *Graduate education: a critique and a program.* New York: Harper & Row, 1961.

Cartter, Allan. *An assessment of quality in graduate education.* Washington: American Council on Education, 1966, pb.

Education for research in psychology. *American Psychologist,* 1959, 14, 167-179.

Financial aid for guidance and personnel graduate study, 1970-1971. Washington: American Personnel and Guidance Association, 1970. Annual.

Friedberg, Robert, and Fink, P. (Eds.) *Cowles guide to graduate schools.* New York: Cowles, 1968, pb.

Graduate study in college student personnel work, 1968-1969. Washington: American Personnel and Guidance Association, 1969. Annual.

Graduate study in psychology: 1971-1972. Washington: American Psychological Association, 1970. Annual.

Jencks, Christopher, and Riesman, D. *The academic revolution.* New York: Doubleday, 1968.

Livesey, Herbert, and Robbins, G. *Guide to American graduate schools.* New York: Viking Press, 1967, pb.

Lundstedt, Sven (Ed.) *Higher education in social psychology.* Cleveland, Ohio: Case Western Reserve, 1968.

Maxwell, Bernard, and Consler, Russell. *Current financial aids for graduate students.* Peoria, Ill.: College Opportunities Unlimited 1966.

Roe, Anne et al. *Graduate education in psychology.* Washington: American Psychological Association, 1959.

Quick, Robert (Ed.) *Fellowships in the arts and sciences.* (11th ed.) Washington: American Council on Education, 1970.

Quick, Robert (Ed.) *A guide to graduate study: programs leading to the Ph.D. degree.* (4th ed.) Washington: American Council on Education, 1969.

Singletary, Otis, and Newman, J. (Eds.) *American universities and colleges.* (10th ed.) Washington: American Council on Education, 1969.

The grants register: postgraduate awards in the English-speaking world. Chicago: St. James Press, 1969.

Walters, Everett (Ed.) *Graduate education today.* Washington: American Council on Education, 1965.

Wasserman, Elga, and Switzer, E. *The vintage guide to graduate study in the arts and sciences.* New York: Vintage, 1968, pb.

Information for Graduate Students

Arnhoff, Franklyn et al. Subdoctoral education in psychology. *American Psychologist,* 1969, 24, 430-443. See bibliography for further information.

Casebook on ethical standards of psychologists. Washington: American Psychological Association.

Daniel, Robert, and Louttit, C. *Professional problems in psychology.* Englewood Cliffs, N.J.: Prentice-Hall, 1953.

Davitz, Joel, and Davitz, L. *A guide for evaluating research plans in psychology and education.* New York: Teachers College Press, 1967, pb.

Harlow, Harry. Editorial: Fundamental principles for preparing psychology journal articles. *Journal of Comparative and Physiological Psychology,* 1962, 55(6), 893-896.

How to write a review. *Contemporary Psychology,* 1967, 12, 395-396.

Klopfer, Walter. *The psychological report.* New York: Grune and Stratton, 1960.

Knox, Wilma. Obtaining a PhD in Psychology. *American Psychologist,* 1970, 25, 1026-1032.

Koefod, Paul. *The writing requirements for graduate degrees.* Englewood Cliffs, N.J.: Prentice-Hall, 1964.

McKeachie, Wilbert. *Teaching tips.* (6th ed.) Boston: Heath, 1969, pb.

Mechanic, David. *Students under stress: a study in the social psychology of adaptation.* New York: Free Press, 1962.

Publication manual of the American Psychological Association. Washington: American Psychological Association, 1967, pb.

Rogers, Carl. *Freedom to learn.* Columbus, Ohio: Merrill, 1969.

Shaffer, Laurance. *Preparing doctoral dissertations in psychology.* New York: Columbia University Press, 1967, pb.

Standards for educational and psychological tests and manuals. Washington: American Psychological Association.

Stenger, Charles. A realistic appraisal of existing and future job opportunities for psychologists. *American Psychologist,* 1970, 25, 959-961.

Stewart, George. *The doctor's oral.* New York: Random House, 1939.

Walker, E., and McKeachie, W. *Some thoughts about teaching the beginning course in psychology.* Belmont, Calif.: Brooks/Cole, 1967, pb.

What is a good review. *Contemporary Psychology,* 1963, 8, 43-44.

Appendix II

Library of Congress Classifications Relevant to Psychology

B	1-8	Philosophy periodicals
	818	Evolution
	819	Existentialism
BC		Logic
	53	Relation of logic to psychology
	141	Logic of chance. Probability. See HA 29-33, QA 273.
	173	Proof
	175	Fallacies
	177	Reasoning, argumentation
	181	Propositions, prediction, judgment
	183	Hypothesis
BD	100-241	Epistemology
	300-331	Ontology
	420-423	The soul. Immortality. See BF 1001-1042.
	428	Soul of animals. See BF 660-685.
	621-638	Cosmology—space, matter, time
BF		Psychology
	1-8	Periodicals. See B 1-8, BF 1001-1008, QP 351.
	11-18	Societies
	20	Congresses
	21-28	Collections. Collected works.
	30	Directories. Yearbooks.
	31	Dictionaries
	32	Terminology

431-433	Mental efficiency, ability, intelligence, mental tests, testing. See LB 1131.
432	By race
435-437	Mental deficiency
441	Comparison, judgment, reasoning, abstraction. BC, BD 235.
455-463	Thought and thinking. Psychology of language, speech, meaning.
456	Psychology of reading, spelling
458	Symbolism
467-475	Psychology of time, space, causality. See BD 621-638.
481	Work and fatigue. See BJ 1498, LB 1075, QP 421.
485	Laziness
491-493	Normal illusions. See BF 1001-1499, QP 495.
495-499	Synesthesia
511-593	Affection. Feeling. Emotion.
515	Pleasure and pain. See BJ 1481-1491.
521	The feelings. Sensibility.
531-593	Emotion
585-593	Expression of the emotions
608-635	Will. Volition. Choice.
620-628	Freedom of the will. See BV 741, JC 571.
632	Training of the will.
633	Brainwashing
634	Confession
635	Diseases of the will.
636-637	Applied psychology. See HV 6543-6548, LC 6519.
638-645	New thought. Menticulture.
660-789	Comparative, genetic psychology.
660-687	Comparative psychology. Animal and human psychology. See QL 785.
685	Instinct. See QL 781.
692	Sex psychology. See HQ, QH 471-475, 481, QP 251.
693	Psychology of women
697	Differential psychology. Individuality.
698	Personality. See BD 331, BF 311.

700-755	Genetic psychology. See B 818, GN 451-453, HM 106-136, QH 361-371.
717	Psychology of play ⁄
721-723	Child psychology. See HQ 771-785, LB 1051-1140.
724	Adolescence. Youth. See HQ 35, LB 1135.
724.5	Adulthood
724.6	Middle age
724.8	Old age
725-727	Class psychology
730-738	Race and ethnic psychology. See CB 195-281, E 185.625, GN 270-273.
751-755	Psychology of nations
761-768	Psychology of evidence. See BF 365-441.
773	Psychology of belief, faith. See BL 53.
774	Psychology of influence
775	Psychology of the marvelous
778	Psychology of worth, value, meaning. See BD 232.
789	Psychology of other special subjects: ambition, color, death, disasters, drowning, fire, funerals, gifts, justice, mountains, motion pictures, self-multilation, suffering, and water.
795-811	Temperament
818-839	Character
840-861	Physiognomy
866-885	Phrenology
889-905	Graphology. Study of handwriting.
908-940	The hand
990	Miscellaneous. Curiosa.
1001-1404	Parapsychology
1001-1008	Periodicals
1010-1018	Societies
1025	Dictionaries
1026-1027	Biography
1028	History
1029-1030	Reports of commissions, investigations.
1031-1038	General works. See BF 638-649.
1048-1063	Hallucinations. Illusions. ⌣
1068-1073	Sleep. Somnambulism. See BF 1111-1156, 1321-1353.

	1074-1099	Dreams and dreaming
	1100-1108	Visions.
	1111-1156	Hypnotism. Suggestion. Animal magnetism. Mesmerism. Subliminal projection. See BF 1628.3, RZ 430.
	1161-1171	Telepathy. Mind reading.
	1211-1218	Multiple consciousness. Dissociation of personality.
	1228-1389	Spiritualism
	1321-1353	Trance and analogous states. Ecstasy. Sensory and motor automatism.
	1325	Clairvoyance
	1331	Crystal gazing
	1338	Clairaudience
	1343	Automatic writing. Planchette.
	1347	Automatic drawing and painting.
	1352	Trance utterance
	1353	Polyglot mediumship
	1371	Physical phenomena of spiritualism. Telekinesis.
	1378	Materialization
	1383	Dematerialization. Fourth dimension.
	1385	Levitation
	1389	Other
BJ	1409	Ethics—pain and suffering
	1460-1468	Ethics—freedom of the will. See BF 620-628.
	1471	Conscience
	1472	Intuition
	1474	Altruism and egotism
	1475	Sympathy. Compassion. See BF 575.59.
	1480-1491	Ethics—happiness, joy, sorrow, grief, hedonism. See BF 515, BJ 1409.
	1498	Ethics—work, idleness, leisure. See BF 481, GN 14.
BL	53	Psychology of religion. See BR 110, HQ 61.
BR	110	Psychology of religious experience, conversion. See BL 53.

BV	235	Psychology of prayer
	741	Religious liberty
	5083	Psychology of mysticism
CB	195-281	Races. Nationalities.
E	98.P95	Psychology of the Indians of North America
	185.625	Psychosocial effects of the race problem on Negroes
GN		Anthropology
	221-265	Physiological anthropology. See QP.
	270-279	Psychological anthropology. See BF 730-755, HM 251-299, GN 451-453, LB 1101-1139.
	451-477	Psychic life of primitive people. See BF 700-755, GN 270-279.
GT	521	Psychology of clothing
GV	1448	Psychology of chess
	1595	Psychology of dancing
HA	29-33	Theory and method of statistics. See QA 276.
HF	5353	Psychology of business
	5386	Success literature. See HF 5548.8.
	5548.8	Industrial psychology. See BF 481.
	5822	Psychology of advertising.
HM	27	Relation of sociology to psychology. See BF 57.
	106-136	Evolution (Sociology)
	133	Small groups
	251-291	Social psychology
	253	Sociometry
	255	Instinct in social psychology
	258	Communication
	261	Public opinion
	263	Publicity. Propaganda. Public relations.
	267	Tradition
	271	Authority and freedom
	276	Liberalism. Toleration
	278	Passive resistance

281-299	Crowds. Tumults. Revolutions.
281	Theory
283	History
291	Other special
299	Miscellaneous special
HQ	Social groups: the family. Marriage. Women.
35	Adolescents and sex. See BF 724, LB 1135.
61	Religious emotion and eroticism
71-449	Abnormal sex relations
73	Sexual perversion in women
76	Homosexuality
79	Sadism. Masochism. Fetishism.
750-799	Eugenics. Child culture. Child study.
768-792	Children. See LB 1101-1135.
773	Problem children
773.5	Gifted children
773.5	Retarded children
796-799	Youth. Adolescence. See HQ 35.
1060-1064	Aged. Gerontology (social aspects). Retirement. See BF 724.8.
HV	Social pathology
689	Psychiatric social work
5045-5047	Psychology of alcoholism
5725-5770	Tobacco habit
5800-5840	Drug habits. See RC 369-371.
6080-6113	Criminal psychology. See HM 281-283.
6133	Psychopathology and crime
6278	Regicide
6499-6535	Homicide. Murder. See HV 6278.
6543-6548	Suicide. See RA 1136.
6705-6707	Offenses against public morals. See HQ 71-440, HV 5045-5047, 5725-5770, 5800-5840.
9051-9230	Juvenile offender
JC 571	Political liberty
575	Equality (of individuals, races)
JF 705	Juridical psychology

KF	8922	Forensic psychology
LB	1028	Educational research
	1051-1091	Educational psychology. See BF 81-108, QP 351-499.
	1057	Nervous system
	1059	Formal discipline
	1061	Habit
	1062	Imagination. Abstraction.
	1063	Memory
	1064	Paired-association
	1065	Interest. Attention. Incentive.
	1067	Apperception
	1069	Suggestion and imitation
	1071	Will
	1073	Emotion
	1075	Fatigue
	1076	Rest
	1083	Individuality
	1084	Group behavior.
	1091	Pathological aspects. See LC 4601.
	1101-1139	Child study. See BF 721-724, HQ 750-799, HV 9051-6230.
	1118	Child biography. See HQ 799.
	1121	Psychophysical studies
	1125	Anthropological studies
	1131-1133	Psychical development
	1134	Learning ability
	1135	Adolescence. See BF 724, HQ 35.
	1137	Play, games. See BF 717.
	3013.6	School psychologists
LC	3950-3990	Education of exceptional children
	3991-4000	Education of gifted children
	4001-4801	Education of handicapped children
	4815	Education of feebleminded adults
M	1977.P8	Psychoanalysis (Songs and music)
ML	3830-3838	Psychology of music

N	71	Psychology of the artist
	8237.5	Psychiatry in art. See BF 725-727, ML 3838.
P	37	Relation of philology and linguistics to psychology
	101-105	Origins of language. See BF 455.
PN	2058	Psychology of the actor
	3448.P8	Psychological novel
	6231.P78	Psychoanalysis (Wit and humor collections)
QA	273	Mathematic probability
	276	Mathematical statistics
QH	361-371	Evolution (Biology)
	431	Heredity
	471-489	Reproduction
	546	Adaptation
QL	775	Social relations of animals
	781	Instinct
	785	Animal intelligence
QP	251-281	Physiology of sex
	351-499	Nervous system and the senses, including physiological psychology
	361-375	Nervous system
	376-425	Brain
	431-499	The senses
	901-981	Experimental pharmacology
RA	790-790.7	Mental hygiene. See BF 635-645, RC 351, 460, 490-499, RZ 400-406.
	1123	Homicide. See HV 6499-6535.
	1136	Suicide. See HV 6543-6548.
	1141	Sexual offenses, diseases. See HQ 71-471.
	1148	Forensic psychology
	1151	Forensic psychiatry
RC	49	Psychosomatic medicine. See RC 435-576.
	321-576	Neurology and psychiatry. Neuropsychiatry.
	346-429	Neurology. Diseases of the nervous system. See QP 351-425, RD 593-595.

	532	Hysteria
	533	Obsessive-compulsive states
	534	Hallucinations
	535	Phobias. Fear.
	537	Psychogenic depression. Neurotic-depressive state.
	539-544	Psychoneuroses with somatic symptoms
	547	Sleep disturbances
	548	Insomnia
	550	War neuroses
	552	Other psychoneuroses
	554-576	Disorders of character, behavior, and intelligence
	555	Pathological personality. Psychopathic personality.
	557	Sexual deviation. See HQ 71-79, RA 1141.
	558	Homosexuality
	559	Sadism
	560	Other disorders
	562-564	Immature personality
	565	Alcoholism
	566	General works on narcotic habits and drug addiction
	567	Tobacco habit
	568	Other habits
	570	Mental deficiency
	571	Idiocy. Mongolism.
	572	Imbecility.
	573	Feeble-mindedness
	574	Other disorders of character, behavior and intelligence
	576	After-care of mental patients. Rehabilitation.
	1085	Aviation psychology
	1090	Aviation psychiatry
RD	593-595	Neurosurgery
RE	912	Psychogenic disturbances of vision
	918	Color perception tests. See BF 789.C7, QP 481.

RF	291	Psychology of the deaf
	293	Psychogenic and neuorgenic deafness. See RC 544.
RG	560	Psychology of pregnancy
RJ	91	Supposed prenatal influence
	101	Hygiene and care of children. See BF 721, RA 790.
	111	Mental hygiene.
	125-135	Physiology of children
	131	Growth and development. See BF 721-723.
	140	Physiology of adolescents. See BF 724.
	486-506	Pediatric neuropsychiatry
	499-506	Child psychiatry. See BF 1091, RJ 111.
	503	Adolescent psychiatry
	504	Adolescent psychiatry
RL	701-751	Diseases due to psychomatic and nerve disorders
RZ	400-406	Mental healing. See RC 49, 435-576.
	430	Mesmerism, animal magnetism. See BF 1111-1156, RC 490-499.
UB	275-277	Psychological warfare. Propaganda. See HM 263.
UH	629-629.5	Military psychiatry.
Z	5001-8000	Subject bibliographies
	5814.C5	Child psychology
	5814.P8	Educational psychology
	5814.P8	Psychological tests
	6663.P8	Physiological
	6664.N5	Psychiatry and pathological psychology
	6724.P8	Psychological warfare
	6878.P8	Psychical research
	7201-7205	Psychology
	7204.P8	Psychoanalysis